MySQL Database Usage & Administration

Vikram Vaswani

D1261805

New York   Chicago   San Francisco
Lisbon   London   Madrid   Mexico City
Milan   New Delhi   San Juan
Seoul   Singapore   Sydney   Toronto

Library of Congress Cataloging-in-Publication Data

Vaswani, Vikram.
    MySQL database usage & administration / Vikram Vaswani.
        p.   cm.
    ISBN 978-0-07-160549-6 (alk. paper)
    1. MySQL (Electronic resource)   2. Relational databases.   3. Client/server
computing.   I. Title.
    QA76.9.D3V394   2010
    005.75'85—dc22   2009034540

McGraw-Hill books are available at special quantity discounts to use as premiums and sales promotions, or for use in corporate training programs. To contact a representative, please e-mail us at bulksales@mcgraw-hill.com.

MySQL Database Usage & Administration

1 2 3 4 5 6 7 8 9 0   DOC DOC   0 1 9

ISBN   978-0-07-160549-6
MHID   0-07-160549-5

Sponsoring Editor Jane K. Brownlow	**Technical Editor** Chris Cornutt	**Composition** Glyph International
Editorial Supervisor Patty Mon	**Copy Editor** Lisa McCoy	**Illustration** Glyph International
Project Manager Ekta Dixit, Glyph International	**Proofreader** Claire Splan	**Art Director, Cover** Jeff Weeks
Acquisitions Coordinator Joya Anthony	**Indexer** Robert Swanson	**Cover Designer** Jeff Weeks
	Production Supervisor Jean Bodeaux	

For Farah and Tonka:
I couldn't have got this far without you!

About the Author

Vikram Vaswani is the founder and CEO of Melonfire (www.melonfire.com), a consultancy firm with special expertise in open-source tools and technologies. He is a passionate proponent of the open-source movement and frequently contributes articles and tutorials on open-source technologies—including Perl, Python, PHP, MySQL, and Linux—to the community at large. His previous books include *MySQL: The Complete Reference* (www.mysql-tcr.com), *PHP: A Beginner's Guide* (www.php-beginners-guide.com), and *PHP Programming Solutions* (www.php-programming-solutions.com).

Vikram has more than eight years' experience interacting with the MySQL RDBMS as a user, administrator, and application developer. He has deployed MySQL in a variety of different environments, including corporate intranets, high-traffic websites, and mission-critical thin client applications, and is a vocal advocate of MySQL in his role as a software consultant.

A Felix Scholar at the University of Oxford, England, Vikram combines his interest in Web application development with various other activities. When not dreaming up plans for world domination, he amuses himself by reading crime fiction, watching old movies, playing squash, blogging, and keeping an eye out for unfriendly agents. Read more about him and *MySQL Database Usage & Administration* at www.mysql-usage.com.

About the Technical Editor

Chris Cornutt has been involved in the PHP community for more than eight years. Soon after discovering the language, he started up his news site, www.PHPDeveloper.org, to share the latest happenings and opinions from other PHPers from around the world. Chris has written for publications such as php|architect and the international PHP magazines on topics ranging from geocoding to trackbacks. He is also a coauthor of *PHP String Handling* (Wrox Press, 2003). Chris lives in Frisco, Texas, with his wife and son, where he works for a large natural-gas distributor maintaining their website and developing PHP-based applications.

Contents at a Glance

Contents

Part II   Administration

Foreword

MySQL is nearly 15 years old, and now it is the ubiquitous database system for websites and many other environments. MySQL really is everywhere. Yet, it remains remarkably easy to get started with MySQL. If you just need to run it on a home system for an application that requires it, you can simply install MySQL with no further worries. But this apparent simplicity can be deceiving!

When you build a website with it or otherwise use it for aspects of a business, you need to get things better than "just running." MySQL offers many features and quite a few settings, and there are plenty of issues to consider in and around database-driven systems.

Many businesses get an expert to help with setup and keeping an eye on things as the system grows over time; however, many people are interested in knowing a bit more about the systems they work with—or at least rely on. Chances are you're one of those people, since you're holding this book.

Unlike a reference manual containing all features in "dry" form, *MySQL Database Usage & Administration* provides practical and easy-to-read information to look up and use while you work on something. Building on his earlier work, *MySQL: The Complete Reference*, Vikram covers the basics as well as many advanced and new features of MySQL 5.1, with examples and clarifications. It's a valuable resource you'll want to keep within reach on your bookshelf.

Arjen Lentz
Founder, Open Query
openquery.com
Brisbane, Australia

Acknowledgments

MySQL is a complex piece of software, and writing a book about it is *not*—as I found out over the last seven months—a particularly simple task. Fortunately, I was aided in this process by a diverse and dynamic group of people, all of whom played an important part in getting this book into your hands.

First and foremost, I would like to thank my wife, who encouraged and supported me through the entire process and made sure I had a comfortable and stress-free working environment. I am pretty sure that I would not have been able to do this without her help. Thanks, babe!

The editorial and marketing team at McGraw-Hill Professional deserves an honorable mention here as well. This is my fifth book with them and, as usual, they have been an absolute pleasure to work with. Acquisitions coordinator Joya Anthony, technical editor Chris Cornutt, and executive editor Jane Brownlow all guided this book through the development process and played no small part in making it the polished and professional product you hold in your hands. I would like to thank them for their expertise, dedication, and efforts on my behalf.

Finally, for making the entire book-writing process more enjoyable than it usually is, thanks to: Patrick Quinlan, Ian Fleming, Bryan Adams, the Stones, Peter O'Donnell, *MAD Magazine*, Scott Adams, FHM, Gary Larson, VH1, Britney Spears, George Michael, Kylie Minogue, *Buffy the Vampire Slayer*, Farah Malegam, Stephen King, Shakira, Anahita Marker, John le Carre, The Saturdays, Barry White, Gwen Stefani, Robert Crais, Robert B. Parker, Baz Luhrmann, Stefy, Anna Kournikova, John Connolly, Wasabi, Omega, Pidgin, Cal Evans, Ling's Pavilion, Tonka and his evil twin Bonka, Din Tai Fung, HBO, Mark Twain, Tim Burton, Harish Kamath, Madonna, John Sandford, Iron Man, the Tube, Dido, Google.com, *The Matrix*, Lee Child, Michael Connelly, Antonio Prohias, Quentin Tarantino, Alfred Hitchcock, Woody Allen, Kinokuniya, Percy Jackson, Jennifer Hudson, Mambo's and Tito's, Easyjet, Humphrey Bogart, Thai Pavilion, Wikipedia, Amazon.com, U2, The Three Stooges, Pacha, Oscar Wilde, Hugh Grant, Punch, Kelly Clarkson, Scott Turow, Slackware Linux, Calvin and Hobbes, Blizzard Entertainment, Alfred Kropp, Otto, Pablo Picasso, Popeye and Olive Oyl, Dennis Lehane, Trattoria, Dire Straits, Bruce Springsteen, David Mitchell, *The West Wing*, Santana, Rod Stewart, and all my friends, at home and elsewhere.

Introduction

Chances are, you've already heard of MySQL: It's a high-performance database system built around a client-server architecture. Over the last few years, this fast, robust, and user-friendly product has become the de facto choice for both business and personal use, notably on account of its advanced suite of data management tools, its friendly licensing policy, and its worldwide support community of users and engineers.

As a reliable, feature-rich database server, MySQL also has applications in business, education, science, and engineering—a fact amply demonstrated by its customer list, which includes such names as Motorola, Sony, NASA, HP, Xerox, and Silicon Graphics. According to the MySQL website, more than 100 million copies of MySQL have been downloaded and distributed to date, and 50,000 more are added to that total *every day*.

These are impressive statistics, but what is even more impressive is that MySQL is—and always has been—an open-source project, with both source and binary code freely available under the terms of the GNU General Public License (MySQL earns revenue through the sale of commercial support packages). This is a key benefit, since it allows users to download and use the product at no cost; however, it also places the responsibility of learning, managing, and securing the resulting installation squarely on the shoulders of those same users.

That's where this book comes in. If you're one of the many millions of users who've downloaded and installed MySQL, found it interesting, and are now wondering how to maximize your usage of the product, this is the book for you. It takes a close look at some of MySQL's most important features—transactions, stored routines, triggers, etc.—and shows you how to use them in a practical context. It also includes information on everything you need to know to function as an effective MySQL system administrator, from securing user accounts to backing up and restoring data. In short, it gives you the knowledge you need to make the most of your MySQL experience.

Who Should Read This Book

MySQL Database Usage & Administration is intended for beginner-to-intermediate MySQL users, particularly those who already have some (limited) experience of using MySQL and are interested in taking their skills to the next level. Users who have cut their teeth on other database systems will also be able to make use of the book, as the first two chapters include a fast introduction to MySQL's dialect of SQL.

If you're an experienced MySQL user, administrator or developer—say, if you've been using MySQL for two years or more—it's quite likely that you'll find this book much less useful than the reader segment described previously.

What This Book Covers

MySQL Database Usage & Administration contains information on the MySQL 5.1 RDBMS and provides one-stop coverage of common topics related to MySQL usage and administration. This includes topics such as views, triggers, transactions, stored routines, security, data backup, performance optimization, and replication. Each chapter also includes practical code examples that readers can "follow along with" to gain a practical understanding of the material being discussed.

The following outline describes the contents of the book and shows how it is broken down into task-focused chapters.

Part I: Usage

Chapter 1: An Introduction to MySQL discusses MySQL's history and evolution, looks at its feature set, and explains why it offers such a compelling value proposition. It also examines MySQL's technical architecture and explains the various MySQL subsystems.

Chapter 2: Understanding Basic Commands provides a quick reference to basic database concepts and MySQL's dialect of SQL, explaining the basic SQL commands to create, modify, and query databases.

Chapter 3: Making Design Decisions offers a thorough discussion of important issues to be considered when designing a MySQL database. It includes coverage of MySQL's data types, storage engines, and handling of primary keys, foreign keys, and indexes.

Chapter 4: Using Joins, Subqueries, and Views discusses MySQL's support for multitable queries, nested queries, and virtual tables, which offer different ways of exploiting table relationships and viewing data.

Chapter 5: Using Transactions examines MySQL's ability to group a series of SQL statements into a single unit and execute them atomically, or undo the entire set of changes in the event of an error.

Chapter 6: Using Stored Procedures and Functions examines MySQL's support for server-side stored routines, discussing important concepts such as conditional tests, loops, cursors, and error handlers.

Chapter 7: Using Triggers and Scheduled Events discusses two relatively recent additions to MySQL, triggers and scheduled events, which provide a framework for automating database operations.

Chapter 8: Working with Data in Different Formats discusses MySQL's built-in tools for importing and exporting data in different formats, including comma-separated, tab-delimited, and XML formats.

Chapter 9: Optimizing Performance offers tips and tricks to squeeze the maximum performance out of your MySQL server, including information on how to fine-tune queries; optimize cache and buffer settings; and maximize performance of stored routines, transactions, and subqueries.

Part II: Administration

Chapter 10: Performing Basic Server Administration explores common server administration tasks, including starting and stopping the server, obtaining server status, using the MySQL log files, and using the new *information_schema* database.

Chapter 11: Managing Users and Controlling Access discusses the MySQL security and privilege system, and the management of user accounts and passwords (including what do to if you forget the MySQL superuser password).

Chapter 12: Performing Maintenance, Backup, and Recovery provides instructions and information on how to back up and restore a MySQL database and use MySQL-supplied utilities to recover data from a damaged database.

Chapter 13: Replicating Data discusses MySQL's replication features, which provide the ability to automatically synchronize databases across multiple hosts.

The appendix includes reference material for the information presented in the first two parts.

Appendix: Installing MySQL and the Sample Database discusses the process of obtaining, installing, and configuring MySQL on both Windows and UNIX.

Conventions

This book uses different types of formatting to highlight special advice. Here's a list:

NOTE *Additional insight or information on the topic*

TIP *A technique or trick to help you do things better*

CAUTION *Something to watch out for*

Q&A *A frequently asked question and its answer*

In the code listings in this book, text highlighted in bold is a command to be entered at the prompt. For example, in the following listing:

```
mysql> INSERT INTO movies (mtitle, myear) VALUES ('Rear Window', 1954);
Query OK, 1 row affected (0.06 sec)
```

the line in bold is a query that you would type at the command prompt. You can use this as a guide to try out the commands in the book.

PART I
Usage

CHAPTER 1

An Introduction to MySQL

In today's interconnected world, it's almost impossible to find a business that doesn't depend on information in some form or another. Be it marketing data, financial movements, or operational statistics, businesses today live or die by their ability to manage, massage, and filter information flow in order to achieve a competitive advantage.

More often than not, all this data finds a home in a business' relational database management system (RDBMS), a software tool that assists in organizing, retrieving, and cross-referencing information. A large number of such systems are currently available, and you've probably already heard of some of them: Oracle, Sybase, Microsoft Access, and PostgreSQL are well-known names. These database systems are powerful, feature-rich software applications, capable of organizing and searching millions of records at high speeds; as such, they're widely used by businesses and government offices, often for mission-critical purposes.

Recently, though, more and more attention has focused on a relatively new entrant in this field: MySQL.

MySQL is a high-performance, multithreaded, multiuser RDBMS built around a client-server architecture. Over the last few years, this fast, robust, and user-friendly database system has become the de facto choice for both business and personal use, notably on account of its advanced suite of data management tools, its friendly licensing policy, and its worldwide support community of users and engineers. This introductory chapter will gently introduce you to the world of MySQL by taking you on a whirlwind tour of MySQL's history, features, and technical architecture.

History

MySQL came into being in 1979, when Michael "Monty" Widenius created a database system named UNIREG for the Swedish company TcX. UNIREG didn't, however, have a Structured Query Language (SQL) interface—something that caused it to fall out of favor with TcX in the mid-1990s. So TcX began looking for alternatives. One of those alternatives was mSQL, a competing DBMS created by David Hughes.

mSQL didn't work for TcX either, however, so Widenius decided to create a new database server customized to his specific requirements. That system, completed and released to a small group in May 1996, became the first version of what is today known as MySQL.

A few months later, MySQL 3.11 saw its first public release as a binary distribution for Solaris. Linux source and binaries followed shortly; an enthusiastic developer community and a friendly, General Public License (GPL)-based licensing policy took care of the rest. Today, MySQL is available for a wide variety of platforms, including Linux, MacOS, and Windows, in both source and binary form.

A few years later, TcX spun off MySQL AB, a private company that had sole ownership of the MySQL server source code and trademark, and was responsible for maintenance, marketing, and further development of the MySQL database server. It was managed by Michael Widenius, David Axmark, and Allan Larsson, supported by both a full-time staff and the active support of a worldwide developer community.

In 2008, MySQL AB was formally acquired by Sun Microsystems, and in 2009, Sun Microsystems was in turn acquired by Oracle, which today owns and develops the MySQL database engine. Although Oracle operates commercially in a number of different markets, the MySQL source code remains available to the community under the GNU General Public License (users can, however, purchase commercial support from MySQL).

Unique Features

MySQL's popularity is due to a particular combination of unique features: speed, reliability, extensibility, and open-source code. The following sections discuss these features in greater detail.

Speed

In an RDBMS, speed—the time it takes to execute a query and return the results to the caller—is everything. By any standards, MySQL is fast, often orders of magnitude faster than its competition. Benchmarks available on the MySQL website show that MySQL outperforms almost every other database currently available, including commercial counterparts like Microsoft SQL Server 2000 and IBM DB2. For example, an eWeek study in February 2002 that compared IBM DB2, Microsoft SQL Server, MySQL, Oracle9i, and Sybase concluded that "MySQL has the best overall performance and that MySQL scalability matches Oracle ... MySQL had the highest throughput, even exceeding the numbers generated by Oracle."[1]

Reliability

Most of the time, high database performance comes at a price: low reliability. MySQL is, however, designed to offer maximum reliability and uptime, and it has been tested and certified for use in high-volume, mission-critical applications. MySQL supports transactions, which ensure data consistency and reduce the risk of data loss, and replication and clustering, two techniques that significantly reduce downtime in the event of a server failure. Finally, MySQL's large user base assists in rapidly locating and resolving bugs and in testing the software in a variety of environments; this proactive approach has resulted in software that is virtually bug-free.

Scalability

MySQL can handle extremely large and complex databases without too much of a performance drop. Tables of several gigabytes containing hundreds of thousands of records are not uncommon, and the MySQL website itself claims to use databases containing 50 million records. A 2005 test by MySQL Test Labs demonstrated that

---

[1] "A Look at MySQL 5.0 Performance Benchmarks: MySQL Technical White Paper"; http://www.mysql.com; May 2006.

What Makes MySQL so Fast?

Part of the reason for MySQL's blazing performance is its fully multithreaded architecture, which allows multiple concurrent accesses to the database. This multithreaded architecture is the core of the MySQL engine, allowing multiple clients to read the same database simultaneously and providing a substantial performance gain. The MySQL code tree is also structured in a modular, multilayered manner, with minimum redundancies and special optimizers for such complex tasks as joins and indexing.

MySQL also includes a *query cache*, which can substantially improve performance by caching the results of common queries and returning this cached data to the caller without having to re-execute the query each time. This is different from competing systems such as Oracle, in that those systems merely cache the execution plan, not the results. However, they still need to execute the query, including all joins, and re-retrieve the query results on every run. MySQL benchmarks claim that this feature improves performance by more than 200 percent, with no special programming required on the part of the user[2].

It is worth noting that MySQL's designers initially left out many of the features that cause performance degradation on competing systems, including transactions, referential integrity, and stored procedures. These features typically add complexity to the server and result in a performance hit. User requests for these features have, however, resulted in their inclusion in newer versions of the product.

"MySQL shows near-linear scalability in a multi-CPU environment,"[3] with performance increasing in proportion to the number of CPUs added to the system. This ability to scale with demand has made MySQL popular with businesses like Eli Lilly, Alstom, Dun & Bradstreet, Epson, and the *New York Times*; high-volume websites such as Google, Facebook, and Slashdot; and government organizations such as NASA, the U.S. Census Bureau, and the Swedish National Police.

Ease of Use

MySQL is so easy to use that even a novice can pick up the basics in a few hours, and the software is well supported by a detailed manual, a large number of free online tutorials, a knowledgeable developer community, and a fair number of books. While most interaction with MySQL takes place through a command-line interface, a number of graphical tools, both browser-based and otherwise, are also available to simplify the task of managing and administering the MySQL database server. Finally, unlike its proprietary counterparts, which have literally hundreds of adjustable parameters,

---

[2] The MySQL manual; http://dev.mysql.com/doc/refman/5.0/en/query-cache.html

[3] The MySQL website; http://www.mysql.com/why-mysql/white-papers/performance.php

MySQL is fairly easy to tune and optimize for even the most demanding applications. For commercial environments, MySQL is fully supported in terms of professional MySQL training, consultancy, and technical support.

Portability and Standards Compliance

MySQL supports most of the important features of the ANSI (American National Standards Institute) SQL standard, and often extends the ANSI standard with custom extensions, functions, and data types designed to improve portability and provide users with enhanced functionality. MySQL is also available for both UNIX and non-UNIX operating systems, including Linux; Solaris; FreeBSD; OS/2; MacOS; and Windows 95, 98, Me, 2000, XP, NT, and Vista; and it runs on a range of architectures, including Intel x86, Alpha, SPARC, PowerPC, and IA64.

Multiuser Support

MySQL is a full multiuser system, which means that multiple clients can access and use one (or more) MySQL database(s) simultaneously; this is of particular significance during development of web-based applications, which are required to support simultaneous connections by multiple remote clients. MySQL also includes a powerful and flexible privilege system that allows administrators to protect access to sensitive data using a combination of user- and host-based authentication schemes.

Internationalization

As a program that is used by millions of users in countries across the globe, it would be unusual indeed if MySQL did not include support for various languages and character sets. MySQL offers full Unicode support, as well as full support for most important character sets (including Latin, Chinese, and European character sets). Character sets are taken into account when sorting, comparing, and saving data.

Wide Application Support

MySQL exposes application programming interfaces (APIs) to many programming languages, thereby making it possible to write database-driven applications in the language of your choice. Currently, MySQL provides hooks to C, C++, Eiffel, Java, Perl, PHP, Python, Ruby, and Tcl, and connectors are available for JDBC, ODBC, and .NET applications.

Open-Source Code

The MySQL source code is freely available under the terms of the GNU General Public License—a key benefit, since it allows users to download and modify the application to meet their specific needs. This unique licensing policy has fuelled MySQL's popularity, creating an active and enthusiastic global community of MySQL developers and users. This community plays an active role in keeping MySQL ahead of its competition, both by crash-testing the software for reliability on millions of installations worldwide and extending the engine to stay abreast of the latest technologies.

High-volume, well-informed mailing lists and user groups assist in the rapid resolution of questions and problems, and a global network of committed MySQL users and developers provides knowledgeable advice, bug fixes, and third-party utilities. All of this has paid off: A code inspection study by Reasoning, Inc. concluded that the code quality of MySQL was six times better than that of comparable proprietary code[4].

NOTE *It is worth noting that if your MySQL-powered application is not licensed under the GPL or other MySQL-approved open-source license and you intend to redistribute it (whether internally or externally), you are required to purchase a commercial license for this use. Oracle earns revenue both from the sale of these licenses and by providing support, training, and consultation services for the MySQL database server.*

Product Family

In addition to the core MySQL database server, Oracle makes available a number of MySQL-related products and tools. This section introduces you to some of the other members of the MySQL product family.

MySQL Server

This core product consists of a high-performance database server, which is the main software engine responsible for creating and managing databases, executing queries and returning query results, and maintaining security. This core product also includes a number of client-side tools, such as a command-line SQL client; tools to manage user permissions; and utilities to import, export, copy, and repair databases.

MySQL Cluster

MySQL Cluster is a version of the MySQL database server that supports "clustering," a technology that allows data to be transparently distributed across two or more physical servers to increase redundancy. This clustering technology plays an important role in high-availability applications, as it ensures continuous data availability even if one of the nodes in the cluster fails. At the time of this writing, MySQL Cluster supports up to 255 nodes in a single cluster and uses synchronous replication to copy data between nodes.

MySQL Proxy

MySQL Proxy is a proxy server that serves as a "gatekeeper" between the MySQL database server and connecting clients. It includes the ability to intercept and rewrite queries, modify result sets, implement query queues, analyze query traffic for reporting purposes, and perform load balancing tasks.

---

[4] The MySQL website; http://www.mysql.com/why-mysql/quality

> ### Are there Different Versions of the MySQL Database Server?
>
> MySQL's core database server comes in two flavors: Community and Enterprise. The Community server is "free": Users can download and use it at no cost under the terms of the GNU GPL, but by the same token, are required to perform all maintenance and administrative tasks themselves, with no support from the MySQL development team. For companies and individuals looking for a greater level of support, the Enterprise server is a commercial offering that provides regular updates and bug fixes, consultancy services and advice from MySQL engineers, and proprietary database-monitoring software in return for a subscription fee.

MySQL Administrator

MySQL Administrator is an all-in-one control center for a MySQL database server, allowing database administrators to track server status in real time. It includes visual tools for user administration, database backup and restore, and log analysis, as well as server fine-tuning.

MySQL Query Browser

MySQL Query Browser is a visual tool for graphically constructing queries and viewing the results. It includes tools to manage database connections, databases, and tables, as well as a debugger (with breakpoint support) to assist in optimizing and troubleshooting complex queries.

MySQL Workbench

MySQL Workbench is a visual design tool that enables database administrators and developers to graphically design and validate data models, generate database schema code, and manage changes to database schemas. It also includes the ability to visually compare and synchronize two versions of a database and create import/export scripts to transfer data from one system to another.

MySQL Migration Toolkit

The MySQL Migration Toolkit is a graphical, wizard-driven tool to port databases from other RDBMS products to MySQL. It includes support for Oracle, Microsoft SQL Server, and Microsoft Access, and provides automated tools to remap and rebuild table schemas; copy records; and transfer indexes, views, triggers, and stored procedures.

MySQL Embedded Server

MySQL Embedded Server is a low-footprint version of the MySQL database server that is intended specifically for use in embedded applications, such as networking equipment, diagnostic tools, or point-of-sale (POS) systems. This embedded database also includes a number of useful administrative features: automatic space expansion, auto-restart, and dynamic reconfiguration.

MySQL Drivers and Connectors

MySQL provides drivers and connectors for many different programming languages, thereby making it possible to build database-driven applications using any one of several different development toolkits. Currently, MySQL provides drivers and connectors for C, C++, Java, Perl, PHP, Python, Ruby, JDBC, ODBC, and .NET applications.

Technical Architecture

MySQL is based on a tiered architecture, consisting of both primary subsystems and support components that interact with each other to read, parse, and execute queries, and to cache and return query results.

Subsystems

There are three primary subsystems within the MySQL architecture, as discussed in the following sections.

Memory and Connection Management

This subsystem manages user connections, via modules for network connection management with clients, and synchronizes competing tasks and processes, via modules for multithreading, thread locking, and performing thread-safe operations. It also handles all memory management issues between requests for data by the query subsystem and the data storage subsystem.

Query Parsing and Execution

Query parsing and execution is handled by two interrelated components: the syntax parser and the query optimizer. The syntax parser decomposes the SQL commands it receives from calling programs into a form that can be understood by the MySQL engine. It also checks the objects being referenced to ensure that the privilege level of the calling program allows it to use them. The query optimizer then prepares the most efficient plan for query execution, making decisions about table-versus-index scans, join methods, and range optimization, and using a bottom-up methodology to detect the optimal execution plan.

Data Storage

The data storage subsystem interfaces with the operating system (OS) to write to disk all of the data in the user tables, indexes, and logs, as well as the internal system data. MySQL 5.1 also introduced a new pluggable architecture, which allows developers to create new table storage mechanisms and "plug them in" to the server at run-time. This pluggable architecture also creates a level of abstraction between the data storage subsystem and the rest of the MySQL server, making it possible for developers to add new data storage engines that interact with the other MySQL subsystems through a standard API.

Connectivity

MySQL is designed on the assumption that the vast majority of its applications will be running on a TCP/IP (Transmission Control Protocol/Internet Protocol) network. This is a fairly good assumption, given that TCP/IP is not only highly robust and secure, but is also common to UNIX, Windows, OS/2, and almost any other serious operating system you'll likely encounter. When the client and the server are on the same UNIX machine, MySQL uses TCP/IP with UNIX sockets, which operate in the UNIX domain; that is, they are generally used between processes on the same UNIX system, as opposed to Internet sockets, which operate between networks.

Standards Compliance

The Structured Query Language (SQL) is an open standard that has been maintained by the American National Standards Institute (ANSI) since 1986. Although it's true that the implementation of this standard does differ in varying degrees from vendor to vendor, it's fair to say that SQL is today one of the most widely used cross-vendor languages. As with other implementations, such as SQL Server's T-SQL (Transact-SQL) and Oracle's SQL, MySQL has its own variations of the SQL standard that add power beyond what is available within the standard. Beginning with v5.1, MySQL also includes support for data import and export using Extensible Markup Language (XML), a widely accepted, vendor-neutral format for data markup and sharing.

Transactions

In the SQL context, a transaction consists of one or more SQL statements that operate as a single unit. Each SQL statement in such a unit is dependent on the others, and the unit as a whole is indivisible. If one statement in the unit does not complete successfully, the entire unit will be rolled back, and all the affected data will be returned to the state it was in before the transaction was started. Thus, a transaction is said to be successful only if all the individual statements within it are executed successfully.

The MySQL transaction system fully satisfies the ACID tests for transaction safety via its InnoDB and BDB table types (older table types, such as the MyISAM type, do not support transactions).

- *Atomicity* is handled by storing the results of transactional statements (the modified rows) in a memory buffer and writing these results to disk and to the binary log from the buffer only once the transaction is committed. This ensures that the statements in a transaction operate as an indivisible unit and their effects are seen either collectively or not at all.

- *Consistency* is primarily handled by MySQL's logging mechanisms, which record all changes to the database and provide an audit trail for transaction recovery. In addition to the logging process, MySQL provides locking mechanisms that ensure that all of the tables, rows, and indexes that make up the transaction are locked by the initiating process long enough to either commit the transaction or roll it back.

- Server-side semaphore variables and locking mechanisms act as traffic managers to help programs manage their own *isolation* mechanisms. MySQL's BDB table handler, for example, uses page-level locking to safely handle multiple simultaneous transactions, while the InnoDB table handler uses a more fine-grained row-level locking.

- MySQL implements *durability* by maintaining a binary transaction log file that tracks changes to the system during the course of a transaction. In the event of a hardware failure or abrupt system shutdown, recovering lost data is a relatively straightforward task by using the last backup in combination with the log when the system restarts.

Because transactional tables incur some performance overhead, it's also possible to specify whether to use transactions on a per-table basis.

Query Caching

If a query returns a given set of records, repeating the same query should return the same set of records, unless the underlying data has somehow changed. As obvious as this sounds, few of the other major RDBMS vendors provide features that take advantage of this principle. Other database products are efficient in storing optimized access plans that detail the process by which data is retrieved; such plans allow queries similar to those that have been issued previously to bypass the process of analyzing indexes yet again to get to the data.

Result-set caching takes this principle a step further by storing the result sets themselves in memory, thus circumventing the need to search the database at all. The data from a query is simply placed in a cache, and when a similar query is issued, this data is returned as if in response to the query that created it in the first place.

The MySQL engine uses an extremely efficient result set–caching mechanism, known as the Query Cache, that dramatically enhances response times for queries that are called upon to retrieve the exact same data as a previous query. This mechanism is so efficient that a major computing publication declared MySQL queries to be faster than those of Oracle and SQL Server (which are both known for their speed). If implemented properly, decision support systems using MySQL with canned reports or data-driven web pages can provide response speeds far beyond those that would be expected without the Query Cache.

Extensibility

In keeping with its open-source roots, MySQL makes the original source code available as part of the distribution, which permits developers to add new functions and features that are compiled into the engine as part of the core product. MySQL also allows separate C and C++ libraries to be loaded in the same memory space as the engine when MySQL starts up.

MySQL also allows developers to add new functions at run-time through a special user-defined function interface. User-defined functions are created initially as special C/C++ libraries and are then added and removed dynamically by means of the CREATE FUNCTION and DROP FUNCTION statements.

Symmetric Multiprocessing Support

To take advantage of multiprocessor architecture, MySQL is built using a multithreaded design, which allows threads to be allocated between processors to achieve a higher degree of parallelism. This is important to know not only for the database administrator, who needs to understand how MySQL takes best advantage of processing power, but also for developers, who can extend MySQL with custom functions. All custom functions must be *thread-safe*—that is, that they must not interfere with the workings of other threads in the same process as MySQL.

MySQL makes use of various thread packages, depending on the platform. POSIX threads are used on most UNIX variants, such as FreeBSD and Solaris. LinuxThreads are used for Linux distributions. For efficiency reasons, Windows threads are used on the Windows platform, but the code that handles them is designed to simulate POSIX threads.

Because MySQL is a threaded application, it is able to let the operating system take over the task of coordinating the allocation of threads to balance the workload across multiple processors. MySQL uses a global connection thread to handle all connection requests and creates a new dedicated thread to handle authentication and SQL query processing for each connection. In addition, in replication, master-host synchronization is handled by separate threads.

Of course, another way to take advantage of multiprocessing is to run multiple instances of MySQL on the same machine, thereby spawning a separate process for each instance. This approach is especially practical for hosting companies and even for internal hosting within corporate environments. By running multiple instances of MySQL on the same computer, you can easily accommodate multiple user bases that need different configuration options.

Security

The process of accessing a MySQL database can be broken down into two tasks: connecting to the MySQL server itself and accessing individual objects, such as tables or columns, in a database. MySQL has built-in security to verify user credentials at both stages.

- MySQL manages user authentication through user tables, which check not only that a user has logged on correctly with the proper username and password, but also that the connection is originating from an authorized TCP/IP address.

- Once a user is connected, a system administrator can bestow user-specific privileges on objects and on the actions that can be taken in MySQL. For example, you might allow *fred@thiscompany.com* to perform only SELECT queries against an inventory table, while allowing *anna@thatcompany.net* to run INSERT, UPDATE, and DELETE statements against the same table.

The actual data that travels over a network, such as query results, isn't encrypted and is, therefore, open to viewing by a hacker. To secure your data, you can use one of the Secure Shell (SSH) protocols; you'll need to install it on both the client applications and the operating system you're using. If you're using MySQL 4.0 or later, you can also use the Secure Socket Layer (SSL) encryption protocol, which can be configured to work from within MySQL, making it safe for use over the Internet or other public network infrastructures.

Application Programming Interfaces

For application developers, MySQL provides a client library that is written in the C programming language and a set of APIs that provide an understandable set of rules by which host languages can connect to MySQL and send commands. Using an API protects client programs from any underlying changes in MySQL that could affect connectivity.

Currently, MySQL provides hooks to C, C++, Eiffel, Java, Perl, PHP, Python, Ruby, and Tcl, and connectors are also available for JDBC, ODBC, and .NET applications.

Applications

MySQL's technical architecture, built as it is around the three tenets of performance, reliability, and ease of use, have made the product extremely popular, both on and off the Web. According to the MySQL website, more than 100 million copies of MySQL have been downloaded and distributed to date, and 50,000 more are added to that total every day. MySQL software today powers a variety of applications, including Internet websites, e-commerce applications, search engines, data warehouses, embedded applications, high-volume content portals, and mission-critical software systems.

Web Applications

It should come as no surprise that MySQL's primary applications today lie in the arena of the Web. As websites and web-based distributed applications grow ever more complex, it becomes more and more important that data be managed efficiently to improve transactional efficiency, reduce response time, and enhance the overall user experience. Consequently, a pressing need exists for a data management solution that is fast, stable, and secure—one that can be deployed and used with minimal fuss and that provides solid underpinnings for future development.

MySQL fits the bill for a number of reasons. Its proven track record generates confidence in its reliability and longevity; its open-source roots ensure rapid bug fixes and a continued cycle of enhancements (not to mention a lower overall cost); its portability and support for various programming languages and technologies make it suitable for a wide variety of applications; and its low cost/high performance value proposition makes it attractive to everyone from home users to small- and medium-sized businesses and government organizations. For these reasons and more, MySQL is a key component of modern web applications, particularly those built on the popular LAMP stack.

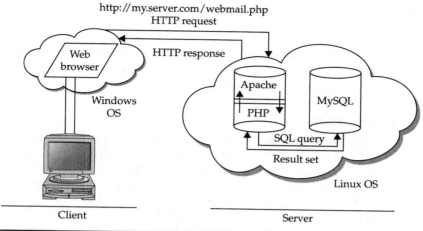

FIGURE 1-1   The LAMP development framework

Wondering what a LAMP stack is? Well, the term refers to a set of open-source software components that are commonly used in conjunction with each other to build web-based applications. These components are

- A base operating system and server environment (**Linux**)
- A web server (**Apache**) to intercept HTTP requests and either serve them directly or pass them on to the PHP interpreter for execution
- A database engine (**MySQL**) that holds application data, accepts connections from the application layer, and modifies or retrieves data from the database
- A programming toolkit (**PHP**, **Perl**, or **Python**) that parses and executes program code, processes database results, and returns results to the client

Figure 1-1 illustrates the four elements of the LAMP framework in action.

Data Warehouses

As the opening paragraph in this chapter notes, businesses are becoming more and more intelligent in how they store, filter, and use information. Data warehouses are a key source of this business intelligence. Typically, data in a data warehouse is gathered from an enterprise's internal information systems, linked, and stored for long periods of time. In its simplest form, this data merely provides a record of past events; however, it can also be "mined" to detect patterns, which serve as input into an organization's decision-making. Speed of data retrieval is thus one crucial component of a data warehouse; long-term reliability is another.

MySQL scores high on both counts. It supports engine-level data integrity through the use of primary key and foreign key constraints. An extremely efficient query-caching mechanism dramatically enhances response times for queries that are called upon to retrieve the exact same data as a previous query. MySQL InnoDB table format uses asynchronous I/O and a sequential read-ahead buffer to improve data retrieval speed, and a "buddy algorithm" and Oracle-type tablespaces for optimized file and memory management. For data storage reliability, MySQL supports replication, a data distribution mechanism that places copies of tables and databases in remote locations to reduce downtime in case of a server failure.

Business Applications

As a reliable, feature-rich database server, MySQL also has applications in business, education, science, and engineering—a fact amply demonstrated by its customer list, which includes such names as Motorola, Sony, NASA, HP, Xerox, and Silicon Graphics. Whether it is small, embedded applications or high-availability data processing systems, MySQL offers the scalability and performance needed to achieve business objectives. The MySQL website states that "MySQL scales to deal with billions of rows and terabytes of data, making it suitable for a wide range of transactional and analytic applications."

To take advantage of multiprocessor architecture, MySQL is built using a multithreaded design, which allows threads to be allocated between processors to achieve a higher degree of parallelism. MySQL's clustering technology allows data to be distributed across multiple nodes to achieve greater redundancy, while its fully ACID-compliant transactional engine provides a high degree of safety from undetected data loss. At the other end of the scale, MySQL's embedded server library has a 1-MB memory/4-MB disk space footprint and provides a multithreaded, cross-platform data storage engine for use in kiosk-style applications or appliances. Finally, MySQL uses a two-tier privilege system (at the connection level and at the individual object level) to ensure the security and integrity of its data, and supports the SSL encryption protocol for client/server communication.

Summary

This chapter provided a gentle introduction to the world of MySQL, discussing the history and evolution of the product and highlighting some of its unique features and advantages vis-à-vis competing alternatives. It explained the various components of the MySQL architecture, discussed some of the key technical features of the MySQL engine, and illustrated how they interact with each other. Finally, it discussed some of MySQL's real-world applications, notably with regard to web application development, data warehousing, and industrial applications.

If you'd like to learn more about the topics discussed in this chapter, consider visiting the following links:

- A more detailed history of MySQL at http://www.linuxjournal.com/article.php?sid=3609
- The MySQL development roadmap at http://dev.mysql.com/doc/refman/5.1/en/roadmap.html

- The MySQL manual at http://dev.mysql.com/doc
- An overview of MySQL's technical architecture at http://dev.mysql.com/doc/refman/5.1/en/pluggable-storage-overview.html
- MySQL case studies at http://www.mysql.com/why-mysql/case-studies
- MySQL customer listings at http://www.mysql.com/customers
- MySQL market share and usage statistics at http://www.mysql.com/why-mysql/marketshare
- MySQL performance benchmarks at http://www.eweek.com/article2/0,3959,293,00.asp and http://www.mysql.com/why-mysql/benchmarks
- Awards won by MySQL at http://www.mysql.com/why-mysql/awards

CHAPTER 2

Understanding Basic Commands

You already know that an electronic database management system (DBMS) is a
tool that helps you organize information efficiently so it becomes easier to find
exactly what you need. A relational database management system (RDBMS) like
MySQL takes things a step further by enabling you to create links between the various
pieces of data in a database and use the relationships to analyze the data in different
ways.

Most of the time, your primary tool to perform these tasks is a language known as
Structured Query Language (SQL). To use MySQL effectively, you'll need to be able to
speak SQL fluently—it's your primary means of interacting with the database server,
and it plays a very important role in helping you get to the data you need rapidly and
efficiently.

This chapter, which is aimed primarily at users new to MySQL, explains some of
the basic SQL commands to manipulate database structures and records. If you've
never used a database before, this chapter should give you the basic information you
need to understand the more advanced material in subsequent chapters. Alternatively,
if you're familiar with another flavor of RDBMS, you can use this chapter as a quick-
and-dirty refresher, or flip through it to understand how MySQL's dialect of SQL
differs from other database systems.

Understanding Basic Concepts

To truly understand how a database works, you need to move from abstract theoretical
concepts to practical real-world examples. This section does just that, by using a simple
example database to explain some of the basic concepts you must know before
proceeding further in this book.

Databases, Tables, and Records

Every database is composed of one or more tables. These tables, which structure data
into rows and columns, are what lend organization to the data.

Figure 2-1 illustrates what a typical table looks like.

AirportID	AirportCode	AirportName	CityName	CountryCode	NumRunways	NumTerminals
34	ORY	Paris-Orly Airport	Paris	FR	3	2
48	LGW	Gatwick Airport	London	UK	2	2
56	LHR	Heathrow Airport	London	UK	2	5
59	CIA	Rome Ciampino Airport	Rome	IT	1	1
62	AMS	Schiphol Airport	Amsterdam	NL	6	1
72	BCN	Barcelona International Airport	Barcelona	ES	3	3
74	MUC	Franz Josef Strauss Airport	Munich	DE	3	2
83	LIS	Lisbon Airport	Lisbon	PT	2	2
87	BUD	Budapest Ferihegy International	Budapest	HU	2	2
92	ZRH	Zurich Airport	Zurich	CH	3	1
126	BOM	Chhatrapati Shivaji International	Bombay	IN	2	2
132	MAD	Barajas Airport	Madrid	ES	4	4

FIGURE 2-1   A table containing airport information

As you can see, a table divides data into rows, with a new entry (or record) on every row. The data in each row is further broken down into columns (or fields), each of which contains a value for a particular attribute of that data. For example, consider the record for Heathrow Airport, and you'll see that the record is clearly divided into separate fields for the airport code, name, city, country, number of runways, and number of terminals.

TIP *Think of a table as a drawer containing files. A record is the electronic representation of a file in the drawer.*

Primary and Foreign Keys

Records within a table are not arranged in any particular order—they can be sorted alphabetically, by ID, by member name, or by any other criteria you choose to specify. Therefore, it becomes necessary to have some method of identifying a specific record in a table. In the previous example, each airport record is identified by a unique number, and this unique field is referred to as the *primary key* for that table. Primary keys don't appear automatically; you have to explicitly mark a field as a primary key when you create a table.

TIP *Think of a primary key as a label on each file that tells you what it contains. In the absence of this label, the files would all look the same and it would be difficult for you to identify the one(s) you need.*

With a relational database system like MySQL, it's also possible to link information in one table to information in another. When you begin to do this, the true power of an RDBMS becomes evident. So let's add one more table, this one listing flight routes between airport pairs (Figure 2-2).

If you take a close look at this second table, you'll see that it lists flight routes between different pairs of airports using the airport codes from the first table. Thus, you can see that route 1003 links Bombay and London (a distance of 7200 km), while route 1176 links London and Madrid (a distance of 1267 km).

Let's now add two more tables to define the flight schedule for the routes described previously (Figure 2-3).

These tables add a further level of detail by linking flight routes with the actual flight schedule for those routes. Thus, we see that flight 876 flies the London-Madrid route on Mondays, Tuesdays, Wednesdays, Thursdays, and Fridays, while flight 535 operates the Paris-London route on Tuesdays and Thursdays only.

FIGURE 2-2
A table listing routes between airport pairs

RouteID	From	To	Distance	Duration	Status
1003	126	56	7200	550	1
1005	34	48	343	85	1
1176	56	132	1267	150	1
1175	132	56	1267	150	1

FlightID	RouteID	AircraftID
535	1005	3451
876	1175	3467
652	1018	3465

FlightID	DepDay	DepTime
535	2	15:30:00
535	4	15:30:00
876	1	7:10:00
876	2	7:10:00
876	3	7:10:00
876	4	7:10:00
876	5	7:10:00
652	1	14:10:00
652	2	14:10:00
652	3	14:10:00
652	4	14:10:00
652	5	14:10:00
652	6	17:45:00
652	7	17:45:00

FIGURE 2-3   Two tables listing flight schedules for various routes

To understand these relationships visually, look at Figure 2-4.

Relationships such as those described previously form the foundation of a relational database system. The common fields used to link the tables together are called *foreign keys*, and when every foreign key value is related to a field in another table, this relationship being unique, the system is said to be in a state of *referential integrity*. In other words, if the *AirportID* field is present once and only once in each table that uses it, and if a change to the *AirportID* field in any single table is reflected in all other tables, referential integrity is said to exist.

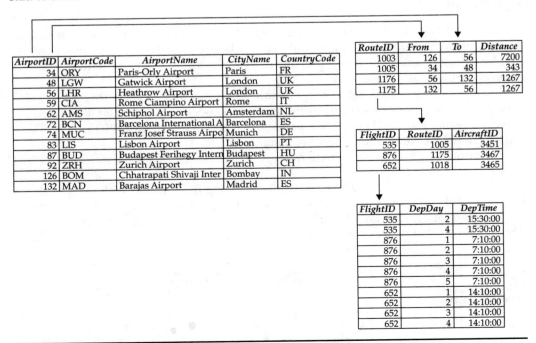

FIGURE 2-4   The inter-relationships between airports, routes, and flights

Once one or more relationships are set up between tables, it is possible to extract a subset of the data (a *data slice*) to answer specific questions. The act of pulling out this data is referred to as a *query*, and the resulting data is referred to as a *result set*. And it's in creating these queries, as well as in manipulating the database itself, that SQL truly comes into its own.

Referential Integrity

Referential integrity is a basic concept with an RDBMS, and one that becomes important when designing a database with more than one table. When foreign keys are used to link one table to another, referential integrity, by its nature, imposes constraints on inserting new records and updating existing records. For example, if a table only accepts certain types of values for a particular field, and other tables use that field as their foreign key, this automatically imposes certain constraints on the dependent tables. Similarly, referential integrity demands that a change in the field used as a foreign key—a deletion or new insertion—must immediately be reflected in all dependent tables.

Many of today's databases take care of this automatically—if you've worked with Microsoft Access, for example, you'll have seen this in action—but some don't. In the latter case, the task of maintaining referential integrity becomes a manual one in which the values in all dependent tables have to be updated manually whenever the value in the primary table changes. Because using foreign keys can degrade the performance of your RDBMS, MySQL leaves the choice of activating such automatic updates (and losing some measure of performance) or deactivating foreign keys (and gaining the benefits of greater speed) to the developer by making it possible to choose a different type for each table.

Structured Query Language (SQL)

SQL began life as SEQUEL, the Structured English Query Language, a component of an IBM research project called System/R. System/R was a prototype of the first relational database system; it was created at IBM's San Jose laboratories in 1974, and SEQUEL was the first query language to support multiple tables and multiple users. The name SEQUEL was later changed to SQL for legal reasons.

In the late 1970s, SQL made its first appearance in a commercial role as the query language used by the Oracle RDBMS. This was quickly followed by the Ingres RDBMS, which also used SQL, and by the 1980s, SQL had become the de facto standard for the rapidly growing RDBMS industry. In 1989, SQL became an ANSI standard commonly referred to as SQL89; this was later updated in 1992 to become SQL92 or SQL2, the standard in use on most of today's commercial RDBMSs (including MySQL).

NOTE   *Although most of today's commercial RDBMSs do support the SQL92 standard, many of them also take liberties with the specification, extending SQL with proprietary extensions and enhancements. MySQL is an example of one such RDBMS. Most often, these enhancements are designed to improve performance or add extra functionality to the system; however, they can cause substantial difficulties when migrating from one DBMS to another.*

As a language, SQL was designed to be "human-friendly"; most of its commands resemble spoken English, making it easy to read, understand, and learn. Commands are formulated as statements, and every statement begins with an "action word." The following examples demonstrate this:

```
CREATE DATABASE toys;
USE toys;
SELECT id FROM toys WHERE targetAge > 3;
DELETE FROM toys WHERE productionStatus = "Revoked";
```

As these examples illustrate, SQL syntax is close to spoken English, and this makes it quite easy for novice programmers to learn and use. SQL statements can be divided into three broad categories, each concerned with a different aspect of database management.

- **Statements used to define the structure of a database**   These statements define the relationships among different pieces of data; definitions for database, table, and column types; and database indexes. In the SQL specification, this component is referred to as Data Definition Language (DDL).

- **Statements used to manipulate data**   These statements control adding and removing records, querying and joining tables, and verifying data integrity. In the SQL specification, this component is referred to as Data Manipulation Language (DML).

- **Statements used to control the permissions and access level to different pieces of data**   These statements define the access levels and security privileges for databases, tables, and fields, which may be specified on a per-user and/or per-host basis. In the SQL specification, this component is referred to as Data Control Language (DCL).

Typically, every SQL statement ends in a semicolon, and white space, tabs, and carriage returns are ignored by the SQL processor. The following two statements are equivalent, even though the first is on a single line and the second is split over multiple lines.

```
DELETE FROM toys WHERE productionStatus = "Revoked";

DELETE FROM
        toys
   WHERE productionStatus =

"Revoked";
```

Database Normalization

An important part of designing a database is a process known as normalization. *Normalization* refers to the activity of streamlining a database design by eliminating redundancies and repeated values. Most often, redundancies are eliminated by placing repeating groups of values into separate tables and linking them through foreign keys.

This not only makes the database more compact and reduces the disk space it occupies, but it also simplifies the task of making changes. In non-normalized databases, because values are usually repeated in different tables, altering them is a manual (and error-prone) find-and-replace process. In a normalized database, because values appear only once, making changes is a simple one-step UPDATE.

The normalization process also includes validating the database relationships to ensure that there aren't any crossed wires and to eliminate incorrect dependencies. This is a worthy goal, because when you create convoluted table relationships, you add greater complexity to your database design ... and greater complexity translates into slower query time as the optimizer tries to figure out how best to handle your table joins.

A number of so-called *normal forms* are defined to help you correctly normalize a database. A *normal form* is simply a set of rules that a database must conform to. Five such normal forms exist, ranging from the completely non-normalized database to the fully normalized one.

Working with Databases and Tables

Now that you have an understanding of basic RDBMS concepts, let's put the theory into practice. The following sections will guide you through a fast-paced tutorial that introduces you to the MySQL command-line client and shows you how to create a database, add tables and records to it, and write queries to retrieve data from it.

Using the MySQL Command-Line Client

The MySQL RDBMS consists of two primary components: the MySQL database server itself and a suite of client-side programs, including an interactive client and utilities to manage MySQL user permissions, view and copy databases, and import and export data. If you installed and tested MySQL according to the procedure outlined in Appendix A of this book, you've already met the MySQL command-line client. This client is your primary means of interacting with the MySQL server, and this section will get you started with it.

To begin, ensure that your MySQL server is running and then connect to it by entering the command *mysql* at your command prompt to invoke the command-line client. Remember to send a valid password with your username, or else MySQL will reject your connection attempt. (Throughout this section and the ones that follow, boldface type is used to indicate commands that you should enter at the prompt).

```
[user@host]# mysql -u root -p
Password: ******
```

If all went well, you'll see a prompt like this:

```
Welcome to the MySQL monitor.  Commands end with ; or \g.
Your MySQL connection id is 70 to server version: 5.0.15
Type 'help;' or '\h' for help. Type '\c' to clear the buffer.
mysql>
```

The mysql> you see is an interactive prompt, where you enter SQL statements. Statements entered here are transmitted to the MySQL server using a proprietary client-server protocol, and the results are transmitted back using the same format.

Try this out by sending the server a simple statement:

```
mysql> SELECT 6*3;
+------+
| 6*3 |
+------+
|  18 |
+------+
1 row in set (0.01 sec)
```

Here, the SELECT statement is used to perform an arithmetic operation on the server and return the results to the client. Statements entered at the prompt must be terminated with either a semicolon or a \g signal, followed by a carriage return, to send the statement to the server. Statements can be entered in either uppercase or lowercase type.

The response returned by the server is displayed in tabular form as rows and columns. The number of rows returned, as well as the time taken to execute the statement, is also printed. If you're dealing with extremely large databases, this information can come in handy to analyze the speed of your queries.

White space, tabs, and carriage returns in SQL statements are ignored. In the MySQL command-line client, typing a carriage return without ending the statement correctly simply causes the client to jump to a new line and wait for further input. The continuation character -> is displayed in such situations to indicate that the statement is not yet complete.

You can close the connection to the server and exit the client at any time by typing **quit** at the mysql> prompt.

```
mysql> quit
Bye
```

Don't quit just yet, though—there's a database waiting to be created!

Creating Databases

Because all tables are stored in a database, the first statement you need to know is the CREATE DATABASE statement, which initializes an empty database. Try it out by creating a database called db1:

```
mysql> CREATE DATABASE db1;
Query OK, 1 row affected (0.05 sec)
```

Databases in MySQL are represented as directories on the disk, and tables are represented as files within those directories. Therefore, database names must comply with the operating system's (OS) restrictions on which characters are permissible within directory names. Database names cannot exceed 64 characters, and names that contain special characters or consist entirely of digits or reserved words must be quoted with the backtick (`) operator.

TIP *To simplify moving databases and tables between different operating systems, lowercase all database and table names, and ensure they consist of only alphanumeric and underscore characters. Try to avoid using reserved MySQL keywords as database names.*

To select a particular database as the default for all subsequent statements, use the USE statement. Here's an example:

```
mysql> USE db1;
Database changed
```

Creating Tables

Once you've got a database, the next step is to add some tables to it. To create a table, use the CREATE TABLE statement, as in the following listing:

```
mysql> CREATE TABLE airport (
    ->    AirportID smallint(5) unsigned NOT NULL,
    ->    AirportCode char(3) NOT NULL,
    ->    AirportName varchar(255) NOT NULL,
    ->    CityName varchar(255) NOT NULL,
    ->    CountryCode char(2) NOT NULL,
    ->    Runways INT(11) unsigned NOT NULL,
    ->    NumTerminals tinyint(1) unsigned NOT NULL,
    ->    PRIMARY KEY  (AirportID)
    -> ) ENGINE=InnoDB;
Query OK, 0 rows affected (0.38 sec)
```

The CREATE TABLE statement begins with the table name, followed by a set of parentheses. These parentheses enclose one or more *field definitions,* separated by commas. Each field definition contains the field name, its data type, and any special modifiers or constraints that apply. Following the closing parenthesis is an optional *table type specifier,* which tells MySQL which storage engine to use for this table.

Table and field names must conform to the same rules that apply to database names. MySQL tables are stored as files within the database directory and, as such, are subject to the host operating system's rules on filenames.

Specifying Field Data Types

When creating a MySQL table, specifying a data type for every field is necessary. This data type plays an important role in enforcing the integrity of the data in a MySQL database and in making this data easier to use and manipulate. MySQL offers a number of different data types, which are summarized in Table 2-1.

Type	Used For
TINYINT, SMALLINT, MEDIUMINT, INT, BIGINT	Integer values
FLOAT	Single-precision floating-point values
DOUBLE	Double-precision floating-point values
DECIMAL	Decimal values
BIT	Bit-field values
CHAR	Fixed-length strings up to 255 characters
VARCHAR	Variable-length strings up to 255 characters
TINYBLOB, BLOB, MEDIUMBLOB, LONGBLOB	Binary data
TINYTEXT, TEXT, MEDIUMTEXT, LONGTEXT	Text blocks
DATE	Date values
TIME	Time values or durations
YEAR	Year values
DATETIME, TIMESTAMP	Combined date and time values
ENUM, SET	Predefined sets of values

TABLE 2-1   MySQL Data Types

These data types are discussed in greater detail later in Chapter 3.

Adding Field Modifiers and Keys

A number of additional constraints, or modifiers, can be applied to a field to increase the consistency of the data that will be entered into it and to mark it as "special" in some way. These modifiers can either appear as part of the field definition, if they apply only to that specific field (for example, a default value for a field), or after all the field definitions, if they relate to multiple fields (for example, a multicolumn primary key).

- To specify whether the field is allowed to be empty or if it must necessarily be filled with data, place the NULL and NOT NULL modifiers after each field definition.

- To specify a default value for a field, use the DEFAULT modifier. This default value is used if no value is specified for that field when inserting a record. In the absence of a DEFAULT modifier for NOT NULL fields, MySQL automatically inserts a nonthreatening default value into the field.

- To have MySQL automatically generate a number for a field (by incrementing the previous value by 1), use the AUTO_INCREMENT modifier. This is particularly useful to generate row numbers for each record in the table. However, the AUTO_INCREMENT modifier can only be applied to numeric fields that are both NOT NULL and belong to the PRIMARY KEY. A table may only contain one AUTO_INCREMENT field.

- To specify the character set for fields containing string values, use the CHARACTER SET modifier.

- To *index* a field, use the INDEX modifier. When a field is indexed in this manner, MySQL no longer needs to scan each row of the table for a match when performing queries; instead, it can simply look up the index. Indexing is recommended for fields that frequently appear in the WHERE, ORDER BY, and GROUP BY clauses of SELECT queries and for fields used to join tables together.

- A variant of the INDEX modifier is the UNIQUE modifier, which is a special type of index used to ensure that values entered into a field must be either unique or NULL.

- To specify a primary key for the table, use the PRIMARY KEY modifier. The PRIMARY KEY constraint can best be thought of as a combination of the NOT NULL and UNIQUE constraints because it requires values in the specified field to be neither NULL nor repeated in any other row. It thus serves as a unique identifier for each record in the table, and it should be selected only after careful thought has been given to the inter-relationships between tables.

- To specify a foreign key for a table, use the FOREIGN KEY modifier. The FOREIGN KEY modifier links a field in one table to a field (usually a primary key) in another table, setting up a base for relationships. However, foreign keys are only supported in MySQL's InnoDB storage engine; the FOREIGN KEY modifier is simply ignored in all other engines.

TIP Indexes, primary keys, and foreign keys play an important role in determining both the performance and integrity of your database. These topics are discussed in greater detail in Chapter 3.

Selecting a Storage Engine

Following the field definitions and modifiers come one or more table modifiers, which specify table-level attributes. Of these, the most frequently used one is the ENGINE modifier, which tells MySQL which *storage engine*, or table type, to use. A number of such engines are available, each with different advantages. Table 2-2 has a list.

Type	Description
ISAM	Legacy engine
MYISAM	Revision of ISAM engine with support for dynamic-length fields
INNODB	ACID-compliant transactional engine with support for foreign keys
MEMORY	Memory-based engine with support for hash indexes
CSV	Text-based engine for CSV recordsets

TABLE 2-2 MySQL Storage Engines

Type	Description
ARCHIVE	Engine with compression features for large recordsets
FEDERATED	Engine for remote tables
NDB	Engine for clustered tables
MERGE	Engine for merged tables
BLACKHOLE	Bitbucket engine

TABLE 2-2   MySQL Storage Engines *(continued)*

These storage engines are discussed in greater detail later in Chapter 3.

Using Other Table Modifiers

The TYPE attribute isn't the only option available to control the behavior of the table being created. A number of other MySQL-specific attributes are also available. Here's a list of the more interesting ones.

- The AUTO_INCREMENT modifier specifies the starting value to use for AUTO_INCREMENT fields in the table.

- The CHARACTER SET and COLLATE modifiers specify the table character set and collation.

- The CHECKSUM modifier controls whether table checksums should be calculated and stored.

- The COMMENT modifier saves a descriptive label for the table.

- The MAX_ROWS and MIN_ROWS modifiers specify the maximum and minimum number of rows the table is likely to have.

- The PACK_KEYS modifier controls whether table indexes are compressed. Compressing indexes reduces the table's size on disk, but can affect performance (as indexes need to be uncompressed every time they are updated).

- The DELAY_KEY_WRITE modifier controls whether table indexes are updated only after all writes to the table are complete. This can improve performance for tables that see a high frequency of writes.

- The UNION modifier specifies a list of tables to be merged (only useful with the MERGE storage engine).

- The DATA DIRECTORY and INDEX DIRECTORY modifiers specify custom paths for the table data and index files.

Altering Tables

Table definitions created with the CREATE TABLE statement are not set in stone—it's easy to alter them at a later date as well. The SQL statement to do this is the ALTER TABLE statement. It is used to add or delete fields; alter field types; add, remove, or modify keys; alter the table type; and change the table name (among other things). The following sections discuss these capabilities in greater detail.

Altering Table Names

To alter a table name, use an ALTER TABLE statement with a supplementary RENAME clause. The following example demonstrates by renaming table bills to invoices:

```
mysql> ALTER TABLE airport RENAME TO cities;
Query OK, 0 rows affected (0.28 sec)
```

An alternative is to use the RENAME TABLE statement, which does the same thing. Here's an example, which reverses the previous operation:

```
mysql> RENAME TABLE cities TO airport;
Query OK, 0 rows affected (0.06 sec)
```

Altering Field Names and Properties

A CHANGE clause can be used to alter a field's name, type, and properties, simply by using a new field definition instead of the original one. Here's an example, which changes the field named *Runways* defined as INT(11) to a field named *NumRunways* with definition TINYINT(1):

```
mysql> ALTER TABLE airport CHANGE Runways NumRunways TINYINT(1);
Query OK, 0 rows affected (0.23 sec)
Records: 0  Duplicates: 0  Warnings: 0
```

When a field is changed from one type to another, MySQL will automatically attempt to convert the data in that field to the new type. If the data in the field is inconsistent with the new field definition—for example, a field defined as NOT NULL contains NULL values, or a field marked as UNIQUE contains duplicate values—MySQL will generate an error. To alter this default behavior, add an IGNORE clause to the ALTER TABLE statement that tells MySQL to ignore such inconsistencies.

Adding and Removing Fields and Keys

To add a new field to a table, place an ADD clause in your ALTER TABLE statement. The following example demonstrates by adding a field named *StartYear* to the *airports* table:

```
mysql> ALTER TABLE airport ADD StartYear YEAR NOT NULL;
Query OK, 0 rows affected (0.26 sec)
Records: 0  Duplicates: 0  Warnings: 0
```

To do the reverse—delete an existing field from a table—use a DROP clause instead of an ADD clause. The following example removes the field added in the previous operation (along with any data it might have contained):

```
mysql> ALTER TABLE airport DROP StartYear;
Query OK, 0 rows affected (0.18 sec)
Records: 0  Duplicates: 0  Warnings: 0
```

To delete a table's primary key, use the DROP PRIMARY KEY clause, as illustrated here:

```
mysql> ALTER TABLE airport DROP PRIMARY KEY;
Query OK, 0 rows affected (0.06 sec)
```

To add a new primary key, use the ADD PRIMARY KEY clause, as illustrated here:

```
mysql> ALTER TABLE airport ADD PRIMARY KEY (AirportID);
Query OK, 0 rows affected (0.05 sec)
```

TIP *A table's primary key must always be* NOT NULL.

Altering Table Types

To alter the table's storage engine, add an ENGINE clause to the ALTER TABLE statement with the name of the new storage engine, as in the following example:

```
mysql> ALTER TABLE airport ENGINE = INNODB;
Query OK, 6 rows affected (0.11 sec)
```

CAUTION *To execute an* ALTER TABLE *statement, MySQL first creates a copy of the original table, changes it, and then deletes the original table and replaces it with the changed copy. For this reason,* ALTER TABLE *operations on large tables may take a fair amount of time.*

Removing Tables and Databases

To remove a database, use the DROP DATABASE statement, which deletes the named database and all its tables permanently. Similarly, to delete a table, use the DROP TABLE statement. Try this out by creating and dropping a database and a table:

```
mysql> CREATE DATABASE music;
Query OK, 1 row affected (0.05 sec)
mysql> CREATE TABLE member ( MemberID INT NOT NULL );
Query OK, 0 rows affected (0.00 sec)
mysql> DROP TABLE member;
Query OK, 0 rows affected (0.00 sec)
mysql> DROP DATABASE music;
Query OK, 0 rows affected (0.49 sec)
```

These DROP statements will immediately wipe out the target, along with all the data it contains—so use them with care!

TIP *If what you actually intended was to empty the table of all records, use the* TRUNCATE TABLE *statement instead, which internally* DROP-s *the table and then re-creates it. The* AUTO_INCREMENT *counter, if one exists, is automatically reset in* TRUNCATE TABLE *operations (this does not happen if you simply delete all the records in the table with a* DELETE *statement).*

Working with Records

Once databases and tables are defined, the next step is to begin using them by populating them with records and performing queries on the data stored inside them. This section discusses the SQL statements to add, edit, and delete records to a table and then perform different types of queries on that data to retrieve a result set of records that satisfy the query.

Creating Records

Once you've created a table, it's time to begin entering data into it. The SQL statement to accomplish this is the INSERT statement. The syntax of the INSERT statement is illustrated in the following example:

```
mysql> INSERT INTO airport (AirportID, AirportCode, AirportName,
    -> CityName, CountryCode, NumRunways, NumTerminals)
    -> VALUES (34, 'ORY', 'Orly Airport', 'Paris', 'FR', 3, 2);
Query OK, 1 row affected (0.09 sec)
```

The INSERT statement is followed by the optional keyword INTO, a table name, and a field list, in parentheses, which indicates which fields the values are to be inserted into. A VALUES clause completes the statement by specifying the values to be inserted into the previously named fields.

MySQL also allows multiple records to be inserted into a table at once by using multiple VALUES() clauses within the same INSERT statement. To see how this works, try running the following statements:

```
mysql> INSERT INTO airport (AirportID, AirportCode, AirportName,
    -> CityName, CountryCode, NumRunways, NumTerminals)
    -> VALUES
    -> (48, 'LGW', 'Gatwick Airport',
    ->    'London', 'GB', 3, 1),
    -> (56, 'LHR', 'Heathrow Airport',
    ->    'London', 'GB', 2, 5),
    -> (59, 'CIA', 'Rome Ciampino Airport',
    ->    'Rome', 'IT', 1, 1),
    -> (72, 'BCN', 'Barcelona International Airport',
    ->    'Barcelona', 'ES', 3, 3);
Query OK, 4 rows affected (0.05 sec)
Records: 4  Duplicates: 0  Warnings: 0


mysql> INSERT INTO airport (AirportID, AirportCode, AirportName,
    -> CityName, CountryCode, NumRunways, NumTerminals)
    -> VALUES
    -> (62, 'AMS', 'Schiphol Airport',
    ->    'Amsterdam', 'NL', 6, 1),
    -> (74, 'MUC', 'Franz Josef Strauss Airport',
    ->    'Munich', 'DE', 3, 2),
```

```
        -> (83, 'LIS', 'Lisbon Airport',
        ->    'Lisbon', 'PT', 2, 2),
        -> (87, 'BUD', 'Budapest Ferihegy International Airport',
        ->    'Budapest', 'HU', 2, 2),
        -> (92, 'ZRH', 'Zurich Airport ',
        ->    'Zurich', 'CH', 3, 1),
        -> (126, 'BOM', 'Chhatrapati Shivaji International Airport ',
        ->    'Bombay', 'IN', 2, 2),
        -> (129, 'BRS', 'Bristol International Airport',
        ->    'Bristol', 'GB', 1, 1),
        -> (132, 'MAD', 'Barajas Airport',
        ->    'Madrid', 'ES', 4, 4),
        -> (165, 'NCE', 'Nice CÙte d''Azur Airport ',
        ->    'Nice', 'FR', 2, 2),
        -> (201, 'SIN', 'Changi Airport',
        ->    'Singapore', 'SG', 3, 3);
Query OK, 10 rows affected (0.07 sec)
Records: 10   Duplicates: 0   Warnings: 0
```

MySQL can automatically perform the following operations:

- For AUTO_INCREMENT fields, entering a NULL value automatically increments the previously generated field value by 1.
- For the first TIMESTAMP field in a table, entering a NULL value automatically inserts the current date and time.
- For UNIQUE or PRIMARY KEY fields, entering a value that already exists causes MySQL to generate an error.

TIP *When inserting string and some date values into a table, enclose them in quotation marks so that MySQL doesn't confuse them with variable or field names. Quotation marks within the values themselves can be "escaped" by preceding them with the backslash (\) symbol.*

Removing and Modifying Records

Just as you INSERT records into a table, so, too, can you remove records with the DELETE statement. You can select a specific subset of rows to be deleted by adding the WHERE clause to the DELETE statement. The following example would only delete records for those airports with three or more terminals:

```
mysql> DELETE FROM airport WHERE NumTerminals >= 3;
Query OK, 4 rows affected (0.05 sec)
```

Omitting the WHERE clause in a DELETE statement would delete all the records from the table.

CAUTION *It is not possible to reverse a* DELETE *operation in MySQL (unless you're in the middle of an InnoDB transaction that hasn't yet been committed). Therefore, be extremely careful when using* DELETE *commands, both with and without* WHERE *clauses—a small mistake and the contents of your entire table will be lost for good.*

Data in a database usually changes over time, which is why SQL includes an UPDATE statement designed to change existing values in a table. As with DELETE, UPDATE can be used to change all the values in a particular field, or to change only those values matching a particular condition. To illustrate how this works, consider the following example, which changes the country code 'GB' to 'UK.'

```
mysql> UPDATE airport SET CountryCode = 'UK'
    -> WHERE CountryCode = 'GB';
Query OK, 3 rows affected (0.24 sec)
Rows matched: 3   Changed: 3  Warnings: 0
```

Thus, the SET clause specifies the field name, as well as the new value for the field; the WHERE clause is used to identify which rows of the table to change. In the absence of this clause, all the rows of the table are updated with the new value.

To update multiple fields at once, simply use multiple SET clauses. The following example illustrates by updating the record for Gatwick Airport with new values:

```
mysql> UPDATE airport SET NumTerminals = 2,
    -> NumRunways = 2 WHERE AirportCode = 'LGW';
Query OK, 1 row affected (0.10 sec)
Rows matched: 1   Changed: 1  Warnings: 0
```

Retrieving Records

Just as you can add records to a table with the INSERT statement, you can retrieve them with the SELECT statement. The SELECT statement is one of the most versatile and useful statements in SQL. It offers tremendous flexibility in extracting specific subsets of data from a table.

In its most basic form, the SELECT statement can be used to evaluate expressions and functions, or as a "catch-all" query that returns all the records in a specific table. Here is an example of using SELECT to evaluate mathematical expressions:

```
mysql> SELECT 75 / 15, 61 + (3 * 3);
+---------+---------------+
| 75 / 15 | 61 + (3 * 3)  |
+---------+---------------+
|    5.00 |            70 |
+---------+---------------+
1 row in set (0.05 sec)
```

And here is an example of using SELECT to retrieve all the records in a table:

```
mysql> SELECT * FROM airport\G


*************************** 1. row ***************************
      AirportID: 34
    AirportCode: ORY
    AirportName: Orly Airport
       CityName: Paris
    CountryCode: FR
     NumRunways: 3
   NumTerminals: 2
*************************** 2. row ***************************
      AirportID: 48
    AirportCode: LGW
    AirportName: Gatwick Airport
       CityName: London
    CountryCode: UK
     NumRunways: 2
   NumTerminals: 2
*************************** 3. row ***************************
      AirportID: 56
    AirportCode: LHR
    AirportName: Heathrow Airport
       CityName: London
    CountryCode: UK
     NumRunways: 2
   NumTerminals: 5
*************************** 4. row ***************************
      AirportID: 59
    AirportCode: CIA
    AirportName: Rome Ciampino Airport
       CityName: Rome
    CountryCode: IT
     NumRunways: 1
   NumTerminals: 1
*************************** 5. row ***************************
      AirportID: 62
    AirportCode: AMS
    AirportName: Schiphol Airport
       CityName: Amsterdam
    CountryCode: NL
     NumRunways: 6
   NumTerminals: 1
*************************** 6. row ***************************
      AirportID: 72
    AirportCode: BCN
    AirportName: Barcelona International Airport
       CityName: Barcelona
```

```
 CountryCode: ES
  NumRunways: 3
NumTerminals: 3
*************************** 7. row ***************************
    AirportID: 74
  AirportCode: MUC
  AirportName: Franz Josef Strauss Airport
     CityName: Munich
  CountryCode: DE
   NumRunways: 3
 NumTerminals: 2
*************************** 8. row ***************************
    AirportID: 83
  AirportCode: LIS
  AirportName: Lisbon Airport
     CityName: Lisbon
  CountryCode: PT
   NumRunways: 2
 NumTerminals: 2
*************************** 9. row ***************************
    AirportID: 87
  AirportCode: BUD
  AirportName: Budapest Ferihegy International Airport
     CityName: Budapest
  CountryCode: HU
   NumRunways: 2
 NumTerminals: 2
*************************** 10. row ***************************
    AirportID: 92
  AirportCode: ZRH
  AirportName: Zurich Airport
     CityName: Zurich
  CountryCode: CH
   NumRunways: 3
 NumTerminals: 1
*************************** 11. row ***************************
    AirportID: 126
  AirportCode: BOM
  AirportName: Chhatrapati Shivaji International Airport
     CityName: Bombay
  CountryCode: IN
   NumRunways: 2
 NumTerminals: 2
*************************** 12. row ***************************
    AirportID: 129
  AirportCode: BRS
  AirportName: Bristol International Airport
     CityName: Bristol
```

```
     CountryCode: UK
      NumRunways: 1
    NumTerminals: 1
*************************** 13. row ***************************
        AirportID: 132
      AirportCode: MAD
      AirportName: Barajas Airport
         CityName: Madrid
      CountryCode: ES
       NumRunways: 4
     NumTerminals: 4
*************************** 14. row ***************************
        AirportID: 165
      AirportCode: NCE
      AirportName: Nice Côte d'Azur Airport
         CityName: Nice
      CountryCode: FR
       NumRunways: 2
     NumTerminals: 2
*************************** 15. row ***************************
        AirportID: 201
      AirportCode: SIN
      AirportName: Changi Airport
         CityName: Singapore
      CountryCode: SG
       NumRunways: 3
     NumTerminals: 3
15 rows in set (0.02 sec)
```

Retrieving Specific Fields

The asterisk (*) in the previous example indicates that the records returned by the SELECT query should contain all the fields present in the table. To return only one or two specific fields, specify their name(s) in the SELECT statement, like this:

```
mysql> SELECT AirportName, NumTerminals FROM airport;
+------------------------------------------------+--------------+
| AirportName                                    | NumTerminals |
+------------------------------------------------+--------------+
| Orly Airport                                   |            2 |
| Gatwick Airport                                |            2 |
| Heathrow Airport                               |            5 |
| Rome Ciampino Airport                          |            1 |
| Schiphol Airport                               |            1 |
| Barcelona International Airport                |            3 |
| Franz Josef Strauss Airport                    |            2 |
| Lisbon Airport                                 |            2 |
| Budapest Ferihegy International Airport        |            2 |
```

```
| Zurich Airport                              |              1 |
| Chhatrapati Shivaji International Airport    |              2 |
| Bristol International Airport                |              1 |
| Barajas Airport                             |              4 |
| Nice Cote d'Azur Airport                    |              2 |
| Changi Airport                              |              3 |
+---------------------------------------------+----------------+
15 rows in set (0.00 sec)
```

Filtering Records with a WHERE Clause

To restrict which records appear in the result set, add a WHERE clause to your SELECT statement. This WHERE clause is used to define specific criteria used to filter records from the result set. Records that do not meet the specified criteria will not appear in the result set.

The following example filters the record set to only display airports in the United Kingdom:

```
mysql> SELECT AirportName FROM airport
    -> WHERE CountryCode = 'UK';
+------------------------------+
| AirportName                  |
+------------------------------+
| Gatwick Airport              |
| Heathrow Airport             |
| Bristol International Airport |
+------------------------------+
3 rows in set (0.00 sec)
```

Using Operators

The = symbol previously used is an equality operator, used to test whether the left side of the expression is equal to the right side. MySQL comes with numerous such operators that can be used in the WHERE clause for comparisons and calculations. Table 2-3 lists the important operators in MySQL by category.

Here is an example of using a comparison operator in the WHERE clause to list airports with three or more terminals:

```
mysql> SELECT AirportName FROM airport
    -> WHERE NumTerminals >= 3;
+---------------------------------+
| AirportName                     |
+---------------------------------+
| Heathrow Airport                |
| Barcelona International Airport  |
| Barajas Airport                 |
| Changi Airport                  |
+---------------------------------+
4 rows in set (0.00 sec)
```

TABLE 2-3 MySQL
Operators

Operator	What It Does
Arithmetic operators	
+	Addition
-	Subtraction
*	Multiplication
/	Division; returns quotient
%	Division; returns modulus
Comparison operators	
=	Equal to
<> aka !=	Not equal to
<=>	NULL-safe equal to
<	Less than
<=	Less than or equal to
>	Greater than
>=	Greater than or equal to
BETWEEN	Exists in specified range
IN	Exists in specified set
IS NULL	Is a NULL value
IS NOT NULL	Is not a NULL value
LIKE	Wildcard match
REGEXP aka RLIKE	Regular expression match
Logical operators	
NOT aka !	Logical NOT
AND aka &&	Logical AND
OR aka ||	Logical OR
XOR	Exclusive OR

Multiple conditions can be combined with the AND or OR logical operators. This next example lists all airports with more than two runways outside the United Kingdom:

```
mysql> SELECT AirportName FROM airport WHERE
    -> NumRunways > 2 AND CountryCode != 'UK';
+----------------------------------+
| AirportName                      |
+----------------------------------+
| Orly Airport                     |
| Schiphol Airport                 |
```

```
| Barcelona International Airport |
| Franz Josef Strauss Airport    |
| Zurich Airport                 |
| Barajas Airport                |
| Changi Airport                 |
+--------------------------------+
7 rows in set (0.00 sec)
```

The LIKE operator can be used to perform queries using wildcards, which comes in handy when you're not sure what you're looking for. Two types of wildcards are allowed when using the LIKE operator: the % wildcard, which is used to signify zero or more occurrences of a character, and the _ wildcard, which is used to signify exactly one occurrence of a character.

This next example uses the LIKE operator with the logical OR operator to list all airports containing the letters *h* or *b*:

```
mysql> SELECT AirportName FROM airport
    -> WHERE AirportName LIKE '%h%'
    -> OR AirportName LIKE '%b%';
+------------------------------------------+
| AirportName                              |
+------------------------------------------+
| Heathrow Airport                         |
| Schiphol Airport                         |
| Barcelona International Airport           |
| Lisbon Airport                           |
| Budapest Ferihegy International Airport  |
| Zurich Airport                           |
| Chhatrapati Shivaji International Airport |
| Bristol International Airport            |
| Barajas Airport                          |
| Changi Airport                           |
+------------------------------------------+
10 rows in set (0.01 sec)
```

Sorting Records and Eliminating Duplicates

To see the data from a table ordered by a specific field, attach the ORDER BY clause to the SELECT statement. This clause enables you to specify both the field name and the sort direction (ASCending or DESCending).

Here is an example of sorting the airport list by three-letter code in ascending order:

```
mysql> SELECT AirportCode, AirportName FROM airport
    -> ORDER BY AirportCode ASC;
```

```
+-------------+------------------------------------------------+
| AirportCode | AirportName                                    |
+-------------+------------------------------------------------+
| AMS         | Schiphol Airport                               |
| BCN         | Barcelona International Airport                |
| BOM         | Chhatrapati Shivaji International Airport      |
| BRS         | Bristol International Airport                  |
| BUD         | Budapest Ferihegy International Airport        |
| CIA         | Rome Ciampino Airport                          |
| LGW         | Gatwick Airport                                |
| LHR         | Heathrow Airport                               |
| LIS         | Lisbon Airport                                 |
| MAD         | Barajas Airport                                |
| MUC         | Franz Josef Strauss Airport                    |
| NCE         | Nice Cote d'Azur Airport                       |
| ORY         | Orly Airport                                   |
| SIN         | Changi Airport                                 |
| ZRH         | Zurich Airport                                 |
+-------------+------------------------------------------------+
15 rows in set (0.06 sec)
```

And here is the same table sorted by city name in descending order:

```
mysql> SELECT CityName, AirportName FROM airport
    -> ORDER BY CityName DESC;
+-----------+------------------------------------------------+
| CityName  | AirportName                                    |
+-----------+------------------------------------------------+
| Zurich    | Zurich Airport                                 |
| Singapore | Changi Airport                                 |
| Rome      | Rome Ciampino Airport                          |
| Paris     | Orly Airport                                   |
| Nice      | Nice Cote d'Azur Airport                       |
| Munich    | Franz Josef Strauss Airport                    |
| Madrid    | Barajas Airport                                |
| London    | Gatwick Airport                                |
| London    | Heathrow Airport                               |
| Lisbon    | Lisbon Airport                                 |
| Budapest  | Budapest Ferihegy International Airport        |
| Bristol   | Bristol International Airport                  |
| Bombay    | Chhatrapati Shivaji International Airport      |
| Barcelona | Barcelona International Airport                |
| Amsterdam | Schiphol Airport                               |
+-----------+------------------------------------------------+
15 rows in set (0.00 sec)
```

To eliminate duplicate records in a table, add the DISTINCT keyword. Consider the following example, which illustrates the use of this keyword by printing a list of all the unique country codes in the airport list:

```
mysql> SELECT DISTINCT CountryCode FROM airport;
+-------------+
| CountryCode |
+-------------+
| FR          |
| UK          |
| IT          |
| NL          |
| ES          |
| DE          |
| PT          |
| HU          |
| CH          |
| IN          |
| SG          |
+-------------+
11 rows in set (0.00 sec)
```

Limiting Results

To limit the number of records returned by MySQL, use the LIMIT clause, as illustrated in the following:

```
mysql> SELECT AirportCode, AirportName, NumTerminals
    -> FROM airport LIMIT 0,3;
+-------------+------------------+--------------+
| AirportCode | AirportName      | NumTerminals |
+-------------+------------------+--------------+
| ORY         | Orly Airport     |            2 |
| LGW         | Gatwick Airport  |            2 |
| LHR         | Heathrow Airport |            5 |
+-------------+------------------+--------------+
3 rows in set (0.08 sec)
```

It is also possible to combine the ORDER BY and LIMIT clauses to return a sorted list restricted to a certain number of values. The following example illustrates by listing the top three airports by number of terminals:

```
mysql> SELECT AirportCode, AirportName, NumTerminals
    -> FROM airport ORDER BY NumTerminals DESC
    -> LIMIT 0,3;
```

```
+----------------+-------------------+---------------+
| AirportCode    | AirportName       | NumTerminals  |
+----------------+-------------------+---------------+
| LHR            | Heathrow Airport  |             5 |
| MAD            | Barajas Airport   |             4 |
| SIN            | Changi Airport    |             3 |
+----------------+-------------------+---------------+
3 rows in set (0.02 sec)
```

Using Built-in Functions

MySQL comes with more than 100 built-in functions to help perform calculations and process the records in a result set. These functions can be used in a SELECT statement, either to manipulate field values or in the WHERE clause. The following example illustrates by using MySQL's COUNT() function to return the total number of airport records:

```
mysql> SELECT COUNT(AirportID) FROM airport;
+------------------+
| COUNT(AirportID) |
+------------------+
|               15 |
+------------------+
1 row in set (0.00 sec)
```

You can calculate string length with the LENGTH() function, as in the following:

```
mysql> SELECT DISTINCT CityName, LENGTH(CityName)
    -> FROM airport LIMIT 0,5;
+-----------+-------------------+
| CityName  | LENGTH(CityName)  |
+-----------+-------------------+
| Paris     |                 5 |
| London    |                 6 |
| Rome      |                 4 |
| Amsterdam |                 9 |
| Barcelona |                 9 |
+-----------+-------------------+
5 rows in set (0.00 sec)
```

You can use the DATE() function to format date and time values into a human-readable form, as illustrated in the following:

```
mysql> SELECT DATE_FORMAT(NOW(), '%W %d %M %Y');
+-----------------------------------+
| DATE_FORMAT(NOW(), '%W %d %M %Y') |
+-----------------------------------+
| Thursday 02 October 2008          |
+-----------------------------------+
1 row in set (0.03 sec)
```

Grouping Records

To group records on the basis of a specific field, use MySQL's GROUP BY clause. Each group created in this manner is treated as a single row, even though it internally contains multiple records. The COUNT() function can be used in this context to count the number of records in each group. Consider the following example, which groups and counts airports by country:

```
mysql> SELECT CountryCode, COUNT(AirportID) AS NumAirports
    -> FROM airport GROUP BY CountryCode;
+-------------+-------------+
| CountryCode | NumAirports |
+-------------+-------------+
| CH          |           1 |
| DE          |           1 |
| ES          |           2 |
| FR          |           2 |
| HU          |           1 |
| IN          |           1 |
| IT          |           1 |
| NL          |           1 |
| PT          |           1 |
| SG          |           1 |
| UK          |           3 |
+-------------+-------------+
11 rows in set (0.02 sec)
```

To further filter the groups, add a HAVING clause to the GROUP BY clause. This HAVING clause works much like a regular WHERE clause, making it possible to filter the grouped data by a specific condition. The following example revises the previous one to only return those countries having two or more airports:

```
mysql> SELECT CountryCode, COUNT(AirportID) AS NumAirports
    -> FROM airport GROUP BY CountryCode
    -> HAVING NumAirports >= 2;
+-------------+-------------+
| CountryCode | NumAirports |
+-------------+-------------+
| ES          |           2 |
| FR          |           2 |
| UK          |           3 |
+-------------+-------------+
3 rows in set (0.00 sec)
```

In addition to the COUNT() function, MySQL offers the MIN() and MAX() functions to retrieve the minimum and maximum of a group, the AVG() function to return the average of a group of values, and the SUM() function to return the total of a group of values.

Using Variables

MySQL supports *user-defined variables*, which come in handy when you need to pass values from one SQL statement to another. These variables are session variables—they remain extant for the duration of the client session, and are automatically destroyed once the client disconnects—and are defined using the SET statement. Note that variable names are case-insensitive and must be prefixed with the @ symbol.

Here's an example:

```
mysql> SET @runways = 3;
Query OK, 0 rows affected (0.02 sec)
mysql> SELECT AirportName, NumRunways
    -> FROM airport
    -> WHERE NumRunways >= @runways;
+---------------------------------+------------+
| AirportName                     | NumRunways |
+---------------------------------+------------+
| Orly Airport                    |          3 |
| Schiphol Airport                |          6 |
| Barcelona International Airport  |          3 |
| Franz Josef Strauss Airport     |          3 |
| Zurich Airport                  |          3 |
| Barajas Airport                 |          4 |
| Changi Airport                  |          3 |
+---------------------------------+------------+
7 rows in set (0.01 sec)
```

Another way to define a variable is to write the result of a SELECT statement into it using the SELECT INTO statement. Here's an example, which finds the airport with the maximum number of inward routes, stores the airport identifier into the @aid variable, and then uses the variable to retrieve the airport name:

```
mysql> SELECT `to` INTO @aid
    -> FROM route
    -> GROUP BY `to`
    -> ORDER BY COUNT(`to`)
    -> DESC LIMIT 1;
Query OK, 1 row affected (0.00 sec)

mysql> SELECT AirportName
    -> FROM airport
    -> WHERE AirportID = @aid;
+------------------+
| AirportName      |
+------------------+
| Heathrow Airport |
+------------------+
1 row in set (0.09 sec)
```

Modifying SELECT Behavior

A number of other keywords can be added to the SELECT statement to modify its behavior.

- The SQL_CACHE and SQL_NO_CACHE keywords tell MySQL whether the query results should be cached.

- The SQL_BUFFER_RESULT keyword forces MySQL to store query results in a temporary table. This result buffer eliminates the need for MySQL to lock the tables used by the query while the results are being transmitted to the client, thus ensuring they can be used by other processes in the interim.

- The SQL_BIG_RESULT and SQL_SMALL_RESULT keywords can be used to indicate the expected size of the result set to MySQL and, thereby, help it identify the most optimal way to sort and store the returned records (disk-based or in-memory temporary tables, respectively).

- The SQL_HIGH_PRIORITY keyword raises the priority of the query over competing UPDATE, INSERT, or DELETE statements, thereby resulting in (slightly) faster query execution on busy database servers.

- The SQL_CALC_FOUND_ROWS keyword tells MySQL to calculate the total number of rows matching the query, without taking into account any LIMIT that might have been set. This total number can then be retrieved via a call to the FOUND_ROWS() function.

Appropriate usage of the SQL_CACHE, SQL_BUFFER_RESULT, SQL_BIG_RESULT, SQL_SMALL_RESULT, and SQL_HIGH_PRIORITY keywords can significantly improve the speed of your transactions with the MySQL server. Chapter 9 has more information on some of these keywords.

Viewing Database, Table, and Field Information

MySQL also comes with a full-featured list of SHOW statements to obtain information about all aspects of the server, its databases, and its tables. Here's a quick list:

- The SHOW DATABASES statement displays a list of databases on the server.

- The SHOW TABLES statement displays a list of tables in a database.

- The DESCRIBE statement displays the structure of a table.

- The SHOW CREATE TABLE statement retrieves the SQL statements originally used to create the table.

- The SHOW INDEX statement displays a list of table indexes.

- The SHOW ENGINES statement retrieves a list of available storage engines.

- The SHOW PROCESSLIST statement displays a list of active connections to the server, as well as what each one is doing.

- The SHOW ERRORS and SHOW WARNINGS statements display a list of errors and warnings generated by the server.

- The SHOW STATUS statement displays live server status (including information on server uptime, number of queries processed, and number of connections).

- The SHOW TABLE STATUS statement displays detailed information on the tables in a database (including information on the table type, the number of rows, the date and time of the last table update, and the lengths of indexes and rows).

- The SHOW CHARACTER SET statement displays a list of available character sets.

Summary

This chapter provided a crash course in MySQL's dialect of SQL, showing you how to create databases and tables; insert, modify, and delete records; and execute different types of queries. This introductory chapter on SQL wasn't meant to be deep—rather, it was intended as a broad overview of the things you can do with MySQL and a primer for the more detailed material ahead. The next few chapters will build on this introductory material to discuss some of MySQL's more advanced features.

While this chapter covered a fair bit of ground, it still barely scratched the surface of what you can do with MySQL. For more in-depth information about the topics in this chapter, you should visit the following links:

- The official MySQL tutorial at http://dev.mysql.com/doc/refman/5.1/en/tutorial.html

- A discussion of RDBMS concepts at http://www.melonfire.com/community/columns/trog/article.php?id=52

- Database normalization at http://en.wikipedia.org/wiki/Database_normalization

- More information on the MySQL command-line client at http://dev.mysql.com/doc/refman/5.1/en/mysql.html

- Detailed information on SQL statements discussed in this chapter at http://dev.mysql.com/doc/refman/5.1/en/sql-syntax.html

CHAPTER 3

Making Design Decisions

In the RDBMS world, efficiency (in data storage) and speed (in data retrieval) are the two key goals for any database architect. To achieve these goals, a database architect must consider every aspect of a proposed database design and decide the optimal storage structure for the data within it.

Broadly, there are two main storage decisions facing a database architect when proposing a database design: which data types are best suited to a table's fields, and which storage engine is best suited to a table's intended use. An architect must also make decisions about which fields to index and how best to construct table relationships through the use of foreign and primary keys. These design-time decisions have a far-reaching effect on database performance and require careful thought and consideration. The following sections discuss the issues involved in greater detail.

Selecting Field Data Types

Every field of a MySQL table incorporates a data type as one of its primary attributes. This data type plays an important role in enforcing the integrity of the data in a MySQL database and in making this data easier to use and manipulate.

Intelligent use of data typing can result in smaller databases and tables, efficient indexing, and quicker query execution; indifferent, ham-handed use of types can result in bloated tables, wasted storage space, inefficient indexing, and a gradual deterioration in performance. For example, using a VARCHAR type on a field that is meant for numeric or date values could result in unexpected behavior when you perform calculations on it, just as using a large TEXT field for small string values could lead to a waste of space and inefficient indexing. Wise database architects, therefore, make it a point to be fully aware of the various data types available in a system, together with the limitations and benefits of each, prior to implementing a database-driven application; the alternative can be costly in terms of both time and money.

MySQL supports a number of different data types, as listed in Table 2-1 in Chapter 2. To help you choose the one best suited to the values you expect to enter into a field, the following sections examine each of these types in greater detail.

Numeric Types

For integer values, MySQL offers you a choice of the TINYINT, SMALLINT, MEDIUMINT, INT, and BIGINT types, which differ from each other only in the size of values they can store. Use the TINYINT and SMALLINT types for small integer values, the INT type for larger integer values, and the BIGINT type for extremely large values. For floating-point values, use the FLOAT and DOUBLE types for single-precision and double-precision floating point values, respectively. And, finally, for decimal values, use the DECIMAL data type.

When defining an integer field, you can include a width specifier in parentheses. This *width specifier* controls the padding MySQL applies to the field when retrieving it from the database. For a field defined as BIGINT (20), MySQL will automatically pad the value to 20 characters before displaying it.

When defining floating-point and decimal fields, MySQL enables you to include both a width specifier and a *precision specifier*. For example, the declaration FLOAT (7,4) specifies that displayed values will not contain more than seven digits, with four digits after the decimal point. You can also add the ZEROFILL attribute to pad values with leading zeroes, and the UNSIGNED attribute to force a field to only accept positive values.

CAUTION *By default, MySQL will automatically truncate or round values down to the maximum allowed value for the field they're being placed in. To avoid this and instead have MySQL generate an error, run MySQL in "strict mode." A discussion of MySQL modes can be found in Chapter 10.*

Character and String Types

MySQL lets you store strings up to 255 characters in length as either a CHAR or VARCHAR type. The difference between these two types is simple: CHAR fields are fixed to the length specified at the time of definition, while VARCHAR fields can grow and shrink dynamically, based on the data entered into them. This makes VARCHAR fields more suitable for fields that accept variable-length data, and CHAR fields better for fields that always contain values of the same length.

Both CHAR and VARCHAR type definitions must include a width specifier in parentheses, as with numeric type definitions. Thus, the definition CHAR (10) creates a field whose length remains *exactly 10 characters,* regardless of what is entered into it, while the definition VARCHAR (10) creates a field whose length can range *anywhere between 0 and 10 characters,* depending on what is entered into it.

Text and Binary Types

MySQL enables you to store strings greater than 255 characters in length as either a TEXT or BLOB type. The difference between TEXT and BLOB types is minimal at best: TEXT types are compared in a case-insensitive manner, while BLOB types are compared in a case-sensitive manner. For this reason, BLOBs are usually used to store binary data, while TEXT fields are used to store ASCII data.

Depending on the size of the string you're trying to store, MySQL offers you a choice of the TINYTEXT, TEXT, MEDIUMTEXT, and LONGTEXT types (for ASCII text blocks) and the TINYBLOB, BLOB, MEDIUMBLOB, and LONGBLOB types (for binary data).

Date and Time Types

For simple date and time values, MySQL offers the intelligently named DATE and TIME data types. The DATE type is used to store date values consisting of year, month, and day components, while the TIME type is used for time values or durations consisting of hour, minute, and second components. Both DATE and TIME types can be used for values in either numeric (YYYYMMDD and HHMMSS) or string ('YYYY-MM-DD' and 'HH:MM:SS') format.

If what you need is a combination of the two, consider using the DATETIME or TIMESTAMP types, both of which let you specify both date and time values in a single field. The difference between the two lies in how the values are stored: DATETIME fields are stored in the form 'YYYY-MM-DD HH:MM:SS', and TIMESTAMP fields are stored in the form YYYYMMDDHHMMSS.

How Do I Enter the Current Date and Time into a Field?

When inserting records into a table containing a TIMESTAMP field, MySQL automatically fills that field with the current date and time if no other value was specified. To accomplish the same thing with other date/time fields, use the NOW() function.

Finally, for simple applications that only need to store the year, MySQL offers the special YEAR type, which accepts a four-digit year value. It's worthwhile to use this value if your application deals mostly with the year component of a date value, because a field marked as YEAR occupies 1 byte on disk (as compared to a DATETIME or DATE field, which can occupy up to 8 bytes). MySQL YEAR fields can accept any value in the range 1901 to 2155.

Enumerations

For situations where a field value must be selected from a predefined list of values, MySQL offers the ENUM and SET data types. For both these types, a list of predefined values must be included as part of the type definition. An ENUM field definition can contain up to 65,536 elements, while a SET field definition can hold up to 64 elements.

For a field marked as an ENUM field, only one of the predefined values may be selected, whereas for a field marked as a SET field, zero, one, or more than one of the pre-defined values may be selected. ENUM fields are best suited for mutually exclusive values, while SET fields are best suited for independent values. As an example, the definition ENUM ('red', 'green', 'yellow') forces entry of any one of the three values, while the definition SET ('mon', 'tue', 'wed', 'thu', 'fri') allows entry of none, one, or all of the five values. In addition, SET values are stored as bits, making it possible to perform bitwise comparison and sorting operations on them.

What Happens if I Try Inserting an Unlisted Value into an ENUM or SET Field?

With both ENUM and SET types, attempting to insert a value that does not exist in the predefined list of values will cause MySQL to insert either an empty string or a 0.

Data Type Selection Checklist

To decide the data type for a field, take into account the following factors:

- The range and type of values that the field will hold
- The types of calculations you expect to perform on those values
- The manner in which the data is to be formatted for display purposes

- The manner in which the data is to be sorted and compared against other fields
- The available subtypes for each field and their storage efficiencies

By taking all of these factors into consideration when designing your database, you reduce the chance of incompatibilities and storage inefficiencies later.

Selecting Table Storage Engines

As Table 2-2 in Chapter 2 illustrates, MySQL supports many different storage engines for its tables, each with its own advantages and disadvantages. While all of MySQL's storage engines are reasonably efficient, using the wrong storage engine can hinder your application from achieving its maximum possible performance. For example, using the ARCHIVE engine for a table that will see frequent reads and writes will produce significantly slower performance than using the MYISAM engine for the same table.

To help you choose the most appropriate engine for your table, the following sections discuss each of these engines in greater detail.

The MyISAM Storage Engine

The MyISAM storage engine extends the base ISAM type with a number of additional optimizations and enhancements, and is MySQL's default table type. MyISAM tables are optimized for compression and speed, and are immediately portable between different OSs and platforms (for example, the same MyISAM table can be used on both Windows and UNIX OSs). The MyISAM format supports large table files (up to 256TB in size) and allows indexing of BLOB and TEXT columns. Tables and table indexes can be compressed to save space, a feature that comes in handy when storing large BLOB or TEXT fields. VARCHAR fields can either be constrained to a specific length or adjusted dynamically as per the data within them, and the format supports searching for records using any key prefix, as well as using the entire key.

Because MyISAM tables are optimized for MySQL, it's no surprise that the developers added a fair amount of intelligence to them. MyISAM tables can be either fixed-length or dynamic-length. MySQL automatically checks MyISAM tables for corruption on startup and can even repair them in case of errors. Table data and table index files can be stored in different locations, or even on different file systems. And intelligent defragmentation logic ensures a high-performance coefficient, even for tables with a large number of inserts, updates, and deletions. Large MyISAM tables can also be compressed, or "packed," into smaller read-only tables that take up less disk space, with MySQL's myisampack utility.

The InnoDB Storage Engine

The InnoDB storage engine has been a part of MySQL since MySQL 4.0. InnoDB is a fully ACID-compliant and efficient table format that provides full support for transactions in MySQL without compromising speed or performance. Fine-grained (row- and table-level) locks improve the fidelity of MySQL transactions, and InnoDB also supports nonlocking reads and multiversioning (features previously only available in the Oracle RDBMS). InnoDB tables can grow up to 64TB in size.

Asynchronous I/O and a sequential read-ahead buffer improve data retrieval speed, and a "buddy algorithm" and Oracle-type tablespaces result in optimized file and memory management. InnoDB also supports automatic creation of hash indexes in memory on an as-needed basis to improve performance, and it uses buffering to improve the reliability and speed of database operations. As a result, InnoDB tables match (and, sometimes, exceed) the performance of MyISAM tables.

InnoDB tables are fully portable between different OSs and architectures, and, because of their transactional nature, they're always in a consistent state (MySQL makes them even more robust by checking them for corruption and repairing them on startup). Support for foreign keys and commit, rollback, and roll-forward operations complete the picture, making this one of the most full-featured table formats available in MySQL.

The Archive Storage Engine

The Archive storage engine provides a way to store large recordsets that see infrequent reads into a smaller, compressed format. The key feature of this storage engine is its ability to compress records as they are inserted and decompress them as they are retrieved using the zlib library. These tables are ideally suited for storage of historical data, typically to meet auditing or compliance norms.

Given that this storage engine is not designed for frequent reads, it lacks many of the bells and whistles of the InnoDB and MyISAM engines: Archive tables only support INSERT and SELECT operations, do not allow indexes (and, therefore, perform full table scans during reads), ignore BLOB fields in read operations, and, by virtue of their on-the-fly compression system, necessarily display lower performance. That said, Archive tables are still superior to packed MyISAM tables because they support both read and write operations and produce a smaller disk footprint.

The Federated Storage Engine

The Federated storage engine implements a "stub" table that merely contains a table definition; this table definition is mirrored on a remote MySQL server, which also holds the table data. A Federated table itself contains no data; rather, it is accompanied by connection parameters that tell MySQL where to look for the actual table records. Federated tables thus make it possible to access MySQL tables on a remote server from a local server without the need for replication or clustering.

Federated "stub" tables can point to source tables that use any of MySQL's standard storage engines, including InnoDB and MyISAM. However, in and of themselves, they are fairly limited; they lack transactional support and indexes, cannot use MySQL's query cache, and are less than impressive performance-wise.

The Memory Storage Engine

The Memory storage engine, as the name suggests, implements in-memory tables that use hash indexes, making them at least 30 percent faster than regular MyISAM tables. They are accessed and used in exactly the same manner as regular MyISAM or ISAM tables.

However, the data stored within them is available only for the lifetime of the MySQL server and is erased if the MySQL server crashes or shuts down. Although these tables can offer a performance benefit, their temporary nature makes them unsuitable for uses more sophisticated than temporary data storage and management.

Can I Define How Much Memory a Memory Table Can Use?
Yes, the size of Memory tables can be limited by setting a value for the `max_heap_table_size` server variable.

The CSV Storage Engine

The CSV storage engine provides a convenient way to merge the portability of text files with the power of SQL queries. CSV tables are essentially plain ASCII files, with commas separating each field of a record. This format is easily understood by non-SQL applications, such as Microsoft Excel, and thus allows data to be easily transferred between SQL and non-SQL environments. A fairly obvious limitation, however, is that CSV tables don't support indexing and SELECT operations must, therefore, perform a full table scan, with the attendant impact on performance. CSV tables also don't support the NULL data type.

The MERGE Storage Engine

A MERGE table is a virtual table created by combining multiple MyISAM tables into a single table. Such a combination of tables is only possible if the tables involved have completely identical table structures. Any difference in field types or indexes won't permit a successful union. A MERGE table uses the indexes of its component tables and doesn't maintain any indexes of its own, which can improve its speed in certain situations. MERGE tables permit SELECT, DELETE, and UPDATE operations, and can come in handy when you need to pull together data from different tables or to speed up performance in joins or searches between a series of tables.

The ISAM Storage Engine

ISAM tables are similar to MyISAM tables, although they lack many of the performance enhancements of the MyISAM format and, therefore, don't offer the optimization and performance efficiency of that type. Because ISAM indexes cannot be compressed, they use fewer system resources than their MyISAM counterparts. ISAM indexes also require more disk space, however, which can be a problem in small-footprint environments.

Like MyISAM, ISAM tables can be either fixed-length or dynamic-length, though maximum key lengths are smaller with the ISAM format. The format cannot handle tables greater than 4GB, and the tables aren't immediately portable across different platforms. In addition, the ISAM table format is more prone to fragmentation, which can reduce query speed, and has limited support for data/index compression.

NOTE MySQL versions prior to MySQL 5.1 included the ISAM storage engine primarily for compatibility with legacy tables. This storage engine is no longer supported as of MySQL 5.1.

What Is a Temporary Table? Is It the Same as a Table Created with the Memory Storage Engine?

No. Memory tables, which are created by adding the ENGINE=MEMORY modifier to a CREATE TABLE statement, remain extant during the lifetime of the server. They are destroyed once the server process is terminated; however, while extant, they are visible to all connecting clients.

Temporary tables, which are initialized with the CREATE TEMPORARY TABLE statement, are a different kettle of fish. These tables are client-specific and remain in existence only for the duration of a single client session. They can use any of MySQL's supported storage engines, but they are automatically deleted when the client that created them closes its connection with the MySQL server. As such, they come in handy for transient, session-based data storage or calculations. And, because they're session-dependent, two different client sessions can use the same table name without conflicting.

The NDB Storage Engine

The NDB storage engine implements a high-availability, in-memory table type designed only for use in clustered MySQL server environments. The NDB format supports large table files (up to 384EB in size), variable-length fields, and replication. However, NDB tables don't support foreign keys, savepoints, or statement-based replication, and limit the number of fields and indexes per table to 128.

NOTE A new addition to MySQL is the Blackhole storage engine. As you might guess from the name, this is MySQL's equivalent of a bit bucket: Any data entered into a Blackhole table immediately disappears, never to be seen again. This storage engine isn't just the MySQL development team's idea of a joke, however—it does have some utility as a "cheap" SQL syntax verification tool, a statement logger, or a replication filter.

Storage Engine Selection Checklist

To decide the most appropriate storage engine for a table, take into account the following factors:

- Frequency of reads versus writes
- Whether transactional support is needed

- Whether foreign key support is needed
- Indexing requirements
- Table size and speed at which it will grow
- OS/architecture portability
- Future extendibility requirements and adaptability to changing data requirements

It's worth noting, also, that MySQL lets you mix and match storage engines within a database. So you could use the MyISAM engine for tables that see frequent SELECTs and use InnoDB tables for tables that see frequent INSERTs or transactions. This ability to select storage engines on a per-table basis is unique to MySQL and plays a key role in helping it achieve its blazing performance.

Using Primary and Foreign Keys

Primary keys serve as unique identifiers for the records in a table, while foreign keys are used to link related tables together. When designing a set of database tables, it is important to specify which fields will be used for primary and foreign keys to clarify both in-table structure and inter-table relationships.

Primary Keys

You can specify a primary key for the table with the PRIMARY KEY constraint. In a well-designed database schema, a *primary key* serves as an unchanging, unique identifier for each record. If a key is declared as primary, this usually implies that the values in it will rarely be modified.

The PRIMARY KEY constraint can best be thought of as a combination of the NOT NULL and UNIQUE constraints because it requires values in the specified field to be neither NULL nor repeated in any other row. Consider the following example, which demonstrates by setting the numeric *AirportID* field as the primary key for the *airport* table.

```
mysql> CREATE TABLE airport (
 -> AirportID smallint(5) unsigned NOT NULL,
 -> AirportCode char(3),
 -> AirportName varchar(255) NOT NULL,
 -> CityName varchar(255) NOT NULL,
 -> CountryCode char(2) NOT NULL,
 -> NumRunways INT(11) unsigned NOT NULL,
 -> NumTerminals tinyint(1) unsigned NOT NULL,
 -> PRIMARY KEY (AirportID)
 -> ) ENGINE=MYISAM;
Query OK, 0 rows affected (0.05 sec)
```

In this situation, because the *AirportID* field is defined as the primary key, MySQL won't allow duplication or NULL values in that field. This allows the database administrator to ensure that every airport listed in the table has a unique numeric value, thereby enforcing a high degree of consistency on the stored data.

PRIMARY KEY constraints can be specified for either a single field or for a composite of multiple fields. Consider the following example, which demonstrates by constructing a table containing a composite primary key:

```
mysql> CREATE TABLE flightdep (
    -> FlightID SMALLINT(6) NOT NULL,
    -> DepDay TINYINT(4) NOT NULL,
    -> DepTime TIME NOT NULL,
    -> PRIMARY KEY (FlightID, DepDay, DepTime)
    -> ) ENGINE=MyISAM;
Query OK, 0 rows affected (0.96 sec)
```

In this case, the table rules permit repetition of the flight number, the departure day, or the departure time, but not of all three together. Look what happens if you try:

```
mysql> INSERT INTO flightdep (FlightID, DepDay, DepTime)
    -> VALUES (511,1,'00:01');
Query OK, 1 row affected (0.20 sec)
mysql> INSERT INTO flightdep (FlightID, DepDay, DepTime)
    -> VALUES (511,2,'00:01');
Query OK, 1 row affected (0.00 sec)
mysql> INSERT INTO flightdep (FlightID, DepDay, DepTime)
    -> VALUES (511,1,'00:02');
Query OK, 1 row affected (0.00 sec)
mysql> INSERT INTO flightdep (FlightID, DepDay, DepTime)
    -> VALUES (511,1,'00:01');
ERROR 1062 (23000): Duplicate entry '511-1-00:01:00' for key 'PRIMARY'
```

Composite primary keys can come in handy when a record is to be uniquely identified by a combination of its attributes, rather than by only a single attribute.

Foreign Keys

The fundamental basis of a relational database system like MySQL is its capability to create relationships between the tables that make up the database. By making it possible to easily relate records in different tables to one another, an RDBMS makes it possible to analyze data in different ways while simultaneously keeping it organized in a systematic fashion, with minimal redundancy.

These relationships are managed through the use of *foreign keys*, essentially, fields that have the same meaning in all the tables in the relationship and that serve as points of

FIGURE 3-1
A one-to-one
relationship between
tables

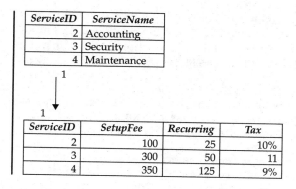

ServiceID	ServiceName
2	Accounting
3	Security
4	Maintenance

ServiceID	SetupFee	Recurring	Tax
2	100	25	10%
3	300	50	11
4	350	125	9%

commonality to link records in different tables together. A foreign key relationship could be one-to-one (a record in one table is linked to one and only one record in another table) or one-to-many (a record in one table is linked to multiple records in another table).

NOTE *Foreign keys are only supported on InnoDB tables.*

Figure 3-1 illustrates a one-to-one relationship: a service and its associated description, with the relationship between the two managed via the unique *ServiceID* field.

Figure 3-2 illustrates a one-to-many relationship: an author and his or her books, with the link between the two maintained via the unique *AuthorID* field.

AuthorID	AuthorName
2	Dennis Lehane
3	Agatha Christie
4	J K Rowling

BookID	BookName	AuthorID
100	Harry Potter and the Goblet of Fire	4
101	Harry Potter and the Deathly Hallows	4
102	Murder on the Orient Express	3
103	Prayers for Rain	2
104	Death on the Nile	3
105	Harry Potter and the Chamber of Secrets	4

FIGURE 3-2 A one-to-many relationship between tables

When creating a table, a foreign key can be defined in much the same way as a primary key, by using the FOREIGN KEY...REFERENCES modifier. The following example demonstrates by creating two InnoDB tables linked to each other in a one-to-many relationship by the aircraft type identifier:

```
mysql> CREATE TABLE aircrafttype (
    -> AircraftTypeID smallint(4) unsigned NOT NULL AUTO_INCREMENT,
    -> AircraftName varchar(255) NOT NULL,
    -> PRIMARY KEY (AircraftTypeID)
    -> ) ENGINE=INNODB;
Query OK, 0 rows affected (0.61 sec)
mysql> CREATE TABLE aircraft (
    -> AircraftID smallint(4) unsigned NOT NULL AUTO_INCREMENT,
    -> AircraftTypeID smallint(4) unsigned NOT NULL,
    -> RegNum char(6) NOT NULL,
    -> LastMaintEnd date NOT NULL,
    -> NextMaintBegin date NOT NULL,
    -> NextMaintEnd date NOT NULL,
    -> PRIMARY KEY (AircraftID),
    -> UNIQUE RegNum (RegNum),
    -> INDEX (AircraftTypeID),
    -> FOREIGN KEY (AircraftTypeID)
    -> REFERENCES aircrafttype (AircraftTypeID)
    -> ) ENGINE=INNODB;
Query OK, 0 rows affected (0.45 sec)
```

In this example, the *aircraft.AircraftTypeID* field is a foreign key, linked to the *aircrafttype.AircraftTypeID* primary key. Note the manner in which this relationship is specified in the FOREIGN KEY...REFERENCES modifier. The FOREIGN KEY part specifies one end of the relationship (the field name in the current table), while the REFERENCES part specifies the other end of the relationship (the field name in the referenced table).

TIP *As a general rule, it's a good idea to use integer fields as foreign keys rather than character fields, as this produces better performance when joining tables.*

Once a foreign key is set up, MySQL only allows entry of those values into the aircraft types into the *aircraft* table that also exist in the *aircrafttype* table. Continuing the previous example, let's see how this works.

```
mysql> INSERT INTO aircrafttype
    -> (AircraftTypeID, AircraftName)
    -> VALUES (503, 'Boeing 747');
Query OK, 1 row affected (0.09 sec)
mysql> INSERT INTO aircraft
    -> (AircraftID, AircraftTypeID, RegNum,
    -> LastMaintEnd, NextMaintBegin, NextMaintEnd)
    -> VALUES
```

```
 -> (3451, 503, 'ZX6488',
 -> '2007-10-01', '2008-10-23', '2008-10-31');
Query OK, 1 row affected (0.04 sec)
mysql> INSERT INTO aircraft
 -> (AircraftID, AircraftTypeID, RegNum,
 -> LastMaintEnd, NextMaintBegin, NextMaintEnd)
 -> VALUES
 -> (3452, 616, 'ZX6488',
 -> '2007-10-01', '2008-10-23', '2008-10-31');
ERROR 1452 (23000): Cannot add or update a child row: a foreign key
constraint fails (`db1`.`aircraft`, CONSTRAINT `aircraft_ibfk_1` FOREIGN KEY
(`AircraftTypeID`) REFERENCES `aircrafttype` (`AircraftTypeID`))
```

Thus, because an aircraft type with identifier 616 doesn't exist in the *aircrafttype*, MySQL rejects the record with that value for the *aircraft* table. In this manner, foreign key constraints can significantly help in enforcing the data integrity of the tables in a database and reducing the occurrences of "bad" or inconsistent field values.

The following three constraints must be kept in mind when linking tables with foreign keys:

- All the tables in the relationship must be InnoDB tables. In non-InnoDB tables, the FOREIGN KEY...REFERENCES modifier is simply ignored by MySQL.

- The fields used in the foreign key relationship must be indexed in all referenced tables (InnoDB will automatically create these indexes for you if you don't specify any).

- The data types of the fields named in the foreign key relationship should be similar. This is especially true of integer types, which must match in both size and sign.

What's interesting to note is this: Even if foreign key constraints exist on a table, MySQL permits you to DROP the table without raising an error (even if doing so would break the foreign key relationships established earlier). In fact, in versions of MySQL earlier than 4.0.13, dropping the table was the only way to remove a foreign key. MySQL 4.0.13 and later does, however, support a less drastic way of removing a foreign key from a table, via the ALTER TABLE command. Here's an example:

```
mysql> ALTER TABLE aircraft DROP FOREIGN KEY aircraft_ibfk_1;
Query OK, 1 row affected (0.57 sec)
Records: 1 Duplicates: 0 Warnings: 0
```

To remove a foreign key reference, use the DROP FOREIGN KEY clause with the internal name of the foreign key constraint. This internal name can be obtained using the SHOW CREATE TABLE statement. And in case you're wondering why you must use the internal constraint name and not the field name in the DROP FOREIGN KEY clause ... well, that's a good question!

Automatic Key Updates and Deletions   Foreign keys can certainly take care of ensuring the integrity of newly inserted records. But what if a record is deleted from the table named in the REFERENCES clause? What happens to all the records in subordinate tables that use this value as a foreign key?

Obviously, those records should be deleted as well, or else you'll have orphan records cluttering your database. MySQL 3.23.50 and later simplifies this task by enabling you to add an ON DELETE clause to the FOREIGN KEY...REFERENCES modifier, which tells the database what to do with the orphaned records in such a situation. Here's a sequence that demonstrates this:

```
mysql> CREATE TABLE aircraft (
 -> AircraftID smallint(4) unsigned NOT NULL AUTO_INCREMENT,
 -> AircraftTypeID smallint(4) unsigned NOT NULL,
 -> RegNum char(6) NOT NULL,
 -> LastMaintEnd date NOT NULL,
 -> NextMaintBegin date NOT NULL,
 -> NextMaintEnd date NOT NULL,
 -> PRIMARY KEY (AircraftID),
 -> UNIQUE RegNum (RegNum),
 -> FOREIGN KEY (AircraftTypeID)
 -> REFERENCES aircrafttype (AircraftTypeID)
 -> ON DELETE CASCADE
 -> ) ENGINE=INNODB;
Query OK, 0 rows affected (0.17 sec)
mysql> INSERT INTO aircraft
 -> (AircraftID, AircraftTypeID, RegNum,
 -> LastMaintEnd, NextMaintBegin, NextMaintEnd)
 -> VALUES
 -> (3451, 503, 'ZX6488',
 -> '2007-10-01', '2008-10-23', '2008-10-31');
Query OK, 1 row affected (0.05 sec)
mysql> DELETE FROM aircrafttype;
Query OK, 1 row affected (0.06 sec)
mysql> SELECT * FROM aircraft;
Empty set (0.01 sec)
```

MySQL 4.0.8 and later also lets you perform these automatic actions on updates by allowing the use of an ON UPDATE clause, which works in a similar manner to the ON DELETE clause. So, for example, adding the ON UPDATE CASCADE clause to a foreign key definition tells MySQL that when a record is updated in the primary table (the table referenced for foreign key checks), all records using that foreign key value in the current table should also be automatically updated with the new values to ensure the consistency of the system.

Table 3-1 lists the four keywords that can follow an ON DELETE or ON UPDATE clause.

Keyword	What It Means
CASCADE	Delete all records containing references to the deleted key value.
SET NULL	Modify all records containing references to the deleted key value to instead use a NULL value (this can only be used for fields previously marked as NOT NULL).
RESTRICT	Reject the deletion request until all subordinate records using the deleted key value have themselves been manually deleted and no references exist (this is the default setting, and it's also the safest).
NO ACTION	Do nothing.

TABLE 3-1   Actions Available in ON DELETE and ON UPDATE Clause

---

CAUTION   *Be aware that setting up MySQL for automatic operations through* ON UPDATE *and* ON DELETE *rules can result in serious data corruption if your key relationships aren't set up perfectly. For example, if you have a series of tables linked together by foreign key relationships and* ON DELETE CASCADE *rules, a change in any of the master tables can result in records, even records linked only peripherally to the original deletion, getting wiped out with no warning. For this reason, you should check (and then double-check) these rules before finalizing them.*

Using Indexes

To speed up searches and reduce query execution time, MySQL lets you index particular fields of a table. The term "index" here means much the same as in the real world. Similar in concept to the index you find at the end of a book, an *index* is a list of sorted field values used to simplify the task of locating specific records in response to queries.

In the absence of an index, MySQL needs to scan each row of the table to find the records matching a particular query. This might not cause a noticeable slowdown in smaller tables, but, as table size increases, a complete table scan can add many seconds of overhead to a query. An index speeds up things significantly: With an index, MySQL can bypass the full table scan altogether by instead looking up the index and jumping to the appropriate location(s) in the table. When looking for records that match a specific search condition, reading an index is typically faster than scanning an entire table. This is because indexes are smaller in size and can be searched faster.

That said, an index does have two important disadvantages: It takes up additional space on disk, and it can affect the speed of INSERT, UPDATE, and DELETE queries because the index must be updated every time table records are added, updated, or deleted. Most of the time, though, these reasons shouldn't stop you from using indexes: Disk storage is getting cheaper every day, and MySQL includes numerous optimization techniques to reduce the time spent on updating indexes and searching them for specific values.

Indexing is typically recommended for fields that frequently appear in the WHERE, ORDER BY, and GROUP BY clauses of SELECT queries, and for fields used to join tables together.

NOTE *With InnoDB tables, MySQL uses intelligent insert buffering to reduce the number of disk writes to InnoDB indexes by maintaining a list of changes in a special insert buffer and then updating the index with all the changes in a single write (rather than multiple simultaneous writes). MySQL also tries to convert the disk-based B-tree indexes into adaptive hash indexes (which can be searched faster), based on patterns in the queries being executed.*

Indexes can be defined either when the table is created or at a later date. To define an index at table creation time, add the INDEX or KEY modifier (the terms are synonymous in MySQL) to the CREATE TABLE statement, as in the following example:

```
mysql> CREATE TABLE airport (
 -> AirportID smallint(5) unsigned NOT NULL,
 -> AirportCode char(3) NOT NULL,
 -> AirportName varchar(255) NOT NULL,
 -> CityName varchar(255) NOT NULL,
 -> CountryCode char(2) NOT NULL,
 -> NumRunways INT(11) unsigned NOT NULL,
 -> NumTerminals tinyint(1) unsigned NOT NULL,
 -> PRIMARY KEY (AirportID),
 -> INDEX (AirportCode),
 -> INDEX (CountryCode)
 -> ) ENGINE=InnoDB;
Query OK, 0 rows affected (0.48 sec)
```

The previous statement builds an index of airport and country codes for the airport list.

To create multifield indexes by concatenating the values of all indexed fields, up to a maximum of 15, specify a comma-separated list of field names in the index modifier, as in the next example:

```
mysql> CREATE TABLE flightdep (
 -> FlightID SMALLINT(6) NOT NULL,
 -> DepDay TINYINT(4) NOT NULL,
 -> DepTime TIME NOT NULL,
 -> INDEX (DepDay,DepTime)
 -> ) ENGINE=MyISAM;
Query OK, 0 rows affected (0.19 sec)
```

Indexes can also be added to an existing table with the CREATE INDEX command. Here's an example, which creates an index on the AirportID field of the *airport* table:

```
mysql> CREATE INDEX AirportID ON airport(AirportID);
Query OK, 15 rows affected (1.02 sec)
Records: 15 Duplicates: 0 Warnings: 0
```

> ### Can I Specify How Much of a Field Should Be Indexed?
>
> Yes, by stating the required index length in parentheses after the field name in a CREATE INDEX statement. For BLOB and TEXT fields, this is mandatory; it is optional for CHAR and VARCHAR fields. Here's an example:
>
> ```
> CREATE INDEX synopsis ON books (synopsis(100));
> ```

TIP *If an index name isn't specified in the INDEX modifier of a CREATE TABLE statement, MySQL automatically names the index using the corresponding field name as the base.*

To remove an index, use the DROP INDEX command, as in the next example:

```
mysql> DROP INDEX AirportID on airport;
Query OK, 15 rows affected (0.24 sec)
Records: 15 Duplicates: 0 Warnings: 0
```

In addition to the "regular" index type, MySQL supports two other important index variants: UNIQUE indexes and FULLTEXT indexes, which are discussed in the following sections.

The UNIQUE Index

You can specify that values entered into a field must be unique, that is, not duplicated in any other row, by adding the UNIQUE modifier to the CREATE TABLE and CREATE INDEX commands. Once a field is marked as UNIQUE in this manner, any attempt to enter duplicate data into it will fail.

```
mysql> CREATE UNIQUE INDEX AirportCode on airport (AirportCode);
Query OK, 0 rows affected (0.27 sec)
Records: 0 Duplicates: 0 Warnings: 0
mysql> INSERT INTO airport (AirportID, AirportCode, AirportName,
  -> CityName, CountryCode, NumRunways, NumTerminals)
  -> VALUES (34, 'ORY', 'Orly Airport', 'Paris', 'FR', 3, 2);
Query OK, 1 row affected (0.04 sec)
mysql> INSERT INTO airport (AirportID, AirportCode, AirportName,
  -> CityName, CountryCode, NumRunways, NumTerminals)
  -> VALUES (35, 'ORY', 'Paris-Orly Airport', 'Paris', 'FR', 3, 2);
ERROR 1062 (23000): Duplicate entry 'ORY' for key 'AirportCode'
```

Note, however, that a UNIQUE field is permitted to store NULL values (so long as the underlying field is not marked NOT NULL).

The FULLTEXT Index

MySQL 3.23.23 and later supports a special type of index designed specifically for full-text searching on MyISAM tables, called a FULLTEXT index. This index, which results in faster queries than the LIKE operator, makes it possible to query the indexed columns for arbitrary text strings and return only those records that contain values similar to the search strings. When performing this type of full-text search, MySQL calculates a similarity score between the table records and the search string, and returns only those records with a high score.

NOTE FULLTEXT *indexes are only supported on MyISAM tables.*

Here's an example:

```
mysql> CREATE FULLTEXT INDEX Synopsis ON books(Synopsis);
Query OK, 15 rows affected (0.11 sec)
Records: 15 Duplicates: 0 Warnings: 0
```

Once the index is created, you can search it with the MATCH() function, providing the search string as an argument to the AGAINST() function. Consider the following example:

```
mysql> SELECT Title, MATCH(Synopsis) AGAINST ('suspense') AS score
    -> FROM books LIMIT 0, 10;
+----------------------------------+------------------+
| Title                            | Score            |
+----------------------------------+------------------+
| The Prometheus Deception         | 0                |
| Dark Hollow                      | 2.5951748101926  |
| Easy Prey                        | 2.703356073143   |
| Prayers For Rain                 | 2.8519631063088  |
| Roses Are Red                    | 2.8209489868374  |
| Personal Injuries                | 0                |
| Demolition Angel                 | 0                |
| Code To Zero                     | 0                |
| Adrian Mole: The Cappuccino Years| 0                |
| The Bear And The Dragon          | 0                |
+----------------------------------+------------------+
10 rows in set (0.11 sec)
```

The argument passed to the MATCH() function must be a field list that maps exactly to some FULLTEXT index on the table. The MATCH() function then calculates a similarity score between the search string and the named fields for every record in the table. According to the MySQL manual, similarity is scored on the basis of a number of parameters, including the following:

- The number of words in the row
- The number of unique words in that row
- The total number of words in the collection
- The number of rows that contain a particular word

A similarity score of 0 indicates that no similarity exists between the values being compared.

> ***Note*** FULLTEXT *indexes are fairly new to MySQL and work best when used with large tables. Small tables don't offer a sufficient spread of data values for the index to operate optimally.*

Words that appear in more than 50 percent of the total records in the table (so-called *stopwords*) are ignored and are treated as having no relevance for the purpose of full-text searching. Similarly, words that appear more frequently are given less weight in the index than words that appear less frequently.

Typically, you would use the MATCH() function in a WHERE clause to retrieve those records with a high similarity score, as in the following example:

```
mysql> SELECT Title, Author FROM books WHERE MATCH (Synopsis)
    -> AGAINST ('suspense');
+------------------+-------------------+
| Title            | Author            |
+------------------+-------------------+
| Prayers For Rain | Dennis Lehane     |
| Roses Are Red    | James Patterson   |
| Easy Prey        | John Sandford     |
| Dark Hollow      | John Connolly     |
+------------------+-------------------+
4 rows in set (0.06 sec)
```

Boolean Searches

In MySQL 4.0.1 and later, you can also execute Boolean searches on a FULLTEXT index by adding the IN BOOLEAN MODE modifier and one or more Boolean operators in the argument passed to the AGAINST() function. The following examples illustrate. The first example returns all those records containing both the words "crime" and "suspense" in the *Synopsis* field, while the second example lists all those records containing the word "romance" but not the words "teenage" or "period" in their synopsis:

```
mysql> SELECT Title, Author FROM books WHERE MATCH (Synopsis)
    -> AGAINST ('suspense');
+------------------+-------------------+
| Title            | Author            |
+------------------+-------------------+
| Prayers For Rain | Dennis Lehane     |
| Roses Are Red    | James Patterson   |
| Easy Prey        | John Sandford     |
| Dark Hollow      | John Connolly     |
+------------------+-------------------+
4 rows in set (0.06 sec)
```

> ***Tip*** *For faster full-text indexing, add a FULLTEXT index to a table after it's been populated with data, with the CREATE INDEX or ALTER TABLE commands, rather than at table creation time itself.*

Summary

Good database design goes a long way towards streamlining the performance of your queries and, by extension, your application. Choosing data types that best match field values, selecting a storage engine that is optimized for the type of queries you intend to use, selecting primary and foreign keys, and applying indexing to commonly used search fields are crucial tasks in achieving a database that is both efficient and fast.

This chapter focused on these key design decisions. It provided detailed information on MySQL's data types and storage engines, explaining the pros and cons of each and offering guidelines to help you choose the best one for your needs. It explained how to define primary keys and discussed the benefits of foreign keys that automatically cascade changes or deletions to subordinate tables. Finally, it examined MySQL's index types, with working examples of the most important ones.

To learn more about the topics in this chapter, consider visiting the following links:

- Detailed information on MySQL's data types at http://dev.mysql.com/doc/refman/5.1/en/data-types.html
- A comparison of MySQL's storage engines at http://dev.mysql.com/tech-resources/articles/storage-engine.html and http://dev.mysql.com/doc/refman/5.1/en/storage-engines.html
- Primary key constraints at http://dev.mysql.com/doc/refman/5.1/en/constraint-primary-key.html
- Foreign key constraints at http://dev.mysql.com/doc/refman/5.1/en/innodb-foreign-key-constraints.html
- Full-text search functions at http://dev.mysql.com/doc/refman/5.1/en/fulltext-search.html

CHAPTER 4

Using Joins, Subqueries, and Views

If you've been following along, you should now understand that the effectiveness of relational database systems lies in their ability to "split" data across multiple tables and dynamically generate different views of this data by linking these tables together as needed. These links, or relationships, between tables are what put the *R* in RDBMS; they not only make it possible to store information more efficiently (by removing redundancies and repetition), but they also enable the discovery of new patterns or causal chains hidden in the data.

This chapter builds on the basic DML concepts discussed earlier and demonstrates how SQL can be used to query multiple tables at once and to combine the data retrieved from them in different ways. Up until MySQL 4.1, the only way to accomplish such multitable queries was with a *join*; however, MySQL now also supports *subqueries*, or nested queries, which provide an alternative to the traditional join. This chapter examines both approaches, with examples that demonstrate their respective utility.

Using Joins

Look back to the previous chapter, and you'll see that the SELECT query examples retrieved data from only a single table. In the real world, however, your SELECT queries will typically be much more sophisticated, requiring records from different tables to be combined to produce the desired result set. The traditional way of doing this is referred to as a *join*, since it involves "joining" different tables at specific points to create new views of the data.

TIP *When using a join, it's recommended that you prefix each field name with the name of the table it belongs to. This reduces ambiguity when dealing with tables that contain identically named fields. To illustrate, in the example database, the* RouteID *field is seen in both* flight *and* route *tables, so to make it clear which one is being referred to at any given time, specify the field name in queries as either* route.RouteID *or* flight.RouteID.

A common misconception is that MySQL, because of its simplicity and/or open-source roots, is "bad" at joins. This is simply not true. MySQL has supported joins well right from its inception and today boasts support for SQL2-compliant join syntax, which makes it possible to combine table records in a variety of sophisticated ways.

A Simple Join

To illustrate how a join works, consider a simple requirement: finding out which aircraft type is used for flight 652 between Orly and Budapest. Look at the example database, and it's clear that this information is split between the *flight, aircraft,* and *aircrafttype* tables, with the *AircraftID* field linking the *flight* and *aircraft* tables and the *AircraftTypeID* field linking the *aircraft* and *aircrafttype* tables (Figure 4-1).

FlightID	RouteID	AircraftID
535	1005	3451
876	1175	3467
652	1018	3465
662	1018	3465
345	1003	3452
877	1176	3467
675	1023	3451
702	1008	3469
708	1006	3469
896	1141	3145

AircraftID	AircraftTypeID	RegNum	LastMaintEnd
3451	616	ZX6488	10/1/2007
3465	616	ZX5373	0000-00-00
3467	616	ZX7283	2/5/2008
3452	617	ZX5464	10/4/2006

AircraftTypeID	AircraftName
503	Boeing 747
504	Boeing 767
615	Airbus A300/310
616	Airbus A330
617	Airbus A340
618	Airbus A380

Figure 4-1   The relationship between flights, aircraft, and aircraft types

By equating these common fields through a join, it's possible to answer this question without too much trouble:

```
mysql> SELECT f.FlightID, at.AircraftName
    -> FROM aircrafttype AS at, aircraft AS a, flight AS f
    -> WHERE a.AircraftID = f.AircraftID
    -> AND a.AircraftTypeID = at.AircraftTypeID
    -> AND f.FlightID=652;
+----------+--------------+
| FlightID | AircraftName |
+----------+--------------+
|      652 | Boeing 747   |
+----------+--------------+
1 row in set (0.00 sec)
```

In this query, the first part of the WHERE clause is used to connect the common fields within the three tables to each other and present a composite picture. The last bit of the WHERE clause further filters the result set to include only those records relevant for flight 652.

How about another? Try finding which of the airline's flights use airplanes from Boeing:

```
mysql> SELECT f.FlightID, at.AircraftName
    -> FROM aircrafttype AS at, aircraft AS a, flight AS f
    -> WHERE a.AircraftID = f.AircraftID
    -> AND a.AircraftTypeID = at.AircraftTypeID
    -> AND at.AircraftName LIKE 'Boeing%';
+----------+--------------+
| FlightID | AircraftName |
+----------+--------------+
|      535 | Boeing 747   |
|      652 | Boeing 747   |
|      662 | Boeing 747   |
|      675 | Boeing 747   |
|      896 | Boeing 747   |
|      898 | Boeing 747   |
|      897 | Boeing 747   |
|      899 | Boeing 747   |
|      812 | Boeing 747   |
|      857 | Boeing 747   |
|      765 | Boeing 767   |
+----------+--------------+
11 rows in set (0.00 sec)
```

Using the COUNT() function will display a count of the records found instead of the individual records:

```
mysql> SELECT COUNT(f.FlightID)
    -> FROM aircrafttype AS at, aircraft AS a, flight AS f
    -> WHERE a.AircraftID = f.AircraftID
    -> AND a.AircraftTypeID = at.AircraftTypeID
    -> AND at.AircraftName LIKE 'Boeing%';
+-----------------------+
| COUNT(flight.FlightID) |
+-----------------------+
|                    11 |
+-----------------------+
1 row in set (0.08 sec)
```

Types of Joins

Now that you have a basic understanding of how joins work, let's move on to a more detailed discussion of the various types of joins supported by MySQL's SQL. The following different join types are possible in MySQL:

- Cross joins, which involve multiplying tables by each other to create a composite table containing all possible permutations
- Inner joins, which produce only those records for which a match exists in all tables
- Outer joins, which produce all the records from one side of the join and fill in the blanks with NULLs
- Self-joins, which involve duplicating a table by means of table aliases and then connecting the copies to each other by means of other joins
- Unions, which involve adding all the records in the tables involved to create one single, composite sum

The following sections examine each of these join types in greater detail, with examples and illustrations.

Cross Joins

The simplest type of join is the *cross join,* which multiplies the tables involved to create an all-inclusive product. Consider the following example, which joins the *aircraft* and *aircrafttype* tables:

```
mysql> SELECT r.RouteID, at.AircraftTypeID,
    -> at.AircraftName FROM route AS r, aircrafttype AS at;
+---------+----------------+-----------------+
| RouteID | AircraftTypeID | AircraftName    |
+---------+----------------+-----------------+
|    1003 |            503 | Boeing 747      |
|    1003 |            504 | Boeing 767      |
|    1003 |            615 | Airbus A300/310 |
|    1003 |            616 | Airbus A330     |
|    1003 |            617 | Airbus A340     |
|    1003 |            618 | Airbus A380     |
|    1005 |            503 | Boeing 747      |
|    1005 |            504 | Boeing 767      |
|    1005 |            615 | Airbus A300/310 |
|    1005 |            616 | Airbus A330     |
|    1005 |            617 | Airbus A340     |
|    1005 |            618 | Airbus A380     |
|    1176 |            503 | Boeing 747      |
|    1176 |            504 | Boeing 767      |
...
+---------+----------------+-----------------+
174 rows in set (0.00 sec)
```

In this case, fields from both tables are combined to produce a result set that contains all possible combinations. This kind of join is referred to as a cross join, and the number of records in the joined table will be equal to the product of the number of records in each of the tables used in the join. Thus, when performing a cross join between two tables, each of which has 10 records, the result set will contain $10 \times 10 = 100$ records. And as you add more tables to the join, the size of the result set increases exponentially.

For this reason, cross joins have huge implications for the performance of your database server. Fortunately, there are only a few cases where a cross join is necessary—one example would be to generate test data, another to create a derived table that can be used for further joins—and in all those cases, it's a good idea to attach a WHERE clause to the join to limit the size of the result set generated and to clearly specify which fields should be returned in the result set.

Inner Joins

Inner joins are the most common type of join and also the most symmetrical, because they require a match in each table that forms a part of the join. Rows that do not match are excluded from the final result set.

The most common example of an inner join is the *equi-join*, where certain fields in the joined tables are equated to each other using the equality (=) operator. In this case, the final result set only includes those rows from the joined tables that have matches in the specified fields.

NOTE *The joins shown in the previous section, "A Simple Join," are equi-joins.*

To illustrate an equi-join, consider the following query, which displays the registration number and type of each of the airline's aircraft, by joining the *aircraft* and *aircrafttype* tables on the common *AircraftTypeID* field:

```
mysql> SELECT a.RegNum, at.AircraftName
    -> FROM aircraft AS a, aircrafttype AS at
    -> WHERE a.AircraftTypeID = at.AircraftTypeID;
+---------+--------------+
| RegNum  | AircraftName |
+---------+--------------+
| ZX6488  | Boeing 747   |
| ZX5373  | Boeing 747   |
| ZX5731  | Boeing 747   |
| ZX5830  | Boeing 747   |
| ZX6821  | Boeing 767   |
| ZX7283  | Airbus A330  |
| ZX5382  | Airbus A330  |
| ZX5921  | Airbus A330  |
| ZX582   | Airbus A330  |
| ZX5173  | Airbus A330  |
| ZX7391  | Airbus A330  |
| ZX5464  | Airbus A340  |
| ZX1386  | Airbus A340  |
| ZX7634  | Airbus A340  |
| ZX7472  | Airbus A340  |
| ZX1037  | Airbus A380  |
+---------+--------------+
16 rows in set (0.01 sec)
```

Here's another example, this one listing routes greater than 5000 kilometers and the flights that operate on them:

```
mysql> SELECT r.RouteID, f.FlightID, r.Distance
    -> FROM route AS r, flight AS f
    -> WHERE r.RouteID = f.RouteID
    -> AND r.Distance > 5000;
+---------+----------+----------+
| RouteID | FlightID | Distance |
+---------+----------+----------+
|    1003 |      345 |     7200 |
|    1133 |      765 |     6336 |
|    1180 |      685 |    10863 |
|    1193 |      724 |    10310 |
|    1192 |      725 |    10310 |
+---------+----------+----------+
5 rows in set (0.00 sec)
```

Although uncommon, inner joins based on inequalities between fields are also possible. However, these types of joins cannot be called equi-joins, as they do not make use of the equality operator. Here's an example:

```
mysql> SELECT a.RegNum, at.AircraftName
    -> FROM aircraft AS a, aircrafttype AS at
    -> WHERE a.AircraftTypeID != at.AircraftTypeID;
+---------+------------------+
| RegNum  | AircraftName     |
+---------+------------------+
| ZX6488  | Boeing 767       |
| ZX6488  | Airbus A300/310  |
| ZX6488  | Airbus A330      |
| ZX6488  | Airbus A340      |
| ZX6488  | Airbus A380      |
| ZX5373  | Boeing 767       |
| ZX5373  | Airbus A300/310  |
| ZX5373  | Airbus A330      |
| ZX5373  | Airbus A340      |
| ZX6488  | Airbus A300/310  |
...
+---------+------------------+
80 rows in set (0.01 sec)
```

PART I

NOTE *For compliance with the SQL standard, MySQL also supports the use of the* INNER JOIN *and* CROSS JOIN *keywords instead of the comma (,) used in those operations. For example, the following two statements both produce a cross join:*

```
SELECT CountryName, StateName FROM country, state;
SELECT CountryName, StateName FROM country CROSS JOIN state;
```

just as the following two statements both create an inner equi-join:

```
SELECT c.CountryName, s.StateName FROM country AS c, state AS s
WHERE s.CountryID = c.CountryID;
SELECT c.CountryName, s.StateName FROM country AS c INNER JOIN state
AS s WHERE s.CountryID = c.CountryID;
```

Outer Joins

From the previous section, it should be clear that inner joins are symmetrical. To be included in the final result set, records must match in all joined tables. Records that do not match are automatically omitted from the result set. *Outer joins,* on the other hand, are asymmetrical—all records from one side of the join are included in the final result set, regardless of whether they match records on the other side of the join.

Depending on which side of the join is to be preserved, SQL defines a left outer join and a right outer join. In a *left outer join,* all the records from the table on the left side of the join matching the WHERE clause appear in the final result set. In a *right outer join,* all the records matching the WHERE clause from the table on the right appear.

To illustrate the difference, first consider the following inner join, which links routes and flights:

```
mysql> SELECT r.RouteID, f.FlightID
    -> FROM route AS r, flight AS f
    -> WHERE r.RouteID = f.RouteID
    -> AND r.RouteID BETWEEN 1050 AND 1175;
+---------+----------+
| RouteID | FlightID |
+---------+----------+
|    1175 |      876 |
|    1141 |      896 |
|    1141 |      898 |
|    1142 |      897 |
|    1142 |      899 |
|    1133 |      765 |
|    1165 |      674 |
|    1123 |      681 |
|    1139 |      688 |
|    1140 |      689 |
|    1097 |      589 |
|    1059 |      857 |
|    1173 |      871 |
|    1173 |      872 |
|    1169 |      671 |
```

```
|     1169 |      672 |
|     1061 |      833 |
+----------+----------+
17 rows in set (0.05 sec)
```

This join only displays those route-and-flight combinations that match on both sides of the join. Routes without flights, or flights without routes, are not displayed. To display this missing information, a left outer join becomes necessary:

```
mysql> SELECT r.RouteID, f.FlightID
    -> FROM route AS r
    -> LEFT JOIN flight AS f
    -> ON r.RouteID = f.RouteID
    -> WHERE r.RouteID BETWEEN 1050 AND 1175;
+----------+----------+
| RouteID  | FlightID |
+----------+----------+
|     1059 |      857 |
|     1061 |      833 |
|     1071 |     NULL |
|     1097 |      589 |
|     1123 |      681 |
|     1133 |      765 |
|     1139 |      688 |
|     1140 |      689 |
|     1141 |      896 |
|     1141 |      898 |
|     1142 |      897 |
|     1142 |      899 |
|     1165 |      674 |
|     1167 |     NULL |
|     1169 |      671 |
|     1169 |      672 |
|     1173 |      871 |
|     1173 |      872 |
|     1175 |      876 |
+----------+----------+
19 rows in set (0.01 sec)
```

In English, this query translates to "select all the records from the left side of the join (*route*) and, for each row selected, either display the matching value from the right side (*flight*) or display a NULL value." This kind of join is known as a left join or, sometimes, a left outer join.

Notice the difference in the result set: The left outer join displays two additional routes, route 1071 and route 1167, for which no flights exist. This is because when processing the left outer join, MySQL begins by retrieving all of the records matching the query conditions from the table on the left of the join, and then proceeds to the table on the right of the join. As a result, records that exist on the left but have no counterpart on the right will still appear in the result set, with NULL values for the missing fields.

Contrast this to the equi-join used previously, which automatically omits these "orphan" records from the result set.

This kind of join comes in handy when you need to see which values from one table are missing in another table: All you need to do is look for the NULL values. In fact, you don't even need to look—you can have SQL do the heavy lifting for you by adding a new condition to handle this in the WHERE clause, as follows:

```
mysql> SELECT r.RouteID, f.FlightID
    -> FROM route AS r
    -> LEFT JOIN flight AS f
    -> ON r.RouteID = f.RouteID
    -> WHERE r.RouteID BETWEEN 1050 AND 1175
    -> AND f.FlightID IS NULL;
+---------+----------+
| RouteID | FlightID |
+---------+----------+
|    1071 |     NULL |
|    1167 |     NULL |
+---------+----------+
2 rows in set (0.00 sec)
```

TIP *When the field being used for the join has the same name in both tables, the USING clause provides a convenient shortcut over the ON syntax. The following two queries are equivalent:*

```
SELECT r.RouteID, f.FlightID
    FROM route AS r LEFT JOIN flight AS f
    ON r.RouteID = f.RouteID
    WHERE r.RouteID BETWEEN 1050 AND 1175;
SELECT r.RouteID, f.FlightID
    FROM route AS r LEFT JOIN flight AS f
    USING (RouteID)
    WHERE r.RouteID BETWEEN 1050 AND 1175;
```

In a similar vein, it's possible to construct a right outer join, wherein all the records in the table on the right side of the join are displayed, regardless of whether or not matching records in the table on the left side of the join exist. To illustrate, consider the following example, which checks if there are any aircraft types that are not currently in use by the airline:

```
mysql> SELECT a.AircraftID, at.AircraftName
    -> FROM aircraft AS a
    -> RIGHT JOIN aircrafttype AS at
    -> ON a.AircraftTypeID = at.AircraftTypeID;
+------------+------------------+
| AircraftID | AircraftName     |
+------------+------------------+
|       3451 | Boeing 747       |
|       3465 | Boeing 747       |
```

```
|     3145 | Boeing 747       |
|     3565 | Boeing 747       |
|     3425 | Boeing 767       |
|     NULL | Airbus A300/310  |
|     3467 | Airbus A330      |
|     3469 | Airbus A330      |
|     3427 | Airbus A330      |
|     3189 | Airbus A330      |
|     3470 | Airbus A330      |
|     3130 | Airbus A330      |
|     3452 | Airbus A340      |
|     3125 | Airbus A340      |
|     3128 | Airbus A340      |
|     3201 | Airbus A340      |
|     3223 | Airbus A380      |
+----------+------------------+
17 rows in set (0.00 sec)
```

In English, this query translates to "select all the records from the right side of the join (*aircrafttype*) and, for each record selected, either display the matching value from the left side (*aircraft*) or display a NULL value." The output is self-explanatory: The airline does not currently operate any Airbus A300/310 airplanes.

NOTE *The terms "left join" and "right join" are interchangeable, depending on where you're standing. A left join can be turned into a right join (and vice versa) simply by altering the order of the tables in the join. To illustrate, consider the following two queries, which are equivalent:*

```
SELECT * FROM c LEFT JOIN a USING (id);
SELECT * FROM a RIGHT JOIN c USING (id);
```

A refinement of the previous example is to use the COUNT() function in combination with the right outer join and a GROUP BY clause to calculate how many airplanes of each type the airline has in operation:

```
mysql> SELECT at.AircraftName, COUNT(a.AircraftID)
    -> FROM aircraft AS a
    -> RIGHT JOIN aircrafttype AS at
    -> ON a.AircraftTypeID = at.AircraftTypeID
    -> GROUP BY a.AircraftTypeID;
+-----------------+---------------------+
| AircraftName    | COUNT(a.AircraftID) |
+-----------------+---------------------+
| Airbus A300/310 |                   0 |
| Boeing 747      |                   4 |
| Boeing 767      |                   1 |
| Airbus A330     |                   6 |
| Airbus A340     |                   4 |
| Airbus A380     |                   1 |
+-----------------+---------------------+
6 rows in set (0.06 sec)
```

Self-Joins

In addition to cross, inner, and outer joins, MySQL supports a fourth type of join, known as a *self-join*. This type of join involves joining a table to itself, and it's typically used when working with results sets where field values contain internal links to each other.

NOTE *Since MySQL 5.0.12, there is a key difference in the output produced by a join created with the comma (,) operator and a join created with the* USING *clause: In the latter case, MySQL will automatically remove redundant join fields, such that these fields appear only once in the result set. To illustrate, compare the number of fields in the output generated by each of the following two joins:*

```
SELECT * FROM aircraft AS a INNER JOIN aircrafttype AS at
USING(AircraftTypeID);
SELECT * FROM aircraft AS a, aircrafttype AS at WHERE
a.AircraftTypeID = at.AircraftTypeID;
```

You'll see that the output of the first query contains only one instance of the common AircraftTypeID *field, while that of the second contains two such instances. This "coalescing" of duplicate join fields is intended for compliance with the SQL-2003 standard.*

To create a self-join, assign the table in question two different aliases and then use these aliases to construct a join, as though the aliases represented two separate tables. To illustrate, let's try querying the route table to identify "round-trip" routes—that is, routes between the same pair of cities. Because the same table contains both the route origin and destination, a simple SELECT won't work and neither will an inner join. The only way to perform such a query is with a self-join, as follows:

```
mysql> SELECT r1.RouteID, r1.From, r1.To, r1.Distance
    -> FROM route AS r1, route AS r2
    -> WHERE r1.From = r2.To
    -> AND r2.From = r1.To
    -> ORDER BY r1.Distance;
+---------+------+------+----------+
| RouteID | From | To   | Distance |
+---------+------+------+----------+
|    1175 |  132 |   56 |     1267 |
|    1176 |   56 |  132 |     1267 |
|    1139 |   83 |   87 |     2474 |
|    1140 |   87 |   83 |     2474 |
|    1142 |  201 |  126 |     3913 |
|    1141 |  126 |  201 |     3913 |
|    1193 |  201 |   92 |    10310 |
|    1192 |   92 |  201 |    10310 |
+---------+------+------+----------+
8 rows in set (0.00 sec)
```

Most of the magic here lies in the table aliasing. The previous query first creates two copies of the *route* table, aliased as *r1* and *r2,* respectively; joining these together with a self-join now becomes a simple matter.

Here's another example that, though not strictly a self-join, displays some interesting elements. The following query creates two aliases for the airport table and joins its *AirportID* fields to the *route* table's *From* and *To* fields in order to display human-readable airport names (origin and destination) for each route instead of numeric airport identifiers:

```
mysql> SELECT r.RouteID, a1.AirportName AS FromAirport,
    -> a2.AirportName AS ToAirport
    -> FROM route AS r, airport AS a1, airport AS a2
    -> WHERE a1.AirportID = r.From
    -> AND a2.AirportID = r.To;
+----------+----------------------+---------------------------+
| RouteID  | FromAirport          | ToAirport                 |
+----------+----------------------+---------------------------+
|     1005 | Orly Airport         | Gatwick Airport           |
|     1176 | Heathrow Airport     | Barajas Airport           |
|     1175 | Barajas Airport      | Heathrow Airport          |
|     1023 | Gatwick Airport      | Rome Ciampino Airport     |
|     1008 | Orly Airport         | Nice Cote d'Azur Airport  |
|     1009 | Orly Airport         | Zurich Airport            |
|     1165 | Zurich Airport       | Rome Ciampino Airport     |
|     1167 | Zurich Airport       | Heathrow Airport          |
|     1123 | Zurich Airport       | Gatwick Airport           |
...
+----------+----------------------+---------------------------+
29 rows in set (0.16 sec)
```

Unions

In addition to joins, MySQL 4.0 and later supports the UNION operator, which is used to combine the output of multiple SELECT queries into a single result set. Most often, this operator is used to add the result sets generated by different queries to create a single table of results.

To illustrate, consider if airport information was separated into two identically structured tables, *airportGB* and *airportFR,* as shown:

```
mysql> CREATE TEMPORARY TABLE airportUK
    -> SELECT * FROM airport WHERE CountryCode = 'UK';
Query OK, 3 rows affected (0.11 sec)
Records: 3  Duplicates: 0  Warnings: 0
mysql> CREATE TEMPORARY TABLE airportFR
    -> SELECT * FROM airport WHERE CountryCode = 'FR';
Query OK, 2 rows affected (0.13 sec)
Records: 2  Duplicates: 0  Warnings: 0
```

Then, the following query would return a combined result set containing the records from both tables:

```
mysql> SELECT AirportID, AirportName FROM airportUK
    -> UNION
    -> SELECT AirportID, AirportName FROM airportFR;
+-----------+------------------------------+
| AirportID | AirportName                  |
+-----------+------------------------------+
|        48 | Gatwick Airport              |
|        56 | Heathrow Airport             |
|       129 | Bristol International Airport |
|        34 | Orly Airport                 |
|       165 | Nice Cote d'Azur Airport     |
+-----------+------------------------------+
5 rows in set (0.00 sec)
```

You can combine as many SELECT queries as you like with the UNION operator, so long as two basic conditions are fulfilled.

- The number of fields returned by each SELECT query must be the same.
- The data types of the fields in each SELECT query must correspond to each other.

TIP *The* UNION *operator automatically eliminates duplicate rows from the composite result set (this behavior is similar to that obtained by adding the* DISTINCT *keyword to a regular* SELECT *query). To see all of the records (including duplicates) in the* UNION, *add the* ALL *keyword to the* UNION *operator, as in the example query:*

```
SELECT * FROM a UNION ALL SELECT * FROM b;
```

To sort the composite result set returned by a UNION operation, add an ORDER BY clause to the end of the query. However, remember to enclose each of the individual SELECTs in parentheses so that MySQL knows the ORDER BY clause is meant for the final result set and not for the last SELECT in the set. The following example illustrates, sorting the combined list of airports in reverse alphabetical order:

```
mysql> (SELECT AirportID, AirportName FROM airportUK)
    -> UNION
    -> (SELECT AirportID, AirportName FROM airportFR)
    -> ORDER BY AirportName DESC;
+-----------+------------------------------+
| AirportID | AirportName                  |
+-----------+------------------------------+
```

```
|        34 | Orly Airport                    |
|       165 | Nice Cote d'Azur Airport        |
|        56 | Heathrow Airport                |
|        48 | Gatwick Airport                 |
|       129 | Bristol International Airport   |
+-----------+--------------------------------+
5 rows in set (0.02 sec)
```

TIP *Adding an* ORDER BY *clause to individual* SELECT *queries within the* UNION *doesn't usually make too much sense because the result set generated by each individual query is never visible to the user; only the final result is visible. It's interesting to note, also, that queries using* UNION ALL *are often faster than queries using only* UNION.

Using Subqueries

Normally, query results are restricted through the addition of a WHERE or HAVING clause, which contains one or more conditional expressions used to filter out irrelevant records from the result set. Most often, these conditional tests use fixed constants—for example, "list all users older than 40" or "show all invoices between January and June"—making them easy to write and maintain.

However, a situation often arises when the conditional test used by a particular query depends on the value generated by another query—for example, "list all users older than the average user age" or "show the largest invoice from the smallest group of customers." In all such cases, the results generated by one query depend on the data generated by another, and the use of a constant value in the outer query's conditional test becomes infeasible. MySQL 4.1 and later support this requirement through subqueries.

NOTE *Subqueries, although useful, can significantly drain your MySQL RDBMS of performance. This is because at press time, subquery performance is suboptimal in MySQL 4.x and MySQL 5.x on data of any significant size. Subqueries can also be problematic to debug when the data sets returned by them are large or complex. Numerous improvements in the subquery processor are expected in MySQL 6.0; for a complete list, visit http://forge. mysql.com/wiki/Subquery_Works.*

A Simple Subquery

A *subquery* is simply a SELECT query that is subordinate to another query. MySQL enables you to nest queries within one another and to use the result set generated by an inner query within an outer one. As a result, instead of executing two (or more) separate queries, you execute a single query containing one (or more) subqueries.

A subquery works just like a regular SELECT query, except that its result set always consists of a single column containing one or more values. A subquery can be used anywhere an expression can be used; it must be enclosed in parentheses; and, like a regular SELECT query, it must contain a field list (as previously noted, this is a single-column list), a FROM clause with one or more table names, and optional WHERE, HAVING, and GROUP BY clauses.

To illustrate a typical subquery, let's go back to an earlier example: displaying which of the airline's routes originate at Heathrow Airport. This can be accomplished with an inner join, as shown:

```
mysql> SELECT r.RouteID
    -> FROM route AS r, airport AS a
    -> WHERE r.From = a.AirportID
    -> AND a.AirportCode='LHR';
+---------+
| RouteID |
+---------+
|    1176 |
|    1209 |
+---------+
2 rows in set (0.00 sec)
```

However, this can also be rewritten as a subquery:

```
mysql> SELECT r.RouteID
    -> FROM route AS r
    -> WHERE r.From =
    ->    (SELECT a.AirportID
    ->    FROM airport AS a
    ->    WHERE a.AirportCode='LHR');
+---------+
| RouteID |
+---------+
|    1176 |
|    1209 |
+---------+
2 rows in set (0.00 sec)
```

Thus, a subquery makes it possible to combine two or more queries into a single statement and to use the results of one query in the conditional clause of the other.

Each subquery must return a single column of results or else MySQL will not know how to handle the result set. Consider the following example, which demonstrates this by having the subquery return a multicolumn result set:

```
mysql> SELECT r.RouteID
    -> FROM route AS r
    -> WHERE r.From =
    ->    (SELECT *
```

```
    ->    FROM airport AS a
    ->    WHERE a.AirportCode='LHR');
ERROR 1241 (21000): Operand should contain 1 column(s)
```

You can nest subqueries to any depth, so long as the basic rules discussed previously are followed. Consider the following example, which demonstrates this by listing the flights operated by a Boeing 747:

```
mysql> SELECT f.FlightID
    -> FROM flight AS f
    -> WHERE f.AircraftID IN
    ->   (SELECT a.AircraftID
    ->   FROM aircraft AS a
    ->   WHERE a.AircraftTypeID =
    ->     (SELECT AircraftTypeID
    ->     FROM aircrafttype AS at
    ->     WHERE at.AircraftName = 'Boeing 747'
    ->     )
    ->   );
+----------+
| FlightID |
+----------+
|      535 |
|      652 |
|      662 |
|      675 |
|      896 |
|      898 |
|      897 |
|      899 |
|      812 |
|      857 |
+----------+
10 rows in set (0.01 sec)
```

CAUTION   *Because MySQL does not yet fully optimize subqueries, deeply nested subqueries can take a long time to execute, especially in certain situations where the outer query returns more records than the inner one.*

Types of Subqueries

Subqueries can be used in a number of different ways.

- Within a WHERE or HAVING clause
  - With comparison and logical operators
  - With the IN membership test
  - With the EXISTS Boolean test

- Within a FROM clause
- With UPDATE and DELETE queries

The following sections examine each of these aspects in greater detail.

Subqueries and the WHERE/HAVING Clause

MySQL enables you to include subqueries in either a WHERE clause (to constrain the records returned by the enclosing SELECT...WHERE) or a HAVING clause (to constrain the groups created by the enclosing SELECT...GROUP BY). The subquery, which is enclosed in parentheses, can be preceded by comparison and logical operators, the IN operator, or the EXISTS operator.

Subqueries and Comparison Operators   If a subquery produces a single value, you can use MySQL's comparison operators to compare it with the conditional expression specified in the outer query's WHERE or HAVING clause. To demonstrate, consider the following subquery, which returns the airline's longest route:

```
mysql>    SELECT r.RouteID
    ->    FROM route AS r
    ->    WHERE r.Distance =
    ->      (SELECT MAX(r.Distance)
    ->      FROM route AS r);
+---------+
| RouteID |
+---------+
|    1180 |
+---------+
1 row in set (0.03 sec)
```

It's also easy to add one more subquery, this one returning the number of the flight(s) operating said route:

```
mysql> SELECT f.FlightID
    -> FROM flight AS f
    -> WHERE f.RouteID =
    ->    (SELECT r.RouteID
    ->    FROM route AS r
    ->    WHERE r.Distance =
    ->      (SELECT MAX(r.Distance)
    ->      FROM route AS r));
+----------+
| FlightID |
+----------+
|      685 |
+----------+
1 row in set (0.00 sec)
```

You can also use inequality operators with a subquery, as illustrated by the following query, which calculates the average distance of the airline's routes and flags all those routes that are above this average:

```
mysql> SELECT r.RouteID, r.Distance
    -> FROM route AS r
    -> WHERE r.Distance >
    ->    (SELECT AVG(distance) FROM route);
+---------+----------+
| RouteID | Distance |
+---------+----------+
|    1003 |     7200 |
|    1133 |     6336 |
|    1141 |     3913 |
|    1142 |     3913 |
|    1180 |    10863 |
|    1193 |    10310 |
|    1192 |    10310 |
+---------+----------+
7 rows in set (0.01 sec)
```

TIP *With subqueries, you can use the* AND *and* OR *logical operators to add further constraints to a conditional test or the* NOT *logical operator to reverse it.*

Subqueries can also be used in the HAVING clause of a GROUP BY aggregation, as illustrated in the following trivial example, which returns the total number of flights operating today:

```
mysql> SELECT COUNT(fd.FlightID)
    -> FROM flightdep AS fd
    -> GROUP BY fd.DepDay
    -> HAVING fd.DepDay =
    ->    (SELECT WEEKDAY(NOW()));
+--------------------+
| COUNT(fd.FlightID) |
+--------------------+
|                 19 |
+--------------------+
1 row in set (0.00 sec)
```

Subqueries and the IN Operator   Comparison operators are appropriate only so long as the subquery returns a result column consisting of a single value. In case the result set returned by a subquery returns a list of values, however, comparison operators must be substituted by the IN operator.

The IN operator makes it possible to test if a particular value exists in the result set and to perform the outer query if the test is successful. To illustrate, consider the following query, which returns all of the flights operating to Changi Airport:

```
mysql> SELECT f.FlightID
    -> FROM flight AS f
    -> WHERE f.RouteID IN
    ->    (SELECT r.RouteID
    ->    FROM route AS r
    ->    WHERE r.To=
    ->      (SELECT a.AirportID
    ->      FROM airport AS a
    ->      WHERE a.AirportCode='SIN')
    ->    )
    -> ORDER BY FlightID DESC;
+----------+
| FlightID |
+----------+
|      898 |
|      896 |
|      725 |
+----------+
3 rows in set (0.06 sec)
```

Another example might involve finding out the number of routes operated by the airline from airports with more than two terminals:

```
mysql> SELECT r.From, COUNT(r.RouteID) FROM route AS r
    -> WHERE r.from IN
    ->    (SELECT a.AirportID FROM airport AS a
    ->    WHERE a.NumTerminals > 2)
    -> GROUP BY r.From;
+------+------------------+
| From | COUNT(r.RouteID) |
+------+------------------+
|   56 |                2 |
|   72 |                2 |
|  132 |                2 |
|  201 |                3 |
+------+------------------+
4 rows in set (0.00 sec)
```

You can bring in the airport names as well with a quick inner join:

```
mysql> SELECT a.AirportName, a.NumTerminals, COUNT(r.RouteID)
    -> FROM route AS r, airport AS a
    -> WHERE r.From = a.AirportID
```

```
    -> AND r.From IN
    ->    (SELECT a.AirportID FROM airport AS a
    ->    WHERE a.NumTerminals > 2)
    -> GROUP BY r.From;
+---------------------+---------------+-------------------+
| AirportName         | NumTerminals  | COUNT(r.RouteID)  |
+---------------------+---------------+-------------------+
| Heathrow Airport    |             5 |                 2 |
| Barcelona Inter...  |             3 |                 2 |
| Barajas Airport     |             4 |                 2 |
| Changi Airport      |             3 |                 3 |
+---------------------+---------------+-------------------+
4 rows in set (0.00 sec)
```

As with comparison operators, you can use the NOT keyword to reverse the results returned by the IN operator—or, in other words, return those records not matching the result collection generated by a subquery. The following example illustrates by reversing the previous query:

```
mysql> SELECT a.AirportName, a.NumTerminals, COUNT(r.RouteID)
    -> FROM route AS r, airport AS a
    -> WHERE r.From = a.AirportID
    -> AND r.From NOT IN
    ->    (SELECT a.AirportID FROM airport AS a
    ->    WHERE a.NumTerminals > 2)
    -> GROUP BY r.From;
+---------------------+---------------+-------------------+
| AirportName         | NumTerminals  | COUNT(r.RouteID)  |
+---------------------+---------------+-------------------+
| Orly Airport        |             2 |                 4 |
| Gatwick Airport     |             1 |                 2 |
| Schiphol Airport    |             1 |                 1 |
| Franz Josef St...   |             2 |                 2 |
| Lisbon Airport      |             2 |                 1 |
| Budapest Ferih...   |             2 |                 1 |
| Zurich Airport      |             1 |                 4 |
| Chhatrapati Sh...   |             2 |                 2 |
| Bristol Intern...   |             1 |                 1 |
| Nice Cote d'Az...   |             2 |                 2 |
+---------------------+---------------+-------------------+
10 rows in set (0.01 sec)
```

Subqueries and the EXISTS Operator   The special EXISTS operator can be used to check if a subquery produces any results at all. This makes it possible to conditionally execute the outer query only if the EXISTS test returns true.

Here's a simple example:

```
mysql> SELECT r.RouteID, r.From, r.To
    -> FROM route AS r
    -> WHERE EXISTS
    ->    (SELECT f.FlightID
    ->    FROM flight AS f, flightdep AS fd
    ->    WHERE f.FlightID = fd.FlightID
    ->    AND fd.DepTime BETWEEN '02:00' and '04:00');
Empty set (0.00 sec)
```

In this case, because the subquery returns an empty result set—there are no flights between 2 and 4 A.M.—the EXISTS test will return false and the outer query will not execute. If, on the other hand, the inner query returns a result set, the EXISTS test will return true, causing the outer query to execute. Here's an example:

```
mysql> SELECT r.RouteID, r.From, r.To
    -> FROM route AS r
    -> WHERE EXISTS
    ->    (SELECT f.FlightID
    ->    FROM flight AS f, flightdep AS fd
    ->    WHERE f.FlightID = fd.FlightID
    ->    AND fd.DepTime BETWEEN '00:00' and '04:00');
+---------+------+-----+
| RouteID | From | To  |
+---------+------+-----+
|    1003 |  126 |  56 |
|    1005 |   34 |  48 |
|    1176 |   56 | 132 |
|    1175 |  132 |  56 |
|    1018 |   34 |  87 |
...
+---------+------+-----+
29 rows in set (0.00 sec)
```

In this case, because there are some flights between 12 and 4 A.M., the inner query returns a result that, in turn, triggers the execution of the outer query.

It must be noted that when used in this manner, the actual content of the inner query is irrelevant; the previous output could just as well have been accomplished with the following:

```
mysql> SELECT r.RouteID, r.From, r.To
    -> FROM route AS r
    -> WHERE EXISTS
    ->    (SELECT 1);
+---------+------+-----+
| RouteID | From | To  |
+---------+------+-----+
```

```
|    1003 |   126 |  56 |
|    1005 |    34 |  48 |
|    1176 |    56 | 132 |
|    1175 |   132 |  56 |
|    1018 |    34 |  87 |
...
+---------+------+-----+
29 rows in set (0.00 sec)
```

The EXISTS operator is most often used with *correlated subqueries*—subqueries that use fields from the outer query in their clause(s). Such a reference, by a subquery to a field in its enclosing query, is called an *outer reference.*

When an outer reference appears within a subquery, MySQL has to reevaluate the subquery once for every record generated by the outer query and, therefore, test the subquery as many times as there are records in the outer query's result set. Here's an example of a correlated subquery:

```
mysql> SELECT * FROM route AS r
    -> WHERE r.RouteID IN
    ->   (SELECT f.RouteID
    ->   FROM flight AS f, flightdep AS fd
    ->   WHERE f.FlightID = fd.FlightID
    ->   AND f.RouteID = r.RouteID
    ->   AND fd.DepTime BETWEEN '00:00' AND '04:00');
+---------+------+-----+----------+----------+--------+
| RouteID | From | To  | Distance | Duration | Status |
+---------+------+-----+----------+----------+--------+
|    1133 |   74 | 126 |     6336 |      470 |      1 |
|    1141 |  126 | 201 |     3913 |      320 |      1 |
+---------+------+-----+----------+----------+--------+
2 rows in set (0.02 sec)
```

In this case, because the inner query contains a reference to a field in the outer query, MySQL cannot run the inner query only once. Rather, it has to run it over and over—once for every record in the outer table—substitute the value of the named field from that record in the subquery, and then decide whether to include that outer record in the final result set on the basis of whether the corresponding subquery returns a result set. This is obviously expensive in terms of performance, and so outer references should be avoided unless absolutely necessary.

For situations where an outer reference is unavoidable, the EXISTS operator comes in handy as a filter for the outer query's result set. Here's an example, which prints those routes for which no flights exist:

```
mysql> SELECT * FROM route AS r
    -> WHERE NOT EXISTS
    ->   (SELECT 1 FROM flight AS f
    ->   WHERE f.RouteID = r.RouteID);
```

```
+---------+------+----+----------+----------+--------+
| RouteID | From | To | Distance | Duration | Status |
+---------+------+----+----------+----------+--------+
|    1167 |   92 | 56 |      777 |       70 |      0 |
|    1071 |  132 | 72 |      505 |       65 |      0 |
+---------+------+----+----------+----------+--------+
2 rows in set (0.00 sec)
```

Subqueries, the IN Operator and Performance

MySQL 4.x and 5.x are particularly bad at optimizing subqueries that use the IN operator. This is because the MySQL optimizer automatically rewrites these subqueries as correlated subqueries, increasing the performance cost by adding unnecessary outer references. As an example, consider that given the following uncorrelated subquery:

```
SELECT r.RouteID, r.From, r.To
FROM route AS r WHERE r.RouteID IN
  (SELECT f.RouteID
  FROM flight AS f WHERE
  f.FlightID BETWEEN 600 AND 700);
```

MySQL will rewrite it to:

```
SELECT r.RouteID, r.From, r.To
FROM route AS r WHERE EXISTS
  (SELECT 1 FROM flight AS f
  WHERE f.RouteID = r.RouteID
  AND f.FlightID BETWEEN 600 AND 700);
```

For this reason, correlated subqueries (or uncorrelated subqueries that you know will be rewritten into correlated form by MySQL) should be avoided as much as possible and alternative methods of combining data (for example, self-joins or unions) should be explored, as they are often less costly in terms of both time and resource usage.

Subqueries and the FROM Clause

You can also use the results generated by a subquery as a table in the FROM clause of an enclosing SELECT statement. For example, consider the following query, which identifies the most popular aircraft type used by the airline:

```
mysql> SELECT MAX(sq.count), sq.AircraftName FROM
    ->    (SELECT COUNT(a.AircraftID) AS count, at.AircraftName
    ->    FROM aircraft AS a, aircrafttype AS at
```

```
    ->    WHERE a.AircraftTypeID = at.AircraftTypeID
    ->    GROUP BY a.AircraftTypeID)
    ->    AS sq;
+-----------------+--------------+
| MAX(sq.count)   | AircraftName |
+-----------------+--------------+
|               6 | Boeing 747   |
+-----------------+--------------+
1 row in set (0.01 sec)
```

Notice that, in this case, the result set generated by the inner query is stored in a temporary table and used in the FROM clause of the outer query. Such a table is referred to as a *derived table* or a *materialized subquery*. Notice also that when using subquery results in this manner, the derived table must be first aliased to a table name or else MySQL will not know how to refer to fields within it. As an example, look what happens if you re-run the previous query without the table alias:

```
mysql> SELECT MAX(sq.count), sq.AircraftName FROM
    ->    (SELECT COUNT(a.AircraftID) AS count, at.AircraftName
    ->    FROM aircraft AS a, aircrafttype AS at
    ->    WHERE a.AircraftTypeID = at.AircraftTypeID
    ->    GROUP BY a.AircraftTypeID);
ERROR 1248 (42000): Every derived table must have its own alias
```

Another example might involve finding out on which days of the week is the number of flights operated by the airline above average. Here, too, a subquery can be used to generate a table containing a count of the number of flights on each day, and this table can then be used (within the outer query's FROM clause) to compare each day's count with the average value:

```
mysql> SELECT x.DepDay FROM
    ->    (SELECT fd.DepDay, COUNT(fd.FlightID) AS c
    ->    FROM flightdep AS fd
    ->    GROUP BY fd.DepDay)
    -> AS x
    -> WHERE x.c >
    ->    (SELECT COUNT(fd.FlightID)/7 FROM flightdep AS fd);
+--------+
| DepDay |
+--------+
|      1 |
|      2 |
|      3 |
|      4 |
|      5 |
+--------+
5 rows in set (0.00 sec)
```

Subqueries and Other DML Statements

The examples you've seen thus far have only used subqueries in the context of a
SELECT statement. However, subqueries can just as easily be used to constrain UPDATE
and DELETE statements. Here's an example that deletes all routes originating from
Changi Airport:

```
mysql> DELETE FROM route
    -> WHERE route.From =
    ->    (SELECT AirportID FROM airport
    ->    WHERE AirportCode = 'SIN');
Query OK, 3 rows affected (0.00 sec)
```

The IN membership test works here, too—consider the next example, which deletes
all routes originating in the United Kingdom:

```
mysql> DELETE FROM route
    -> WHERE route.From IN
    ->    (SELECT AirportID FROM airport
    ->    WHERE CountryCode = 'UK');
Query OK, 5 rows affected (0.05 sec)
```

UPDATEs can be performed in a similar manner. Consider the following query,
which turns all Boeing aircraft into Airbus A330 aircraft:

```
mysql> UPDATE aircraft
    -> SET AircraftTypeID =
    ->    (SELECT AircraftTypeID
    ->    FROM aircrafttype
    ->    WHERE AircraftName = 'Airbus A330')
    -> WHERE AircraftTypeID IN
    ->    (SELECT AircraftTypeID
    ->    FROM aircrafttype
    ->    WHERE AircraftName LIKE 'Boeing%');
Query OK, 5 rows affected (0.01 sec)
Rows matched: 5  Changed: 5  Warnings: 0
```

Another example might involve reading flight departure times from the *flightdep*
table and writing them to the *flight* table, using the flight number as link. Here's how:

```
mysql> ALTER TABLE flight ADD DepTime TIME NOT NULL;
Query OK, 32 rows affected (0.05 sec)
Records: 32  Duplicates: 0  Warnings: 0

mysql> UPDATE flight SET DepTime =
    ->    (SELECT DepTime FROM flightdep
    ->    WHERE flightdep.FlightID = flight.FlightID
    ->    GROUP BY flightdep.FlightID);
Query OK, 32 rows affected (0.02 sec)
Rows matched: 32  Changed: 32  Warnings: 0
```

Circular References in UPDATE and DELETE Statements   MySQL won't let you delete or update a table's data if you're simultaneously reading that same data with a subquery, as doing so raises the possibility that your subquery might reference rows that have already been deleted or altered. Therefore, the table named in an outer DELETE or UPDATE DML statement cannot appear in the FROM clause of an inner subquery.

To illustrate this, consider the situation where the airline needs to remove "orphan" routes—routes without a corresponding flight—from the database. This appears simple at first glance: Find these routes using a LEFT JOIN between the *route* and *flight* tables with an IS NULL clause and then delete them using a subquery. Here's the query:

```
mysql> DELETE FROM route
    -> WHERE RouteID IN
    ->   (SELECT r.RouteID
    ->   FROM route AS r
    ->   LEFT JOIN flight AS f
    ->   USING (RouteID)
    ->   WHERE f.FlightID IS NULL);
ERROR 1093 (HY000): You can't specify target table 'route' for update
in FROM clause
```

MySQL will not permit this operation, as it creates a circular reference. A more appropriate way to accomplish this would be with a correlated subquery, as follows:

```
mysql> DELETE FROM route
    -> WHERE NOT EXISTS
    ->   (SELECT 1 FROM flight
    ->   WHERE flight.RouteID = route.RouteID);
Query OK, 2 rows affected (0.07 sec)
```

Using Views

Joins and subqueries make it easy to combine data from normalized tables and obtain different perspectives of a database. However, in highly normalized databases with multiple foreign key relationships between tables, getting just the data you need is a reasonably complex task requiring a deep understanding of the underlying table relationships.

To illustrate, consider the SQL query you'd write in order to get a flight timetable for the week:

```
mysql> SELECT DISTINCT r.RouteID, a1.AirportCode AS FromAirport,
    -> a2.AirportCode AS ToAirport, f.FlightID,
    -> fd.DepTime, fd.DepDay
    -> FROM route AS r, flight AS f,
    -> flightdep AS fd, airport AS a1,
    -> airport AS a2
    -> WHERE f.FlightID = fd.FlightID
    -> AND r.RouteID = f.RouteID
```

```
    -> AND r.From = a1.AirportID
    -> AND r.To = a2.AirportID;
+----------+-------------+-----------+----------+----------+--------+
| RouteID  | FromAirport | ToAirport | FlightID | DepTime  | DepDay |
+----------+-------------+-----------+----------+----------+--------+
|     1005 | ORY         | LGW       |      535 | 15:30:00 |      2 |
|     1005 | ORY         | LGW       |      535 | 15:30:00 |      4 |
|     1175 | MAD         | LHR       |      876 | 07:10:00 |      1 |
|     1175 | MAD         | LHR       |      876 | 07:10:00 |      2 |
|     1175 | MAD         | LHR       |      876 | 07:10:00 |      3 |
|     1175 | MAD         | LHR       |      876 | 07:10:00 |      4 |
|     1175 | MAD         | LHR       |      876 | 07:10:00 |      5 |
|     1018 | ORY         | BUD       |      652 | 14:10:00 |      1 |
...
+----------+-------------+-----------+----------+----------+--------+
108 rows in set (0.38 sec)
```

This is a reasonably complex join, which collects and presents data from four different tables to answer a specific question. If the question is asked repeatedly, or with minor variations, it makes sense to store this query in the database and expose it to the outside world as a predefined *view* that can be further manipulated by users through standard SQL. These prepackaged views provide a simple interface to complex data sets, and have been supported in MySQL since v5.0.

A Simple View

Think of a view as a "virtual table" whose contours are defined by the parameters of the SELECT statement that was used to generate it. The fields of this table are derived directly from the fields specified in the SELECT statement, while the contents of the table correspond to the set of records returned by the SELECT statement. Because SELECT statements can span multiple tables, a view can (and usually does) contain records from different tables.

Like a regular table, a view has a name; therefore, it can itself be the subject of other SELECT queries and—in some cases—it can even be modified via INSERT, UPDATE, and DELETE statements. To illustrate, consider the following example, which creates a simple view:

```
mysql> CREATE VIEW v_round_trip_routes AS
    ->      SELECT r1.RouteID, r1.From, r1.To, r1.Distance
    ->      FROM route AS r1, route AS r2
    ->      WHERE r1.From = r2.To
    ->      AND r2.From = r1.To;
Query OK, 0 rows affected (0.13 sec)
```

To create a view, MySQL offers the CREATE VIEW command. This command must be followed by the view name, the keyword AS, and the SELECT statement that generates the view. This is illustrated in the previous example, which creates a view named *v_round_trip_routes* to display only round-trip routes.

This view can now be accessed as though it were a regular table:

```
mysql> SELECT v.RouteID, v.From, v.To
    -> FROM v_round_trip_routes AS v;
+---------+------+-----+
| RouteID | From | To  |
+---------+------+-----+
|    1175 |  132 |  56 |
|    1176 |   56 | 132 |
|    1142 |  201 | 126 |
|    1141 |  126 | 201 |
|    1192 |   92 | 201 |
|    1140 |   87 |  83 |
|    1139 |   83 |  87 |
|    1193 |  201 |  92 |
+---------+------+-----+
8 rows in set (0.10 sec)
```

Records from the view can be filtered using a WHERE clause, as with any other table. Consider the next example, which displays round-trip routes with distances greater than 3,000 kilometers:

```
mysql> SELECT v.RouteID, v.From, v.To, v.Distance
    -> FROM v_round_trip_routes AS v
    -> WHERE v.Distance > 3000;
+---------+------+-----+----------+
| RouteID | From | To  | Distance |
+---------+------+-----+----------+
|    1142 |  201 | 126 |     3913 |
|    1141 |  126 | 201 |     3913 |
|    1192 |   92 | 201 |    10310 |
|    1193 |  201 |  92 |    10310 |
+---------+------+-----+----------+
4 rows in set (0.01 sec)
```

The key thing to note about a view is that it automatically reflects changes in its underlying tables. Consider, for example, what happens when a new round-trip route is added:

```
mysql> INSERT INTO route
    -> (RouteID, `From`, `To`, Distance, Duration, Status)
    -> VALUES
    -> (1016, 129, 132, 1235, 150, 1),
    -> (1017, 132, 129, 1235, 150, 1);
Query OK, 2 rows affected (0.02 sec)
Records: 2  Duplicates: 0  Warnings: 0
```

The view automatically reflects the change in the underlying table:

```
mysql> SELECT v.RouteID, v.From, v.To, v.Distance
    -> FROM v_round_trip_routes AS v;
+----------+------+------+----------+
| RouteID  | From | To   | Distance |
+----------+------+------+----------+
|     1175 |  132 |   56 |     1267 |
|     1176 |   56 |  132 |     1267 |
|     1142 |  201 |  126 |     3913 |
|     1141 |  126 |  201 |     3913 |
|     1192 |   92 |  201 |    10310 |
|     1140 |   87 |   83 |     2474 |
|     1139 |   83 |   87 |     2474 |
|     1193 |  201 |   92 |    10310 |
|     1017 |  132 |  129 |     1235 |
|     1016 |  129 |  132 |     1235 |
+----------+------+------+----------+
10 rows in set (0.16 sec)
```

It's also possible to join the fields in a view to other tables, as in this next example, which joins the *airport* table to retrieve airport names for each round-trip route:

```
mysql> SELECT v.RouteID, a.AirportName AS FromAirport
    -> FROM v_round_trip_routes AS v, airport AS a
    -> WHERE v.From = a.AirportID;
+----------+-----------------------------------------------+
| RouteID  | FromAirport                                   |
+----------+-----------------------------------------------+
|     1175 | Barajas Airport                               |
|     1176 | Heathrow Airport                              |
|     1142 | Changi Airport                                |
|     1141 | Chhatrapati Shivaji International Airport      |
|     1192 | Zurich Airport                                |
|     1140 | Budapest Ferihegy International Airport        |
|     1139 | Lisbon Airport                                |
|     1193 | Changi Airport                                |
|     1017 | Barajas Airport                               |
|     1016 | Bristol International Airport                  |
+----------+-----------------------------------------------+
10 rows in set (0.01 sec)
```

A view only allows access to the fields listed in its SELECT statement; any attempt to access other fields, even if they exist in the underlying table, will generate an error. Consider what happens when you try accessing the *route.Status* field, which is not part of the view definition, through the view:

```
mysql> SELECT v.RouteID, a.AirportName AS FromAirport,
    -> v.Status FROM v_round_trip_routes AS v,
    -> airport AS a WHERE v.From = a.AirportID;
ERROR 1054 (42S22): Unknown column 'v.Status' in 'field list'
```

TIP *Looking for an easy way to restrict access to certain table fields? Grant access to a view that contains only the allowed fields while restricting access to the underlying table. MySQL's privilege system, which is the key to defining these access rules, is discussed in Chapter 11.*

Views are listed in the output of the SHOW TABLES command, as shown:

```
mysql> SHOW TABLES;
+--------------------+
| Tables_in_db1      |
+--------------------+
| aircraft           |
| aircrafttype       |
| airport            |
...
| user               |
| v_round_trip_routes |
+--------------------+
13 rows in set (0.00 sec)
```

It's a good idea to prefix your view names with a character or label, such as *v*, *v_*, or *view_*, so that you can identify them easily in the output of the SHOW TABLES command.

However, you can't use the DROP TABLE command to remove a view; instead, use the DROP VIEW command with the view name as an argument. It's worth noting, however, that dropping a table does not automatically remove any views that depend on it.

```
mysql> DROP VIEW v_timetable;
Query OK, 0 rows affected (0.03 sec)
```

To view (pardon the pun) the SELECT statement used for a particular view, use the SHOW CREATE VIEW command with the view name as an argument. Here's an example:

```
mysql> SHOW CREATE VIEW v_round_trip_routes\G
*************************** 1. row ***************************
                View: v_round_trip_routes
         Create View: CREATE ALGORITHM=UNDEFINED
DEFINER=`root`@`localhost` SQL SECURITY DEFINER
VIEW `v_round_trip_routes` AS
SELECT `r1`.`RouteID` AS `RouteID
`,`r1`.`From` AS `From`,`r1`.`To` AS `To`,`r1`.`Distance` AS `Distance`
FROM (`route` `r1` JOIN `route` `r2`) WHERE ((`r1`.`From` = `r2`.`To`))
```

PART I

```
and (`r2`.`From` = `r1`.`To`))
character_set_client: latin1
collation_connection: latin1_swedish_ci
1 row in set (0.01 sec)
```

NOTE *To create a view, a user must have the* CREATE VIEW *privilege. To see the SQL commands used to create a view, a user must have the* SHOW VIEW *privilege. Privileges are discussed in greater detail in Chapter 11.*

View Security

One of the biggest benefits of views is that they make it possible to restrict the amount of raw information users can access. In this context, the CREATE VIEW command supports an additional SQL SECURITY clause, which specifies the user account whose privileges should be considered when granting access to the view: the user who created it (DEFINER) or the user who invoked it (INVOKER). By default, MySQL allows access to the user who created the view (DEFINER).

Here's an example:

```
mysql> CREATE
    -> DEFINER = 'joe'@'localhost' SQL SECURITY DEFINER
    -> VIEW v_round_trip_routes AS
    -> SELECT r1.RouteID, r1.From, r1.To, r1.Distance
    -> FROM route AS r1, route AS r2
    -> WHERE r1.From = r2.To
    -> AND r2.From = r1.To;
Query OK, 0 rows affected, 1 warning (0.00 sec)
```

TIP *MySQL is always able to automatically identify the definer of a view. However, if you have the appropriate administrative privileges, you can change this to reflect a different user by adding a* DEFINER *clause to the* CREATE VIEW *statement. To avoid errors when doing this, make sure that the user registered as* DEFINER *has all the privileges necessary to perform the* SELECT *statement used by the view.*

Multitable Views

As noted earlier, a view can itself contain fields from different tables. To illustrate, here's a view that produces the flight timetable from an earlier example, containing fields from four different tables:

```
mysql> CREATE VIEW v_timetable AS
    ->    SELECT DISTINCT r.RouteID, a1.AirportCode AS FromAirport,
    ->    a2.AirportCode AS ToAirport, f.FlightID,
```

```
    ->    fd.DepTime, fd.DepDay
    ->    FROM route AS r, flight AS f,
    ->    flightdep AS fd, airport AS a1,
    ->    airport AS a2
    ->    WHERE f.FlightID = fd.FlightID
    ->    AND r.RouteID = f.RouteID
    ->    AND r.From = a1.AirportID
    ->    AND r.To = a2.AirportID;
Query OK, 0 rows affected (0.60 sec)
```

And here's an example of using the view to list all flights on Tuesdays:

```
mysql> SELECT v.RouteID, v.FromAirport,
    -> v.ToAirport, v.FlightID, v.DepTime
    -> FROM v_timetable AS v
    -> WHERE v.DepDay = 2 ORDER BY v.DepTime;
+---------+-------------+-----------+----------+----------+
| RouteID | FromAirport | ToAirport | FlightID | DepTime  |
+---------+-------------+-----------+----------+----------+
|    1141 | BOM         | SIN       |      896 | 00:30:00 |
|    1133 | MUC         | BOM       |      765 | 01:45:00 |
|    1175 | MAD         | LHR       |      876 | 07:10:00 |
|    1009 | ORY         | ZRH       |      663 | 09:10:00 |
|    1173 | BCN         | AMS       |      872 | 12:50:00 |
|    1209 | LHR         | CIA       |      826 | 13:45:00 |
|    1018 | ORY         | BUD       |      652 | 14:10:00 |
...
+---------+-------------+-----------+----------+----------+
17 rows in set (0.10 sec)
```

Views can also be generated from SELECT statements that contain subqueries. Here's a simple example, which displays a list of all flights to Changi Airport:

```
mysql> CREATE VIEW v_flights_to_changi AS
    ->    SELECT FlightID, RouteID, AircraftID
    ->    FROM flight AS f
    ->    WHERE f.RouteID IN
    ->      (SELECT r.RouteID
    ->      FROM route AS r
    ->      WHERE r.To=
    ->        (SELECT a.AirportID
    ->        FROM airport AS a
    ->        WHERE a.AirportCode='SIN')
    ->      )
    ->    ORDER BY FlightID DESC;
Query OK, 0 rows affected (0.02 sec)
mysql> SELECT * FROM v_flights_to_changi;
```

```
+----------+---------+------------+
| FlightID | RouteID | AircraftID |
+----------+---------+------------+
|      898 |    1141 |       3145 |
|      896 |    1141 |       3145 |
|      725 |    1192 |       3125 |
+----------+---------+------------+
3 rows in set (0.00 sec)
```

Nested Views

Views can also reference one another. Consider the next example, which builds on an example from the previous section to create a child view that only shows the weekend flight timetable:

```
mysql> CREATE VIEW v_weekend_timetable AS
    ->     SELECT * FROM v_timetable AS vt
    ->     WHERE vt.DepDay = 6 OR vt.DepDay = 7;
Query OK, 0 rows affected (0.00 sec)
mysql> SELECT v.RouteID, v.FromAirport,
    -> v.ToAirport, v.FlightID, v.DepTime, v.DepDay
    -> FROM v_weekend_timetable AS v
    -> ORDER BY v.DepTime;
+---------+-------------+-----------+----------+----------+--------+
| RouteID | FromAirport | ToAirport | FlightID | DepTime  | DepDay |
+---------+-------------+-----------+----------+----------+--------+
|    1141 | BOM         | SIN       |      896 | 00:30:00 |      6 |
|    1141 | BOM         | SIN       |      896 | 00:30:00 |      7 |
|    1133 | MUC         | BOM       |      765 | 01:45:00 |      6 |
...
+---------+-------------+-----------+----------+----------+--------+
22 rows in set (0.02 sec)
```

Note, however, that when two views depend on each other and the parent is dropped, MySQL will generate an error on any attempt to use the child view:

```
mysql> CREATE VIEW v_temp AS
    ->     SELECT * FROM v_weekend_timetable;
Query OK, 0 rows affected (0.02 sec)
mysql> DROP VIEW v_weekend_timetable;
Query OK, 0 rows affected (0.00 sec)
mysql> SELECT * FROM v_temp;
ERROR 1356 (HY000): View 'db1.v_temp' references invalid table(s)
or column(s) or function(s) or definer/invoker of view lack rights to
use them
```

Updatable Views

Under certain conditions, it's also possible to execute INSERT, UPDATE, or DELETE statements on a view and have the resulting changes applied to the underlying table. To illustrate, consider this next view, which generates a subset of the *airport* table:

```
mysql> CREATE VIEW v_small_airports AS
    ->    SELECT * FROM airport
    ->    WHERE NumTerminals <= 2;
Query OK, 0 rows affected (0.00 sec)
mysql> SELECT AirportID, AirportCode, NumTerminals, CityName
    -> FROM v_small_airports;
+-----------+-------------+--------------+-----------+
| AirportID | AirportCode | NumTerminals | CityName  |
+-----------+-------------+--------------+-----------+
|        34 | ORY         |            2 | Paris     |
|        48 | LGW         |            1 | London    |
|        59 | CIA         |            1 | Rome      |
|        62 | AMS         |            1 | Amsterdam |
|        74 | MUC         |            2 | Munich    |
|        83 | LIS         |            2 | Lisbon    |
|        87 | BUD         |            2 | Budapest  |
|        92 | ZRH         |            1 | Zurich    |
|       126 | BOM         |            2 | Bombay    |
|       129 | BRS         |            1 | Bristol   |
|       165 | NCE         |            2 | Nice      |
+-----------+-------------+--------------+-----------+
11 rows in set (0.02 sec)
```

You can add a new record to the underlying table through the view by using an INSERT statement:

```
mysql> INSERT INTO v_small_airports
    ->    (AirportID, AirportCode, AirportName,
    ->    CityName, CountryCode, NumRunways, NumTerminals)
    ->    VALUES
    ->    (198, 'GOI', 'Dabolim Airport',
    ->    'Goa', 'IN', 1, 2);
Query OK, 1 row affected (0.00 sec)
```

In a similar vein, you can update the underlying table, again through the view:

```
mysql> UPDATE v_small_airports
    -> SET NumTerminals = 1
    -> WHERE AirportCode = 'GOI';
Query OK, 1 row affected (0.00 sec)
Rows matched: 1  Changed: 1  Warnings: 0
mysql> SELECT AirportID, AirportCode, NumTerminals, CityName
    -> FROM v_small_airports;
```

```
+-----------+-------------+--------------+-----------+
| AirportID | AirportCode | NumTerminals | CityName  |
+-----------+-------------+--------------+-----------+
|        34 | ORY         |            2 | Paris     |
|        48 | LGW         |            1 | London    |
|        59 | CIA         |            1 | Rome      |
|        62 | AMS         |            1 | Amsterdam |
|        74 | MUC         |            2 | Munich    |
|        83 | LIS         |            2 | Lisbon    |
|        87 | BUD         |            2 | Budapest  |
|        92 | ZRH         |            1 | Zurich    |
|       126 | BOM         |            2 | Bombay    |
|       129 | BRS         |            1 | Bristol   |
|       165 | NCE         |            2 | Nice      |
|       198 | GOI         |            1 | Goa       |
+-----------+-------------+--------------+-----------+
12 rows in set (0.02 sec)
```

And you can also delete records through the view, as shown:

```
mysql> DELETE FROM v_small_airports
    -> WHERE AirportCode = 'GOI';
Query OK, 1 row affected (0.00 sec)
```

In more general terms, a view will allow UPDATE and DELETE operations if it does not make use of:

- Temporary tables
- Group functions and/or the GROUP BY and HAVING clauses
- Unions or outer joins
- Correlated subqueries

In addition, a view allows INSERT statements when all of the fields needed for a successful INSERT are present in the view.

Views that make use of noncorrelated subqueries are also updatable, subject to these conditions. Consider this next example, which adds a new record to the *v_flights_to_changi* view, created in a previous section with a subquery:

```
mysql> INSERT INTO v_flights_to_changi
    -> VALUES (991,1141,3145);
Query OK, 1 row affected (0.00 sec)
mysql> SELECT * FROM v_flights_to_changi;
+----------+---------+------------+
| FlightID | RouteID | AircraftID |
+----------+---------+------------+
```

```
|       898 |    1141 |       3145 |
|       896 |    1141 |       3145 |
|       725 |    1192 |       3125 |
|       991 |    1141 |       3145 |
+-----------+---------+------------+
4 rows in set (0.00 sec)
mysql> DELETE FROM v_flights_to_changi
    -> WHERE FlightID = 991;
Query OK, 1 row affected (0.00 sec)
mysql> SELECT * FROM v_flights_to_changi;
+-----------+---------+------------+
| FlightID  | RouteID | AircraftID |
+-----------+---------+------------+
|       898 |    1141 |       3145 |
|       896 |    1141 |       3145 |
|       725 |    1192 |       3125 |
+-----------+---------+------------+
3 rows in set (0.01 sec)
```

Joins

Multitable views that make use of inner joins can be updated, so long as the INSERT or UPDATE statement references fields from only one of the tables used in the join. However, DELETE statements will fail when executed on a multitable view.

Here's an example:

```
mysql> CREATE VIEW v_fra_join AS
    ->     SELECT f.FlightID, f.RouteID, `From`, `To`,
    ->     Distance, Duration, Status, f.AircraftID,
    ->     AircraftTypeID, RegNum, LastMaintEnd,
    ->     NextMaintBegin, NextMaintEnd FROM
    ->     flight AS f,
    ->     route AS r, aircraft AS a
    ->     WHERE f.RouteID = r.RouteID
    ->     AND f.AircraftID = a.AircraftID;
Query OK, 0 rows affected (0.00 sec)
mysql> INSERT INTO v_fra_join (FlightID, RouteID, AircraftID)
    -> VALUES (901, 1142, 3469);
Query OK, 1 row affected (0.00 sec)
```

The previous INSERT succeeds because the three fields referenced in the INSERT statement all belong to the *flight* table. However, look what happens if you try to insert a record that spans two tables, *flight* and *route*:

```
mysql> INSERT INTO v_fra_join
    -> (RouteID, `From`, `To`, Distance,
    -> Duration, Status) VALUES (1301, 87,
    -> 201, 1000, 150, 1);
ERROR 1393 (HY000): Can not modify more than one base table
```

```
through a join view 'db1.v_fra_join'
mysql> UPDATE v_fra_join SET Distance = 3915,
    -> AircraftTypeID = 626 WHERE FlightID=901;
ERROR 1393 (HY000): Can not modify more than one base table
through a join view 'db1.v_fra_join'
```

View Constraints

The CREATE VIEW statement also supports an additional clause, the WITH CHECK
OPTION clause. This clause can help enforce data integrity by only allowing those
records to be inserted or updated that match the constraints specified in the view.

To illustrate, consider the *v_small_airports* view created in a previous example. This
view generates a list of all airports with two or fewer terminals. However, in its current
incarnation, you can still insert records into this view (and hence into the underlying
airport table) for airports containing more than two terminals:

```
mysql> INSERT INTO v_small_airports
    -> (AirportID, AirportCode, AirportName,
    -> CityName, CountryCode, NumRunways, NumTerminals)
    -> VALUES
    -> (198, 'GOI', 'Dabolim Airport',
    -> 'Goa', 'IN', 1, 5);
Query OK, 1 row affected (0.00 sec)
```

To disallow this and only allow records that match the view constraint (*NumTerminals*
<= 2), re-create the view with the WITH CHECK OPTION clause and then try repeating the
previous INSERT statement:

```
mysql> DROP VIEW v_small_airports;
Query OK, 0 rows affected (0.05 sec)
mysql> CREATE VIEW v_small_airports AS
    ->    SELECT * FROM airport
    ->    WHERE NumTerminals <= 2
    ->    WITH CHECK OPTION;
Query OK, 0 rows affected (0.05 sec)
mysql> INSERT INTO v_small_airports
    -> (AirportID, AirportCode, AirportName,
    -> CityName, CountryCode, NumRunways, NumTerminals)
    -> VALUES
    -> (198, 'GOI', 'Dabolim Airport',
    -> 'Goa', 'IN', 1, 5);
ERROR 1369 (HY000): CHECK OPTION failed 'db1.v_small_airports'
```

However, a record that satisfies the view constraint (*NumTerminals* <= 2) will be
allowed:

```
mysql> INSERT INTO v_small_airports
    -> (AirportID, AirportCode, AirportName,
```

```
    -> CityName, CountryCode, NumRunways, NumTerminals)
    -> VALUES
    -> (198, 'GOI', 'Dabolim Airport',
    -> 'Goa', 'IN', 1, 2);
Query OK, 1 row affected (0.00 sec)
```

By default, MySQL "cascades" the checks performed by the WITH CHECK OPTION clause so that constraints specified both in the target view and its parents are taken into account. To illustrate, consider the next example, which creates a new view for UK airports only, based on the *v_small_airports* view:

```
mysql> CREATE VIEW v_small_airports_uk AS
    ->    SELECT * FROM v_small_airports
    ->    WHERE CountryCode = 'UK'
    ->    WITH CHECK OPTION;
Query OK, 0 rows affected (0.00 sec)
```

Now, MySQL will only allow records to be inserted if they match the constraints specified for this view (*CountryCode = 'UK'*) as well as for the parent view (*NumTerminals <= 2*):

```
mysql> INSERT INTO v_small_airports_uk
    -> (AirportID, AirportCode, AirportName,
    -> CityName, CountryCode, NumRunways, NumTerminals)
    -> VALUES
    -> (199, 'LCY', 'London City Airport',
    -> 'London', 'GB', 1, 2);
ERROR 1369 (HY000): CHECK OPTION failed 'db1.v_small_airports_uk'
mysql> INSERT INTO v_small_airports_uk
    -> (AirportID, AirportCode, AirportName,
    -> CityName, CountryCode, NumRunways, NumTerminals)
    -> VALUES
    -> (199, 'LCY', 'London City Airport',
    -> 'London', 'UK', 1, 5);
ERROR 1369 (HY000): CHECK OPTION failed 'db1.v_small_airports_uk'
mysql> INSERT INTO v_small_airports_uk
    -> (AirportID, AirportCode, AirportName,
    -> CityName, CountryCode, NumRunways, NumTerminals)
    -> VALUES
    -> (199, 'LCY', 'London City Airport',
    -> 'London', 'UK', 1, 2);
Query OK, 1 row affected (0.00 sec)
```

TIP   *To force MySQL to only consider the constraints of the named view (and not its parents), replace the* WITH CHECK OPTION *clause with a* WITH LOCAL CHECK OPTION *clause.*

Summary

This chapter discussed joins, subqueries, and views—three common methods of exploiting relationships between tables and retrieving record subsets. Joins are table combinations created by linking together common fields. Subqueries are nested SELECT queries whose results serve as filters for the queries enclosing them. Views are prepackaged SQL queries that serve as "virtual tables" and that come in handy for repeated use of the same (complex) query. This chapter offered an overview of the different join types—cross joins, inner joins, outer joins, self-joins, and unions—and explored how subqueries and views can be used within the WHERE and FROM clauses of a SELECT statement, as well as with other DML statements such as UPDATE and DELETE.

At press time, MySQL's subquery implementation is still far from perfect, and joins tend to display better performance than subqueries in most cases. Subqueries can also be problematic to debug when the data sets returned by them are large or complex. Therefore, at least for the near future, it's recommended that you use joins, unions, and other SQL constructs to ensure optimal performance of your application and minimal resource wastage on the RDBMS.

To learn more about the topics discussed in this chapter, consider visiting the following links:

- Detailed information on MySQL join syntax at http://dev.mysql.com/doc/refman/5.1/en/join.html

- Information on how MySQL optimizes outer joins and left joins at http://dev.mysql.com/doc/refman/5.1/en/outer-join-simplification.html and http://dev.mysql.com/doc/refman/5.1/en/left-join-optimization.html

- Information on how MySQL optimizes nested joins at http://dev.mysql.com/doc/refman/5.1/en/nested-joins.html

- Detailed information on MySQL subquery syntax at http://dev.mysql.com/doc/refman/5.1/en/subqueries.html

- Restrictions on MySQL subqueries at http://dev.mysql.com/doc/refman/5.1/en/subquery-restrictions.html

- Optimizing MySQL subqueries at http://dev.mysql.com/doc/refman/5.1/en/in-subquery-optimization.html

- Current information on the state of MySQL subquery optimization at http://forge.mysql.com/wiki/Subquery_Works

- Detailed information on MySQL view syntax at http://dev.mysql.com/doc/refman/5.1/en/views.html

- Restrictions on MySQL views at http://dev.mysql.com/doc/refman/5.1/en/view-restrictions.html

CHAPTER 5

Using Transactions

Usually, MySQL queries are executed independently of each other, with little regard for what had gone before or what has yet to come. A series of INSERT or UPDATE statements, for example, is executed sequentially, regardless of whether any of the queries in the series fail or generate errors. This is because MySQL treats each query as a self-contained unit, bearing no relationship to other queries before or after it.

Most often, this stateless approach works well, especially in the case of small- and medium-sized applications associated with simple business logic. In more complex situations, however, where the actions carried out by a set of SQL statements are "all or nothing" propositions, this approach is often less desirable. In such situations, not only are the queries in a sequence dependent on each other (and, thus, impossible to execute in total isolation), but a failure in one query of the sequence means that the entire sequence should be aborted and the changes made by previous queries in the same sequence be reversed so as to return the database to its earlier state.

These requirements are met by MySQL's transaction model, which makes it possible to group a series of SQL statements into a single unit (or *transaction*) and execute them as a collective proposition. While commercial products such as Oracle and Microsoft SQL Server have supported this transaction model for a while, as have open-source alternatives like PostgreSQL, MySQL introduced support for transactions only in version 4.0, and limited it to specific storage engines in order to give users more flexibility and choice.

This chapter takes a closer look at the MySQL transaction model, explaining what it is, how it works, and how it helps in building more robust applications. This chapter also looks at alternative approaches to the native transaction model, explaining how it is possible to achieve similar functionality through the use of MySQL table locks with the older nontransactional table types.

Understanding Transactions

In the SQL context, a transaction consists of one or more SQL statements that operate as a single unit. Each SQL statement in such a unit is dependent on the others, and the unit as a whole is indivisible. If one statement in the unit does not complete successfully, the entire unit will be rolled back and all the affected data will be returned to the state it was in before the transaction was started. Thus, a transaction is said to be successful only if *all* the individual statements within it are executed successfully.

You might find it hard to think of situations where this all-for-one and one-for-all approach would be useful. In reality, transactions abound all around us—in bank transfers, stock trades, web-based shopping carts, inventory control—the list goes on and on. In all these cases, the success of the transaction depends on a number of interdependent actions executing successfully and in harmony with each other. A failure in any of them must cancel the transaction and return the system back to its earlier, pre-transaction state.

The best way to understand this is with a simple example. Consider a stock trade on any stock exchange (Figure 5-1), in which Trader A sells 400 shares in ACME Corp. to Trader B.

FIGURE 5-1
A stock exchange
transaction

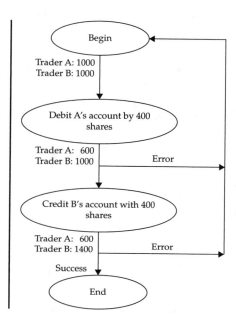

Somewhere behind the hullabaloo of the trading ring is a complex database system tracking all such deals. In this system, a trade such as the previous one is deemed complete only when Trader A's account is debited by 400 ACME Corp. shares and Trader B's account is simultaneously credited with those shares. If either of the previous two steps fail, the exchange would have the unenviable situation of 400 ACME Corp. shares floating around the system with no owner...not very pleasant, I'm sure you'd agree.

Thus, the transfer of 400 ACME Corp. shares from Trader A to Trader B in the previous example can be considered a transaction—a single unit of work that internally encompasses several SQL statements (delete 400 shares from Trader A's account records, add 400 shares to Trader B's records, perform commission calculations for both traders, and save the changes). In keeping with the previous transaction definition, all of these statements should execute successfully. If any one of them fails, the transaction should be reversed so the system goes back to its earlier, stable state. Or, to put it another way, at no point in time should the ownership of the 400 shares be ambiguous.

Let's take another example, this one from our example database: adding a new flight (Figure 5-2). When adding a flight, the airline has to perform three steps: define the flight's source, destination and aircraft; define the flight's departure days and times; and define the number of classes and seats available in each class. At the database level, these operations require three different tables to be modified. If any of these three steps were to fail, the system should cancel *all* the changes made to avoid an inconsistent or incomplete flight record.

Figure 5-2
An airline flight addition

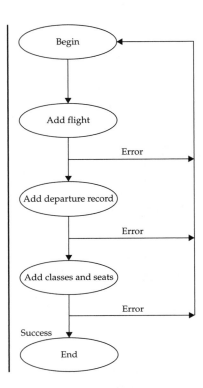

The three previous tasks constitute a single transaction. A failure in any one of them should cause the entire transaction to be cancelled and the system returned to its previous state.

The ACID Properties

The MySQL transaction architecture fully satisfies the ACID tests for transaction safety via its InnoDB storage engine. Older table types, such as the MyISAM type, do not support transactions. Transactions in such systems, therefore, can only be implemented through the use of explicit table locks (although this may not be ACID-compliant).

The term "ACID" is an acronym, stating four properties that every transactional RDBMS must comply with. To qualify for ACID compliance, an RDBMS must exhibit the following characteristics, as described in the following sections.

Atomicity

Atomicity means that every transaction must be treated as an indivisible unit. Given a transaction consisting of two or more tasks, all the statements within it must be successful for the transaction to be considered successful. In the event of a transaction failure, the system should be returned to its pre-transaction state.

With reference to the previous stock exchange example, atomicity means the sale of shares by Trader A and the purchase of the same by Trader B cannot occur independently of each other, and both must take place for the transaction to be considered complete. Similarly, in the airline example, atomicity implies that it would not be possible for the system to add a flight without also adding corresponding departure timings and class/seat information.

For a transaction to meet the atomicity requirement, if any of the statements in the transaction fail, all of the preceding statements must be rolled back to ensure the integrity of the database is unaffected. This is particularly important in mission-critical, real-world applications (like financial systems) that perform data entry or updates and require a high degree of safety from undetected data loss.

Consistency

Consistency means that every transaction must ensure that the database is in a consistent state once it completes executing. Or, to put it another way, consistency means that the database must never reflect a partially completed transaction at any time.

With reference to the previous stock exchange example, consistency means that every debit from a seller's account results in a corresponding and equal credit to a buyer's account. If a transaction reduces Trader A's account by 400 shares, but only credits 300 shares to Trader B's account, the consistency constraint will be violated because the total number of shares in the system changes. Similarly, the consistency property would ensure that if a flight is removed, all data related to that flight, including departure timings and seat/class information, would also be removed.

Isolation

Isolation means that every transaction must occur in its own separate and independent "transaction space," and its impact on the database only becomes visible once the transaction has completed executing (regardless of whether the transaction was successful or not). This is particularly important in multiuser, multitransaction systems, because it implies that the effects of a particular transaction are not "felt" until the transaction is complete. In the absence of the isolation property, two conflicting transactions might quickly produce data corruption, because each transaction would violate the other's integrity.

With reference to the previous stock exchange example, for instance, isolation implies the transaction between the two traders is independent of all other transactions on the exchange and its result is visible to the public at large only once it has been completed. When considering a flight modification, it implies that the list of available flights is updated only once the transaction is complete, and does not reflect other transactions that might still be in process at any given instant.

In reality, of course, the only way to obtain absolute isolation is to ensure that only a single user can access the database at any time. This is not a practical solution at all when dealing with a multiuser RDBMS like MySQL. Instead, most transactional systems use either page-level locking or row-level locking to isolate the changes made by different transactions from each other, at some cost in performance.

Durability

Durability means that changes made by a successful transaction will not be lost, even if the system crashes. Most RDBMS products ensure data durability by keeping a log of all activity that alters data in the database in any way. This database log keeps track of any and all updates made to tables, queries, reports, and so on.

In the event of a system crash or a corruption of the data storage media, the system is able to recover to the last successful update on restart and reflect the changes carried out by transactions that were still in progress when it went down through the use of its logs.

In the context of the previous share transfer example, durability means that once the transfer of shares from Trader A to Trader B has completed successfully, the system should reflect that state, even if a system failure subsequently takes place. Or, when dealing with the airline database, flights that have been added should not vanish from the database in the event of a system failure.

MySQL and the ACID Properties

MySQL fully satisfies the ACID requirements for a transaction-safe RDBMS, as follows:

- *Atomicity* is handled by storing the results of transactional statements (the modified rows) in a memory buffer and writing these results to disk and to the binary log from the buffer only once the transaction is committed. This ensures that the statements in a transaction operate as an indivisible unit and that their effects are seen collectively, or not at all.

- *Consistency* is primarily handled by MySQL's logging mechanisms, which record all changes to the database and provide an audit trail for transaction recovery. In addition to the logging process, MySQL provides locking mechanisms that ensure that all of the tables, rows, and indexes that make up the transaction are locked by the initiating process long enough to either commit the transaction or roll it back.

- Server-side semaphore variables and locking mechanisms act as traffic managers to help programs manage their own *isolation* mechanisms. For example, MySQL's InnoDB engine uses fine-grained row-level locking for this purpose.

- MySQL implements *durability* by maintaining a binary transaction log file that tracks changes to the system during the course of a transaction. In the event of a hardware failure or abrupt system shutdown, recovering lost data is a relatively straightforward task by using the last backup in combination with the log when the system restarts. By default, InnoDB tables are 100 percent durable (in other words, all transactions committed to the system before the crash are liable to be rolled back during the recovery process), while MyISAM tables offer partial durability.

A Simple Transaction

MySQL comes with a number of commands related to beginning, ending, and rolling back transactions. This section examines them in detail.

MySQL supports transactions natively via its InnoDB storage engine, which means the following commands can only be used with those engines. The default type for new tables in MySQL is MyISAM, but you can tell MySQL you want an InnoDB table by adding the optional ENGINE = INNODB clause to your CREATE TABLE command. For existing tables, you can change the table type on the fly through the ALTER TABLE command, again by specifying a new ENGINE clause. Here are some examples:

```
mysql> ALTER TABLE flight ENGINE=INNODB;
Query OK, 32 rows affected (0.06 sec)
Records: 32  Duplicates: 0  Warnings: 0

mysql> ALTER TABLE flightdep ENGINE=INNODB;
Query OK, 108 rows affected (0.09 sec)
Records: 108  Duplicates: 0  Warnings: 0

mysql> ALTER TABLE flightclass ENGINE=INNODB;
Query OK, 7 rows affected (0.06 sec)
Records: 7  Duplicates: 0  Warnings: 0
```

CAUTION *The* ALTER TABLE *command works by backing up the data in the table, erasing it, re-creating it with the specified modifications, and then reinserting the backed-up records. A failure in any of these steps could result in the loss or corruption of your data. Therefore, a good idea is always to create a table backup prior to using the* ALTER TABLE *command.*

To initiate a transaction and tell MySQL that all subsequent SQL statements should be considered a single unit, MySQL offers the START TRANSACTION command to mark the beginning of a transaction.

```
mysql> START TRANSACTION;
Query OK, 0 rows affected (0.00 sec)
```

You can also use the BEGIN or BEGIN WORK commands to initiate a transaction.

Typically, the START TRANSACTION command is followed by the SQL statements that make up the transaction. Let's suppose the transaction here consists of adding a new flight to the system and the steps involved include (1) creating a record for the flight, (2) defining the flight's departure day and time, and (3) defining the flight's class and seat structure.

```
mysql> INSERT INTO flight (FlightID, RouteID, AircraftID)
    -> VALUES (834, 1061, 3469);
Query OK, 1 row affected (0.00 sec)
mysql> INSERT INTO flightdep (FlightID, DepDay, DepTime)
    -> VALUES (834, 4, '16:00');
Query OK, 1 row affected (0.02 sec)
mysql> INSERT INTO flightclass (FlightID, ClassID, MaxSeats,
    -> BasePrice) VALUES (834, 'A', 20, 200);
Query OK, 1 row affected (0.00 sec)
```

Look inside these tables to see if the data has been correctly entered with a quick SELECT query:

```
mysql> SELECT COUNT(FlightID)
    -> FROM flight WHERE FlightID=834;
+-----------------+
| COUNT(FlightID) |
+-----------------+
|               1 |
+-----------------+
1 row in set (0.03 sec)
mysql> SELECT COUNT(FlightID)
    -> FROM flightdep WHERE FlightID=834;
+-----------------+
| COUNT(FlightID) |
+-----------------+
|               1 |
+-----------------+
1 row in set (0.00 sec)
```

Once the SQL statements have all been executed, you can either save the entire transaction to disk with the COMMIT command or undo all the changes made with the ROLLBACK command. Here's an example of rolling it back:

```
mysql> ROLLBACK;
Query OK, 0 rows affected (0.02 sec)
mysql> SELECT COUNT(FlightID)
    -> FROM flightdep WHERE FlightID=834;
+-----------------+
| COUNT(FlightID) |
+-----------------+
|               0 |
+-----------------+
1 row in set (0.02 sec)
mysql> SELECT COUNT(FlightID)
    -> FROM flight WHERE FlightID=834;
+-----------------+
| COUNT(FlightID) |
+-----------------+
|               0 |
+-----------------+
1 row in set (0.00 sec)
```

> **NOTE** *If your transaction involves changes to both transactional and nontransactional tables, the portion of the transaction dealing with nontransactional tables cannot be reversed with a ROLLBACK command. In such a situation, MySQL will return an error notifying you of an incomplete rollback, as in the following:*

```
mysql> ROLLBACK;
ERROR 1196: Some non-transactional changed tables couldn't be rolled back
```

Now, perform the transaction again, this time with a view to saving it.

```
mysql> START TRANSACTION;
Query OK, 0 rows affected (0.00 sec)
mysql> INSERT INTO flight (FlightID, RouteID, AircraftID)
    -> VALUES (834, 1061, 3469);
Query OK, 1 row affected (0.00 sec)
mysql> INSERT INTO flightdep (FlightID, DepDay, DepTime)
    -> VALUES (834, 4, '16:00');
Query OK, 1 row affected (0.02 sec)
mysql> INSERT INTO flightclass (FlightID, ClassID, MaxSeats,
    -> BasePrice) VALUES (834, 'A', 20, 200);
 Query OK, 1 row affected (0.00 sec)
```

There's an interesting experiment you can perform at this point. Open another client connection to the server and check if the previous SQL queries have resulted in any changes to the database.

```
mysql> SELECT COUNT(FlightID)
    -> FROM flight WHERE FlightID=834;
+-----------------+
| COUNT(FlightID) |
+-----------------+
|               0 |
+-----------------+
1 row in set (0.02 sec)
```

This is an example of isolation in action. As noted in the preceding section, isolation means that the results of a transaction become visible only when the transaction is successfully committed. Because the transaction is still in progress and has not yet been saved to disk, it is effectively invisible to any other user of the same database (if visibility between transactions is desired, it can be attained by setting a different transaction isolation level; this is discussed in detail in the section "Transaction Isolation Levels").

The COMMIT command saves the changed records to the database:

```
mysql> COMMIT;
Query OK, 0 rows affected (0.01 sec)
```

The COMMIT command also marks the end of the transaction block. Once the transaction has been committed to the database, the committed data will become visible to other client sessions.

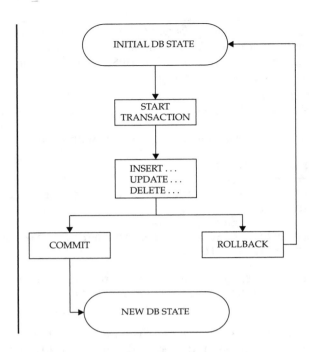

FIGURE 5-3
Transaction life cycle

Figure 5-3 summarizes the life cycle of a transaction with a simple flow diagram.

Can I Start a New Transaction from Within an Existing One?

No. Beginning a second transaction within the first one with START TRANSACTION or BEGIN automatically commits the previous one. In a similar manner, many other MySQL commands will implicitly perform a COMMIT when invoked. Here's a brief list:

```
CREATE DATABASE/CREATE TABLE
DROP DATABASE/TRUNCATE TABLE/DROP TABLE
CREATE INDEX/DROP INDEX
ALTER TABLE/RENAME TABLE
LOCK TABLES/UNLOCK TABLES
CREATE USER/DROP USER/RENAME USER
GRANT/REVOKE/SET PASSWORD
SET AUTOCOMMIT = 1
```

The ADD CHAIN and RELEASE Clauses

By default, once a transaction has completed, MySQL simply awaits the next command. However, MySQL's START TRANSACTION command also supports two additional clauses, which can be used to modify what happens after a transaction completes.

- The ADD CHAIN clause causes MySQL to immediately start a new transaction (with the same isolation level as the previous one) following a commit or rollback.

- The RELEASE clause causes MySQL to terminate the client connection following a commit or rollback.

Adding the NO prefix to either of these two clauses negates the operation.

TIP *It's also possible to modify this behavior by setting the MySQL* completion_type *variable, either on a per-session basis with SET or globally via the MySQL configuration file.*

Savepoints

The InnoDB storage engine supports an additional useful feature: the ability to roll back a transaction partially instead of completely. This is accomplished through the use of savepoints—user-defined points that can be used to mark substages within a transaction. In the event of a transaction failure, these savepoints make it possible to roll back only specific parts of a transaction rather than the entire transaction.

Savepoints within a transaction are set with the SAVEPOINT command, which accepts a user-defined identifier. The ROLLBACK TO SAVEPOINT command can then be used to roll an in-progress transaction back to the named savepoint, reversing all changes made after the savepoint.

Here's an example of savepoints in action:

```
mysql> START TRANSACTION;
Query OK, 0 rows affected (0.02 sec)
mysql> INSERT INTO flight (FlightID, RouteID, AircraftID)
    -> VALUES (834, 1061, 3469);
Query OK, 1 row affected (0.02 sec)
mysql> SAVEPOINT flight1;
Query OK, 0 rows affected (0.04 sec)
mysql> INSERT INTO flightdep (FlightID, DepDay, DepTime)
    -> VALUES (834, 4, '16:00');
Query OK, 1 row affected (0.00 sec)
mysql> SAVEPOINT flight2;
Query OK, 0 rows affected (0.02 sec)
mysql> INSERT INTO flightclass (FlightID, ClassID, MaxSeats,
    -> BasePrice) VALUES (834, 'A', 20, 200);
Query OK, 1 row affected (0.00 sec)
mysql> SAVEPOINT flight3;
Query OK, 0 rows affected (0.01 sec)
```

At this point, there are three savepoints, each one corresponding to a table modification. Verify that the tables have indeed been modified:

```
mysql> SELECT COUNT(FlightID) FROM flightclass
    -> WHERE FlightID=834;
```

```
+-----------------+
| COUNT(FlightID) |
+-----------------+
|               1 |
+-----------------+
1 row in set (0.02 sec)
```

Now, roll back only the last modification:

```
mysql> ROLLBACK TO SAVEPOINT flight2;
Query OK, 0 rows affected (0.02 sec)
```

Check the concerned table to verify the rollback:

```
mysql> SELECT COUNT(FlightID) FROM flightclass
    -> WHERE FlightID=834;
+-----------------+
| COUNT(FlightID) |
+-----------------+
|               0 |
+-----------------+
1 row in set (0.03 sec)
```

Notice that the changes made to other tables persist:

```
mysql> SELECT COUNT(FlightID) FROM flightdep
    -> WHERE FlightID=834;
+-----------------+
| COUNT(FlightID) |
+-----------------+
|               1 |
+-----------------+
1 row in set (0.01 sec)
```

It's important to note that the transaction is still in progress; issuing a ROLLBACK TO SAVEPOINT command doesn't commit or roll back the transaction. Conclude the transaction by rolling back all the remaining changes as well:

```
mysql> ROLLBACK;
Query OK, 0 rows affected (0.05 sec)
mysql> SELECT COUNT(FlightID) FROM flightdep
    -> WHERE FlightID=834;
+-----------------+
| COUNT(FlightID) |
+-----------------+
|               0 |
+-----------------+
1 row in set (0.01 sec)
```

There are some important things to learn about savepoints from the previous example.

- Multiple savepoints can be set per transaction, so long as they each have a unique identifier. Repeating an identifier overwrites previously set savepoints with the same identifier.

- Rolling back to a savepoint does not end the transaction. To end the transaction, use the COMMIT or ROLLBACK commands. However, rolling back to a specified savepoint deletes all savepoints set after that point. If the savepoint specified in the ROLLBACK TO SAVEPOINT command does not exist, MySQL will generate an error.

- A savepoint can be removed using the RELEASE SAVEPOINT command, which accepts a savepoint identifier and removes that savepoint from the stack. Note that this command does not perform an implicit COMMIT or ROLLBACK, so the transaction remains in progress until an explicit COMMIT or ROLLBACK is issued.

Controlling Transactional Behavior

MySQL offers two variables to control transactional behavior—the AUTOCOMMIT variable and the TRANSACTION ISOLATION LEVEL variable. The following sections examine these in greater detail.

Automatic Commits

By default, MySQL implicitly commits the results of every SQL query to the database once it is executed. This is referred to as *autocommit mode* and is the reason you needn't begin every MySQL session with a START TRANSACTION statement or end it with a COMMIT or ROLLBACK. Or, to put it another way, MySQL treats every query as a single-statement transaction.

This default behavior can be modified via the special AUTOCOMMIT variable, which controls MySQL's autocommit mode. The following snippet demonstrates, by turning off the MySQL behavior of internally issuing a COMMIT command after each SQL interaction:

```
mysql> SET AUTOCOMMIT = 0;
Query OK, 0 rows affected (0.02 sec)
```

Subsequent to this, any update to a table will not be saved to the database until an explicit COMMIT command is issued. In fact, terminating a MySQL session without issuing a COMMIT will cause the database to automatically fire a ROLLBACK and undo all the changes made, thereby negating all the work done during the session. The following example demonstrates this:

```
mysql> SET AUTOCOMMIT = 0;
Query OK, 0 rows affected (0.00 sec)
mysql> SELECT COUNT(FlightID)
    -> FROM flight WHERE FlightID=834;
```

```
+------------------+
| COUNT(FlightID)  |
+------------------+
|                0 |
+------------------+
1 row in set (0.02 sec)
mysql> INSERT INTO flight (FlightID, RouteID, AircraftID)
    -> VALUES (834, 1061, 3469);
Query OK, 1 row affected (0.00 sec)
mysql> exit
Bye
```

Start a new session and check the table. It will not contain the changes made, as they were not committed at the end of the last session.

```
mysql> SELECT COUNT(FlightID)
    -> FROM flight WHERE FlightID=834;
+------------------+
| COUNT(FlightID)  |
+------------------+
|                0 |
+------------------+
1 row in set (0.02 sec)
```

To turn autocommit mode back on, reset the AUTOCOMMIT variable to its initial state.

```
mysql> SET AUTOCOMMIT = 1;
Query OK, 0 rows affected (0.00 sec)
```

The AUTOCOMMIT variable is a session variable and always defaults to 1 when a new client session begins.

NOTE *The* AUTOCOMMIT *variable only affects transactional table types like InnoDB. When dealing with nontransactional table types like MyISAM, the* AUTOCOMMIT *variable has no impact and changes to such tables are always saved immediately.*

Transaction Isolation Levels

One of the most important properties of a transaction-capable RDBMS is its capability to "isolate" the different sessions in progress at any given instance on the server. In a single-user environment, this property is largely irrelevant for obvious reasons: There is nothing to isolate because usually only a single session is active at any time. In more complex real-world scenarios, however, it is unlikely this assumption will remain true.

In a multiuser environment, many RDBMS sessions will usually be active at any given time. In the stock trading example discussed previously, for instance, it is unlikely that only a single trade will be taking place at a particular point in time. Far more likely is that hundreds of trades will occur simultaneously. In such a situation, it is essential that the RDBMS isolate transactions so that they do not interfere with each other, while simultaneously ensuring the database's performance does not suffer as a result.

To understand the importance of isolation, consider what would happen if it wasn't enforced. In the absence of transaction isolation, different SELECT statements would retrieve different results within the context of the same transaction because the underlying data was modified by other transactions in the interim. This would create inconsistency and make it difficult to trust a particular result set or use it as the basis for calculations with any degree of confidence. Isolation thus imposes a degree of insulation between transactions, guaranteeing that an application only sees consistent data within the scope of a transaction.

MySQL provides the following four isolation levels in accordance with the ANSI/ISO SQL specification:

```
READ UNCOMMITTED
READ COMMITTED
REPEATABLE READ
SERIALIZABLE
```

These transaction isolation levels determine the degree to which other transactions can "see" inside an in-progress transaction, and are arranged in hierarchical order, beginning with the least secure (and most problematic) level and gradually moving to the most secure level. These isolation levels can be manipulated with the TRANSACTION ISOLATION LEVEL variable, which is discussed in greater detail in the section "Modifying the Transaction Isolation Level."

Let's now look at what each of the isolation levels does.

The READ UNCOMMITTED Isolation Level

The READ UNCOMMITTED isolation level provides the minimum amount of insulation between transactions. In addition to being vulnerable to phantom reads and unrepeatable reads, a transaction at this isolation level can read data that has not yet been committed by other transactions. If this transaction now uses the uncommitted changes made by other transactions as the basis for calculations of its own, and those uncommitted changes are then rolled back by their parent transactions, it can result in massive data corruption.

As an example, consider Figure 5-4. Because the second transaction is able to view the uncommitted changes of the first transaction, the number of flights it sees varies

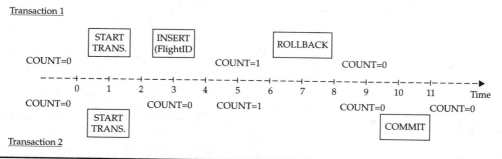

FIGURE 5-4   The READ UNCOMMITTED isolation level and a dirty read

during the lifetime of the first transaction. As a result, at any given instant, the second transaction may be operating on faulty data, depending on whether the first transaction commits or rolls back its changes (hence, the term "dirty read" for this kind of error).

The READ COMMITTED Isolation Level

Even less secure than the REPEATABLE READ isolation level is the READ COMMITTED isolation level. At this level, a transaction can see the committed changes of other transactions during its lifetime. Put another way, this means multiple SELECT statements within the same transaction might return different results if the corresponding tables have been modified by other transactions in the intervening period.

Figure 5-5 shows an example of this. In this case, the second transaction will continue to see zero records during the lifetime of the first transaction. However, once the first transaction commits its changes, the second one will see one flight, even though it is still in progress.

This is obviously a problem—if the second transaction sees two different results for the same operation, it isn't going to know which one to trust as the correct one. Extrapolate a little and assume that instead of a single transaction, many transactions are committing updates to the database, and you'll see every query executed by a transaction could produce a different result set (hence, the term "unrepeatable read" for this kind of situation).

The REPEATABLE READ Isolation Level

For applications that are willing to compromise a little on security for better performance, MySQL offers the REPEATABLE READ isolation level. At this level, a transaction will not see the changes carried out by concurrent transactions until it itself has concluded. Figure 5-6 demonstrates how this works.

In this case, the second transaction can see the new flight added by the first transaction only once both transactions are complete. This is, in fact, the way most users expect transactions to work, and it should come as no surprise that this is MySQL's default transaction isolation level. The InnoDB storage engine accomplishes

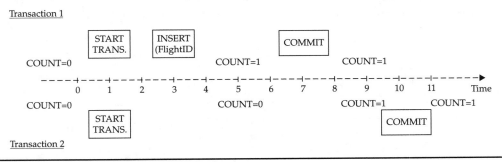

FIGURE 5-5   The READ COMMITTED isolation level

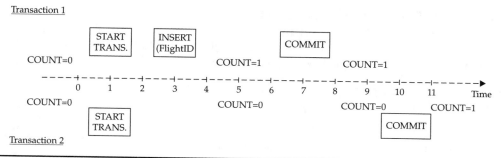

FIGURE 5-6   The REPEATABLE READ isolation level

this by using multiversioning to store a snapshot of the query results when the query is executed for the first time; it then reuses this snapshot for all subsequent queries until the transaction is committed.

The SERIALIZABLE Isolation Level

This SERIALIZABLE isolation level offers the maximum amount of insulation between transactions by treating concurrent transactions as though they were executing sequentially, one after the other. Figure 5-7 illustrates.

Here, the first transaction is adding a new flight to the database, while the second is attempting to view the total number of flights. However, because MySQL is executing these transactions serially, the INSERT operation in the first transaction will lock the table until the transaction is complete. This will force the SELECT operation in the second transaction to wait until the lock is released before it can obtain a result.

This "serialized" approach to handling transactions is the most secure: Sequentially locking and unlocking the table ensures that each transaction only sees data that has actually been committed to the database, with no possibility of dirty or unrepeatable reads. However, this comes at a price: MySQL will take a performance hit if every transaction runs at this isolation level because of the large amount of resources required to handle the various transactional locks at any given instant.

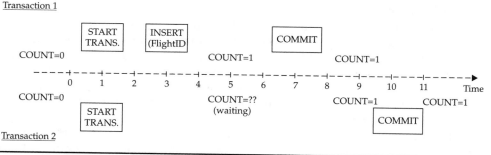

FIGURE 5-7   The SERIALIZABLE isolation level

Modifying the Transaction Isolation Level

Starting from MySQL 4.0.5, you can alter the transaction isolation level using the
TRANSACTION ISOLATION LEVEL variable. MySQL defaults to the REPEATABLE READ
isolation level. You can change this using the SET command, as in the following example:

```
mysql> SET TRANSACTION ISOLATION LEVEL READ COMMITTED;
Query OK, 0 rows affected (0.00 sec)
```

You can obtain the current value of the TRANSACTION ISOLATION LEVEL variable
at any time with a quick SELECT, as in the following:

```
mysql> SELECT @@tx_isolation;
+-----------------+
| @@tx_isolation  |
+-----------------+
| REPEATABLE-READ |
+-----------------+
1 row in set (0.00 sec)
```

By default, this value of the TRANSACTION ISOLATION LEVEL variable is set on a
per-session basis, but you can set it globally for all sessions by adding the GLOBAL
keyword to the SET command line, as shown in the following:

```
mysql> SET GLOBAL TRANSACTION ISOLATION LEVEL READ COMMITTED;
Query OK, 0 rows affected (0.00 sec)
```

You can also set the default transaction isolation level at startup with the special
--transaction-isolation argument to the *mysqld* server process.

NOTE *You need the SUPER privilege to set the global transaction isolation level. Chapter 11
has more information on how to obtain this (and other) privileges in the MySQL access
control system.*

Pseudo-Transactions

So far, you've seen transactions in the context of InnoDB tables, the only native
MySQL storage engine to support ACID-compliant transactions. The older MySQL
table types, still in use in many MySQL installations, do not support transactions, but
MySQL still enables users to implement a primitive form of transactions through the
use of table locks. This section examines these "pseudo-transactions" in greater detail,
with a view to offering some general guidelines on performing secure transactions
with nontransactional tables.

MySQL supports a number of different table types, and the locking mechanisms
available differ from type to type. Therefore, a clear understanding of the different levels

of locking available is essential to implementing a pseudo-transaction environment with MySQL's nontransactional tables.

- **Table locks**   The entire table is locked by a client for a particular kind of access. Depending on the type of lock, other clients will not be allowed to insert records into the table, and could even be restricted from reading data from it.

- **Page locks**   MySQL will lock a certain number of rows (called a *page*) from the table. The locked rows are only available to the thread initiating the lock. If another thread wants to write to data in these rows, it must wait until the lock is released. Rows in other pages, however, remain available for use.

- **Row locks**   Row-level locks offer finer control over the locking process than either table-level locks or page-level locks. In this case, only the rows that are being used by the thread are locked. All other rows in the table are available to other threads. In multiuser environments, row-level locking reduces conflicts between threads, making it possible for multiple users to read and even write to the same table simultaneously. This flexibility must be balanced, however, against the fact that it also has the highest performance overhead of the three locking levels.

The MyISAM table type supports only table-level locking, which offers performance benefits over row- and page-level locking in situations involving a larger number of reads than writes. The InnoDB table type automatically performs row-level locking in transactions.

Table Locks as a Substitute for Transactions

Because MyISAM (and other older MySQL table formats) do not support InnoDB-style COMMIT and ROLLBACK syntax, every change made to the database is immediately saved to disk. As noted previously, in a single-user scenario, this does not present much of a problem; however, in a multiuser scenario, it can cause problems because it is no longer possible to create transaction "bubbles" that isolate the changes made by one user from those made by other users. In such a situation, the only way to ensure consistency in the data seen by different client sessions is a brute-force approach: Prevent other users from accessing the tables being changed for the duration of the change (by locking them), and permit them access only once the changes are complete.

Previous sections of this chapter have already discussed the InnoDB engine, which natively supports row- and page-level locking to safely execute simultaneous transactions. The MyISAM table type, however, does not support these fine-grained locking mechanisms. Instead, explicit table locks have to be set to avoid simultaneous transactions from infringing on each other's space.

The following example sets a read-only lock on the *flight* table:

```
mysql> LOCK TABLE flight READ;
Query OK, 0 rows affected (0.05 sec)
```

Locking more than one table at the same time is not uncommon. This can be easily accomplished by specifying a comma-separated list of table names and lock types after the LOCK TABLES command, as in the following:

```
mysql> LOCK TABLES flight READ, flightdep WRITE
Query OK, 0 rows affected (0.05 sec)
```

The previous statement locks the *flight* table in read mode and the *flightdep* table in write mode.

Tables can be unlocked with a single UNLOCK TABLES command, as in the following:

```
mysql> UNLOCK TABLES;
Query OK, 0 rows affected (0.05 sec)
```

There is no need to name the tables to be unlocked. MySQL automatically unlocks all tables that were locked previously via LOCK TABLES.

There are two main types of table locks: read locks and write locks. Let's take a closer look.

The READ Lock

A READ lock on a table implies that the thread (client) setting the lock can read data from that table, as can other threads. However, no thread can modify the locked table by adding, updating, or removing records for so long as the lock is active.

Here's a simple example you can try to see how READ locks work. Begin by placing a READ lock on the flight table:

```
mysql> LOCK TABLE flight READ;
Query OK, 0 rows affected (0.05 sec)
```

Then, read from it:

```
mysql> SELECT FlightID FROM flight LIMIT 0,4;
+----------+
| flightid |
+----------+
|      345 |
|      535 |
|      589 |
|      652 |
+----------+
4 rows in set (0.00 sec)
```

No problems there. Now, write to it:

```
mysql> INSERT INTO flight (FlightID, RouteID, AircraftID)
    -> VALUES (834, 1061, 3469);
ERROR 1099 (HY000): Table 'flight' was locked with a READ lock and
can't be updated
```

MySQL rejects the INSERT because the table is locked in read-only mode.

What about other threads (clients) accessing the same table? For these threads, reads (SELECTs) will work without a problem. However, writes (INSERTs, UPDATEs, or DELETEs) will cause the initiating thread to halt and wait for the lock to be released before proceeding. Thus, only after the locking thread executes an UNLOCK TABLES command and releases its locks will the next thread be able to proceed with its write.

NOTE *A variant of the* READ *lock is the* READ LOCAL *lock, which differs from a regular* READ *lock in that other threads can execute* INSERT *statements that do not conflict with the thread initiating the lock. This was created for use with the* mysqldump *utility to allow multiple simultaneous* INSERTs *into a table.*

The WRITE Lock

A WRITE lock on a table implies that the thread setting the lock can modify the data in the table, but other threads cannot either read or write to the table for the duration of the lock. Here's a simple example that illustrates how WRITE locks work. Begin by placing a WRITE lock on the *flight* table:

```
mysql> LOCK TABLE flight WRITE;
Query OK, 0 rows affected (0.05 sec)
```

Then, try reading from it:

```
mysql> SELECT FlightID FROM flight LIMIT 0,4;
+----------+
| flightid |
+----------+
|      345 |
|      535 |
|      589 |
|      652 |
+----------+
4 rows in set (0.00 sec)
```

Because a WRITE lock is on the table, writes should take place without a problem.

```
mysql> INSERT INTO flight (FlightID, RouteID, AircraftID)
    -> VALUES (834, 1061, 3469);
```

Now, what about other MySQL sessions? Open a new client session and try reading from the same table while the WRITE lock is still active.

```
mysql> SELECT FlightID FROM flight LIMIT 0,4;
```

The MySQL client will now halt and wait for the first session to release its locks before it can execute the previous command. Once the first session issues an UNLOCK

TABLES command, the SELECT command invoked in the second session will be accepted for processing because the table is no longer locked.

```
mysql> SELECT FlightID FROM flight LIMIT 0,4;
+----------+
| flightid |
+----------+
|      345 |
|      535 |
|      589 |
|      652 |
+----------+
4 rows in set (3 min 32.98 sec)
```

Notice from the output the time taken to execute the simple SELECT command: This includes the time spent waiting for the table lock to be released. This should illustrate one of the most important drawbacks of table locks: If a thread never releases its locks, all other threads attempting to access the locked table(s) are left waiting for the lock to time out, leading to a significant degradation in overall performance.

> ### Which Type of Lock Has Higher Priority?
> In situations involving both WRITE and READ locks, MySQL assigns WRITE locks higher priority to ensure that modifications to the table are saved to disk as soon as possible. This reduces the risk of updates getting lost in case of a disk crash or a system failure.

Implementing a Pseudo-Transaction with Table Locks

This section will now illustrate a transaction through the use of table locks by rewriting one of the earlier transactional examples with locks and MyISAM tables. In the earlier example, the steps included creating a record for the flight, defining the flight's departure day and time, and defining the flight's class and seat structure.

Because each of the three tables concerned will be modified when a new flight is added, they must be locked in WRITE mode so that other threads do not interfere with the transaction.

```
mysql> LOCK TABLES flight WRITE,
    -> flightdep WRITE, flightclass WRITE;
Query OK, 0 rows affected (0.00 sec)
```

As explained previously, WRITE mode implies that other threads will neither be able to read from nor write to the locked tables for so long as the lock is active. Hence, the transaction must be as short and sweet as possible to avoid a slowdown in other requests for data in these tables.

Insert the new records into the various tables:

```
mysql> INSERT INTO flight (FlightID, RouteID, AircraftID)
    -> VALUES (834, 1061, 3469);
Query OK, 1 row affected (0.00 sec)
mysql> INSERT INTO flightdep (FlightID, DepDay, DepTime)
    -> VALUES (834, 4, '16:00');
Query OK, 1 row affected (0.02 sec)
mysql> INSERT INTO flightclass (FlightID, ClassID, MaxSeats,
    -> BasePrice) VALUES (834, 'A', 20, 200);
Query OK, 1 row affected (0.00 sec)
```

Verify the data has been correctly entered with a quick SELECT:

```
mysql> SELECT COUNT(FlightID)
    -> FROM flight WHERE FlightID=834;
+-----------------+
| COUNT(FlightID) |
+-----------------+
|               1 |
+-----------------+
1 row in set (0.02 sec)
```

Unlock the tables, and you're done!

```
mysql> UNLOCK TABLES;
Query OK, 0 rows affected (0.09 sec)
```

Until the tables are unlocked, all other threads trying to access the three locked tables will be forced to wait. The elegance of the transactional approach, in which page- and row-level locks allow other clients to work with the data, even during the course of a transaction, is missing here. That said, however, table locks do help to isolate updates in different client sessions from each other (albeit in a somewhat primitive manner) and, in doing so, help users constrained to older, nontransactional table types to implement an "almost-transactional" environment for their application.

Summary

This chapter discussed transactions, a MySQL feature that lets developers group multiple SQL statements into a single unit and have that unit execute atomically. This feature makes it possible to execute SQL queries in a more secure manner and revert the RDBMS to a previous, stable snapshot in the event of an error.

Transactions can impose a substantial performance drain on an RDBMS because of the resources needed to keep transactions separate from each other in a multiuser environment. As this chapter demonstrated, MySQL is unique in that it lets application developers choose whether to use transactional features on a per-table basis in order to optimize performance. MySQL also exposes a number of variables that developers can adjust to control transactional behavior and performance. Most notable among these is the transaction isolation level, which sets the degree to which transactions are insulated from each other's actions.

To learn more about the topics discussed in this chapter, consider visiting the following links:

- Transactions, at http://dev.mysql.com/doc/refman/5.1/en/commit.html

- Savepoints, at http://dev.mysql.com/doc/refman/5.0/en/savepoints.html

- Pseudo-transactions and table locking, at http://dev.mysql.com/doc/refman/5.1/en/lock-tables.html

- Transaction isolation levels, at http://dev.mysql.com/doc/refman/5.1/en/set-transaction.html

- Deviations between the MySQL transaction model and the ANSI SQL specification, at http://dev.mysql.com/doc/refman/5.1/en/ansi-diff-transactions.html

CHAPTER 6

Using Stored Procedures and Functions

M ost programmers will be familiar with the concept of functions—reusable, independent code segments that encapsulate specific tasks and can be "called upon" as needed from different applications. However, this construct isn't limited only to programming languages: one of the key new features introduced in MySQL 5.0 was its support for stored routines, which bring similar reusability to SQL statements.

Of course, stored routines are not new to the SQL world. Both commercial and open-source alternatives to MySQL have had this feature for many years. When this book went to press, MySQL's implementation of stored routines was not as fully featured or as optimized as that of many of its counterparts, but it improves with each new release. Nevertheless, the material in this chapter, which includes coverage of conditional tests, loops, cursors, and error handlers in the context of MySQL stored routines, should give you more than enough information to get started building some fairly useful stored routines of your own.

Understanding Stored Routines

As your SQL business logic becomes more complex, you might find yourself repeatedly writing blocks of SQL statements to perform the same database operation at the application level—for example, inserting a set of linked records or performing calculations on a particular result set. In these situations, it usually makes sense to turn this block of SQL code into a reusable routine, which resides on the database server (rather than in the application) so that it can be managed independently and invoked as needed from different modules in your application.

Packaging SQL statements into server-side routines has four important advantages.

- A stored routine is held on the database server, rather than in the application. For applications based on a client-server architecture, calling a stored routine is faster and requires less network bandwidth than transmitting an entire series of SQL statements and taking decisions on the result sets. Stored routines also reduce code duplication by allowing developers to extract commonly used SQL operations into a single component. The end result is that application code becomes smaller, more efficient, and easier to read.

- A stored routine is created once but used many times, often from more than one program. If the routine changes, the changes are implemented in one spot (the routine definition) while the routine invocations remain untouched. This fact can significantly simplify code maintenance and upgrades. Debugging and testing an application also becomes easier, as errors can be traced and corrected with minimal impact to the application code.

- Implementing database operations as stored routines can improve application security, because application modules can be denied access to particular tables and only granted access to the routines that manipulate those tables. This not only ensures that an application only sees the data it needs, but also ensures consistent implementation of specific tasks or submodules across the application (because all application modules will make use of the same stored routines rather than attempting to directly manipulate the base tables).

- Using stored routines encourages abstract thinking, because packaging SQL operations into a stored routine is nothing more or less than understanding how a *specific* task may be encapsulated into a *generic* component. In this sense, using stored routines encourages the creation of more robust and extensible application architecture.

It's worth noting also that in the MySQL world, the term "stored routines" is used generically to refer to two different animals: stored procedures and stored functions. While both types of routines contain SQL statements, MySQL imposes several key restrictions on stored functions that are not applicable to stored procedures, as follows:

- Stored functions cannot use SQL statements that return result sets.
- Stored functions cannot use SQL statements that perform transactional commits or rollbacks.
- Stored functions cannot call themselves recursively.
- Stored functions must produce a return value.

NOTE *Stored routines, although useful, are yet to be fully optimized in MySQL 5.x. Therefore, as much as possible, you should avoid using complex stored routines in MySQL, as they can significantly increase overhead. The lack of a fully optimized cache or debugging tools for stored routines are also a hindrance to users and developers.*

Creating and Using Stored Procedures

There are three components to every stored routine (function or procedure).

- Input parameters, or *arguments,* which serve as inputs to the routine
- Output parameters, or *return values,* which are the outputs returned by the routine
- The *body,* which contains the SQL statements to be executed

---

NOTE *To create a stored routine, a user must have the* CREATE ROUTINE *privilege. To execute a stored routine, a user must have the* EXECUTE *privilege. Privileges are discussed in greater detail in Chapter 11.*

To begin with, let's see a simple example of a stored procedure, one that doesn't use either arguments or return values.

```
mysql> DELIMITER //
mysql> CREATE PROCEDURE count_airports()
    -> BEGIN
    ->   SELECT COUNT(AirportID) FROM airport;
    -> END//
Query OK, 0 rows affected (0.62 sec)
```

To define a stored procedure, MySQL offers the CREATE PROCEDURE command. This command must be followed by the name of the stored procedure and parentheses. Input and output arguments, if any, appear within these parentheses, and the main body of the procedure follows. Routine names cannot exceed 64 characters, and names that contain special characters or consist entirely of digits or reserved words must be quoted with the backtick (`) operator.

Can I Override MySQL's Built-in Functions by Creating New Ones with the Same Name?

No. In fact, as a general rule, you should avoid using existing built-in function names as the names for your stored routines; however, if you must do this, MySQL permits it as long as there is an additional space between the procedure or function name and the parentheses that follow it.

The main body of the procedure can contain SQL statements, variable definitions, conditional tests, loops, and error handlers. In the preceding example, it is enclosed within BEGIN and END markers. These BEGIN and END blocks are only mandatory when the procedure body contains complex control structures; in all other cases (such as the previous example, which contains only a single SELECT), they are optional. However, it's good practice to always include them so that the body of the procedure is clearly demarcated.

Notice also in the previous example that the DELIMITER command is used to change the statement delimiter used by MySQL from ; to //. This is to ensure that the ; used to terminate statements within the procedure body does not prematurely end the procedure definition. The delimiter is changed back to normal once the fully defined procedure has been accepted by the server.

Of course, defining a stored procedure is only half the battle—the other half is using it. MySQL offers the CALL command to invoke a stored procedure; this command must be followed with the name of the procedure (and arguments, if any). Here's how:

```
mysql> CALL count_airports();
+------------------+
| COUNT(AirportID) |
+------------------+
|               15 |
+------------------+
1 row in set (0.12 sec)
```

Here's another example, this one using stored procedures to create and drop a table:

```
mysql> DELIMITER //
mysql> CREATE PROCEDURE create_log_table()
    -> BEGIN
    ->    CREATE TABLE log(RecordID INT NOT NULL
    ->    AUTO_INCREMENT PRIMARY KEY, Message TEXT);
    -> END//
```

```
Query OK, 0 rows affected (0.00 sec)
mysql> CREATE PROCEDURE remove_log_table()
    -> BEGIN
    ->    DROP TABLE log;
    -> END//
Query OK, 0 rows affected (0.00 sec)
```

Here's the output when these procedures are invoked:

```
mysql> CALL create_log_table();
Query OK, 0 rows affected (0.13 sec)
mysql> CALL create_log_table();
ERROR 1050 (42S01): Table 'log' already exists
mysql> SHOW TABLES;
+---------------------+
| Tables_in_db1       |
+---------------------+
| aircraft            |
| aircrafttype        |
| airport             |
| flight              |
| flightclass         |
| flightdep           |
| log                 |
| route               |
+---------------------+
8 rows in set (0.00 sec)
mysql> CALL remove_log_table;
Query OK, 0 rows affected (0.05 sec)
mysql> CALL remove_log_table;
ERROR 1051 (42S02): Unknown table 'log'
mysql> SHOW TABLES;
+---------------------+
| Tables_in_db1       |
+---------------------+
| aircraft            |
| aircrafttype        |
| airport             |
| flight              |
| flightclass         |
| flightdep           |
| route               |
+---------------------+
7 rows in set (0.00 sec)
```

To remove a stored procedure, use the DROP PROCEDURE command with the procedure name as argument:

```
mysql> DROP PROCEDURE count_airports;
Query OK, 0 rows affected (0.01 sec)
```

> **Can I Alter the Body of a Procedure After It's Been Created?**
> No. MySQL does offer an ALTER PROCEDURE command, but this currently only permits changes to the characteristics, not the body, of the procedure. To alter the body of a procedure, it is necessary to first drop and then re-create it.

To view the body of a specific stored procedure, use the SHOW CREATE PROCEDURE command with the procedure name as argument. This is a restricted command; it will be executed only if you are the creator of the procedure or have SELECT privileges on the *proc* grant table (privileges are discussed in greater detail in Chapter 11). Here's an example:

```
mysql> SHOW CREATE PROCEDURE create_log_table\G
*************************** 1. row ***************************
           Procedure: create_log_table
            sql_mode: STRICT_TRANS_TABLES
    Create Procedure: CREATE DEFINER=`root`@`localhost`
PROCEDURE `create_log_table`()
BEGIN
  CREATE TABLE log(RecordID INT NOT NULL
  AUTO_INCREMENT PRIMARY KEY, Message TEXT);
END
character_set_client: latin1
collation_connection: latin1_swedish_ci
  Database Collation: latin1_swedish_ci
1 row in set (0.00 sec)
```

To view a list of all stored procedures on the server, use the SHOW PROCEDURE STATUS command. You can filter the output of this command with a WHERE clause, as shown:

```
mysql> SHOW PROCEDURE STATUS WHERE name LIKE '%log%'\G
*************************** 1. row ***************************
                  Db: db1
                Name: create_log_table
                Type: PROCEDURE
             Definer: root@localhost
            Modified: 2008-12-24 13:32:38
             Created: 2008-12-24 13:32:38
       Security_type: DEFINER
             Comment:
character_set_client: latin1
collation_connection: latin1_swedish_ci
  Database Collation: latin1_swedish_ci
*************************** 2. row ***************************
                  Db: db1
                Name: remove_log_table
```

```
             Type: PROCEDURE
          Definer: root@localhost
         Modified: 2008-12-24 13:21:39
          Created: 2008-12-24 13:21:39
    Security_type: DEFINER
          Comment:
character_set_client: latin1
collation_connection: latin1_swedish_ci
 Database Collation: latin1_swedish_ci
2 rows in set (0.01 sec)
```

Using Input and Output Parameters

A stored procedure that always returns the same output is a lot like a radio station that plays the same song all day—not very useful or interesting at all! What you'd really like is the ability to change the music the station plays in response to feedback that you, the listener, provides—in effect, to create an audience-request show. In stored procedure terms, this amounts to creating procedures that can accept input parameters at run-time and use these input parameters to calculate and return different output.

That's where *input parameters* or *arguments* come in. Arguments are "placeholder" variables within a procedure definition; they're replaced at run-time by values provided to the procedure from the calling program. The processing code within the procedure then manipulates these values and generates *output parameters* or *return values*, which are returned to the calling program. Since the input to the procedure will differ each time it is invoked, the output will necessarily differ too.

Input and output parameters are defined within the parentheses that follow a stored procedure name, and are prefixed with one of three keywords—IN, OUT, or INOUT—to define their purpose. IN parameters serve only as inputs to the procedure; OUT parameters represent output values; INOUT parameters can be used both as procedure inputs and outputs. If none of these keywords are specified, MySQL assumes that the parameter is an IN parameter.

IN Parameters   The IN keyword is used to mark input parameters for a stored procedure. It is followed by the parameter name and its data type (which can be any one of MySQL's built-in data types).

The following procedure illustrates the use of input parameters by defining a stored procedure that accepts a numeric airport identifier and returns the corresponding airport name:

```
mysql> DELIMITER //
mysql> CREATE PROCEDURE get_airport_name(IN aid INT)
    -> BEGIN
    ->    SELECT AirportName FROM airport WHERE AirportID = aid;
    -> END//
Query OK, 0 rows affected (0.04 sec)
```

You can now call this procedure with an airport identifier as argument, as shown:

```
mysql> CALL get_airport_name(129);
+-------------------------------+
| AirportName                   |
+-------------------------------+
| Bristol International Airport |
+-------------------------------+
1 row in set (0.01 sec)
```

Change the argument, and the output changes, too:

```
mysql> CALL get_airport_name(201);
+----------------+
| AirportName    |
+----------------+
| Changi Airport |
+----------------+
1 row in set (0.00 sec)
```

You can use multiple IN parameters as well. Here's an example, which uses a stored procedure to insert a new aircraft type record:

```
mysql> DELIMITER //
mysql> CREATE PROCEDURE add_aircraft_type(
    ->    IN aid INT,
    ->    IN atype VARCHAR(255)
    -> )
    -> BEGIN
    ->    INSERT INTO aircrafttype (AircraftTypeID,
    ->    AircraftName) VALUES(aid, atype);
    ->    SELECT AircraftTypeID, AircraftName
    ->    FROM aircrafttype WHERE AircraftTypeID = aid;
    -> END//
Query OK, 0 rows affected (0.10 sec)
mysql> CALL add_aircraft_type(711, 'Boeing 777');
+----------------+--------------+
| AircraftTypeID | AircraftName |
+----------------+--------------+
|            711 | Boeing 777   |
+----------------+--------------+
1 row in set (0.05 sec)
Query OK, 0 rows affected (0.05 sec)
```

TIP *Stored routines are always associated with a specific MySQL database (usually the one in use at the time the routine is defined). To specify that a routine be associated with a different database, or to execute, modify, or delete a routine that belongs to a different database, prefix the database name to the routine name in the format* database-name.routine-name, *in your* CREATE, ALTER, CALL, *or* DROP *commands.*

OUT Parameters The OUT keyword is used to mark a procedure's output parameters. As with the IN keyword, it is followed by a parameter name and data type, and it is automatically initialized to NULL within the body of the procedure. Here's a revision of the previous example, which stores the airport name in an output parameter instead of displaying it:

```
mysql> DELIMITER //
mysql> CREATE PROCEDURE get_airport_name(
    ->    IN aid INT,
    ->    OUT aname VARCHAR(255)
    -> )
    -> BEGIN
    ->   SELECT AirportName INTO aname
    ->   FROM airport WHERE AirportID = aid;
    -> END//
Query OK, 0 rows affected (0.00 sec)
```

Notice that the procedure uses the SELECT INTO command to assign the result of the query to the specified output variable. It's now possible to call the procedure, storing the output in a session variable for later retrieval:

```
mysql> CALL get_airport_name(201, @var);
Query OK, 0 rows affected (0.00 sec)
mysql> SELECT @var;
+----------------+
| @var           |
+----------------+
| Changi Airport |
+----------------+
1 row in set (0.00 sec)
```

Of course, you could also write the output value directly into a session variable within the body of the procedure, if you prefer. Here's a revision of the previous example, which demonstrates this:

```
mysql> DELIMITER //
mysql> CREATE PROCEDURE get_airport_name(
    ->    IN aid INT
    -> )
    -> BEGIN
    ->   SELECT AirportName INTO @aname
    ->   FROM airport WHERE AirportID = aid;
    -> END//
Query OK, 0 rows affected (0.01 sec)
mysql> DELIMITER ;
mysql> CALL get_airport_name(201);
Query OK, 0 rows affected (0.00 sec)
mysql> SELECT @aname;
```

```
+----------------+
| @aname         |
+----------------+
| Changi Airport |
+----------------+
1 row in set (0.00 sec)
```

INOUT Parameters   The INOUT keyword is used for parameters that serve as both input and output, and has the same syntax as the IN and OUT keywords. This is typically used for parameters that are likely to be modified during the course of the procedure. Here's a simple example, which demonstrates this:

```
mysql> DELIMITER //
mysql> CREATE PROCEDURE add_one(
    ->     INOUT num INT
    -> )
    -> BEGIN
    ->    SELECT (num+1) INTO num;
    -> END//
Query OK, 0 rows affected (0.05 sec)
mysql> DELIMITER ;
mysql> SET @a = 9;
mysql> CALL add_one(@a);
Query OK, 0 rows affected (0.00 sec)
mysql> SELECT @a;
+------+
| @a   |
+------+
|   10 |
+------+
1 row in set (0.00 sec)
```

Creating and Using Stored Functions

Stored functions are defined in a similar manner to stored procedures, except that the command to use is the CREATE FUNCTION command. And while it isn't mandatory for a stored procedure to return output to the caller, stored functions must necessarily produce a return value.

Here's a simple example of a stored function, which returns a formatted version of the current date:

```
mysql> DELIMITER //
mysql> CREATE FUNCTION today()
    ->    RETURNS VARCHAR(255)
    ->    BEGIN
    ->       RETURN DATE_FORMAT(NOW(), '%D %M %Y');
    ->    END//
Query OK, 0 rows affected (0.00 sec)
```

As with the CREATE PROCEDURE command, the CREATE FUNCTION command must be followed by the name of the stored function. The same rules that govern procedure names also apply to function names. Input parameters to the function, if any, appear within parentheses following the function name, together with their data type. The function's return value (only a single return value is possible) is represented by a mandatory RETURNS clause that follows the parentheses; this RETURNS clause specifies the data type of the return value.

The main body of the function can contain SQL statements, variable definitions, conditional tests, loops, and error handlers. It must also include a RETURN statement, which specifies the value to return to the caller. However, because stored functions cannot return result sets, take care to ensure that your RETURN statement does not return the output of a SELECT (or any other command that returns a result set).

NOTE *When MySQL encounters a RETURN statement inside a stored function, it halts processing at that point and exits the function with the specified return value.*

To invoke a stored function, you don't need to use the CALL command; instead, use the function name within a SQL statement, as you would for any other built-in function. Here's an example:

```
mysql> SELECT today();
+--------------------+
| today()            |
+--------------------+
| 25th December 2008 |
+--------------------+
1 row in set (0.00 sec)
```

To remove a stored function, use the DROP FUNCTION command with the function name as argument:

```
mysql> DROP FUNCTION today();
Query OK, 0 rows affected (0.01 sec)
```

To view the body of a specific stored function, use the SHOW CREATE FUNCTION command with the function name as argument. This is a restricted command; it will be executed only if you are the creator of the procedure or have SELECT privileges on the *proc* grant table (privileges are discussed in greater detail in Chapter 11). Here's an example:

```
mysql> SHOW CREATE FUNCTION today\G
*********************** 1. row ***********************
            Function: today
            sql_mode: STRICT_TRANS_TABLES
     Create Function: CREATE DEFINER=`root`@`localhost`
FUNCTION `today`() RETURNS varchar(255) CHARSET latin1
```

```
BEGIN
RETURN DATE_FORMAT(NOW(), '%D %M %Y');
END
character_set_client: latin1
collation_connection: latin1_swedish_ci
  Database Collation: latin1_swedish_ci
1 row in set (0.00 sec)
```

To view a list of all stored functions on the server, use the SHOW FUNCTION STATUS command. You can filter the output of this command with a WHERE clause, as shown:

```
mysql> SHOW FUNCTION STATUS WHERE Db='test'\G
*************************** 1. row ***************************
                 Db: test
               Name: get_circle_area
               Type: FUNCTION
            Definer: root@localhost
           Modified: 2008-12-25 16:12:09
            Created: 2008-12-25 16:12:09
      Security_type: DEFINER
            Comment:
character_set_client: latin1
collation_connection: latin1_swedish_ci
  Database Collation: latin1_swedish_ci
1 row in set (0.01 sec)
```

Input Parameters

Because stored functions use a separate RETURNS clause to define their output, all the parameters that appear within the parentheses in the function definition are assumed to be input parameters, and the OUT and INOUT keywords are not required (or supported) for the input argument list. These input parameters can then be manipulated or used for calculations within the function body, as illustrated in the following example:

```
mysql> DELIMITER //
mysql> CREATE FUNCTION get_circle_area(radius INT)
    ->    RETURNS FLOAT
    ->    BEGIN
    ->       RETURN PI() * radius * radius;
    ->    END//
Query OK, 0 rows affected (0.00 sec)
```

You can now pass this function the length of a circle's radius and receive the corresponding circle area, as shown:

```
mysql> SELECT get_circle_area(10);
+--------------------+
| get_circle_area(10) |
+--------------------+
```

```
|      314.15927124023 |
+--------------------+
1 row in set (0.02 sec)
```

You can also read and write directly to session variables from a stored function. Consider the next example, which revises the previous example and uses session variables for both input and output:

```
mysql> DELIMITER //
mysql> CREATE FUNCTION get_circle_area()
    ->    RETURNS INT
    ->    BEGIN
    ->      SET @area = PI() * @radius * @radius;
    ->      RETURN NULL;
    ->    END//
Query OK, 0 rows affected (0.01 sec)
mysql> DELIMITER ;
mysql> SET @radius=2;
Query OK, 0 rows affected (0.00 sec)
mysql> SELECT get_circle_area();
+-------------------+
| get_circle_area() |
+-------------------+
|              NULL |
+-------------------+
1 row in set (0.00 sec)
mysql> SELECT @area;
+-----------------+
| @area           |
+-----------------+
| 12.566370614359 |
+-----------------+
1 row in set (0.03 sec)
```

Stored functions can also manipulate tables, just like stored procedures. Here's an example:

```
mysql> DELIMITER //
mysql> CREATE FUNCTION add_flight_dep(fid INT, depday INT, deptime
TIME)
    ->    RETURNS INT
    ->    BEGIN
    ->      INSERT INTO flightdep (FlightID, DepDay, DepTime)
    ->      VALUES (fid, depday, deptime);
    ->      RETURN 1;
    ->    END//
Query OK, 0 rows affected (0.28 sec)
mysql> DELIMITER ;
mysql> SELECT add_flight_dep(1, 2, '12:35');
```

```
+-------------------------------+
| add_flight_dep(1, 2, '12:35') |
+-------------------------------+
|                             1 |
+-------------------------------+
1 row in set (0.19 sec)
mysql> SELECT DepDay, DepTime FROM flightdep
    -> WHERE FlightID = 1;
+--------+----------+
| DepDay | DepTime  |
+--------+----------+
|      2 | 12:35:00 |
+--------+----------+
1 row in set (0.08 sec)
```

Setting Routine Characteristics

Both the CREATE PROCEDURE and the CREATE FUNCTION commands support additional clauses, which are used to define various characteristics of the stored routine. Here's a list:

- The DETERMINISTIC clause indicates that the routine is "deterministic"—that is, given the same input, it always produces the same output. Routines that make use of random numbers, are tied to the current time, or use functions that return a different value on each invocation, such as CONNECTION_ID(), should instead use the NOT DETERMINISTIC clause.

- The LANGUAGE clause specifies the language for the routine. At the time of this writing, the only legal value for this clause is 'SQL'.

- The CONTAINS SQL clause indicates that the routine contains SQL statements. Valid alternatives for this clause include READS SQL DATA (routine contains statements that read table data), MODIFIES SQL DATA (routine contains statements that write table data), and NO SQL (routine contains no SQL statements).

- The SQL SECURITY clause specifies which user's privileges should be considered when executing the routine: the user who created it (DEFINER) or the user who invoked it (INVOKER).

- The COMMENT clause specifies a human-readable descriptive label for the routine.

Here's an example of how these characteristics can be added to a routine definition:

```
mysql> DELIMITER //
mysql> CREATE PROCEDURE get_airport_name(IN aid INT)
    ->     DETERMINISTIC
    ->     LANGUAGE SQL
    ->     READS SQL DATA
    ->     SQL SECURITY INVOKER
```

```
    ->    BEGIN
    ->      SELECT AirportName FROM airport WHERE AirportID = aid;
    ->    END//
Query OK, 0 rows affected (0.68 sec)
```

How Do I Return a Collection of Values from a Stored Function?

Under MySQL's current implementation, a stored function can only return a single value. However, there is a not-so-pretty workaround: create a temporary table within the function body to store the values returned, and then access this table outside the function. Here's an example:

```
mysql> DELIMITER //
mysql> CREATE FUNCTION get_airport_names(min_terminals INT)
    -> RETURNS INT
    -> BEGIN
    ->   DECLARE count INT DEFAULT 0;
    ->   CREATE TEMPORARY TABLE
    ->     IF NOT EXISTS
    ->     get_airport_names_out (value VARCHAR(255));
    ->   DELETE FROM get_airport_names_out;
    ->   INSERT INTO get_airport_names_out (value)
    ->   SELECT AirportName FROM airport
    ->     WHERE NumTerminals >= min_terminals;
    ->   SELECT COUNT(value) INTO count
    ->     FROM get_airport_names_out;
    ->   RETURN count;
    -> END//
Query OK, 0 rows affected (0.00 sec)
mysql> DELIMITER ;
mysql> SELECT get_airport_names(3);
+----------------------+
| get_airport_names(3) |
+----------------------+
|                    4 |
+----------------------+
1 row in set, 1 warning (0.03 sec)
mysql> SELECT value FROM get_airport_names_out;
+-----------------------------------+
| value                             |
+-----------------------------------+
| Heathrow Airport                  |
| Barcelona International Airport   |
| Barajas Airport                   |
| Changi Airport                    |
+-----------------------------------+
4 rows in set (0.00 sec)
```

Doing More with Stored Routines

MySQL also allows you to use variables, conditional tests, and loops within stored routines, making possible some fairly complex programming. The following sections examine these constructs in greater detail.

Variables

In addition to allowing you to create, access, and manipulate session variables from within a stored procedure, MySQL offers the DECLARE keyword, which can be used to declare variables that are "local" to a given routine. Here's an example:

```
mysql> DELIMITER //
mysql> CREATE PROCEDURE decl()
    -> BEGIN
    ->    DECLARE count INT;
    -> END//
Query OK, 0 rows affected (0.00 sec)
```

A DECLARE statement must be followed by the variable name and its data type. The same rules that govern user-defined variable names also apply to variables in stored routines. Multiple variables of the same type can be initialized in a single DECLARE statement by separating the variable names with commas. Here's how:

```
mysql> DELIMITER //
mysql> CREATE PROCEDURE decl()
    -> BEGIN
    ->    DECLARE count, retval, x INT;
    -> END//
Query OK, 0 rows affected (0.00 sec)
```

The DECLARE statement also supports an optional DEFAULT keyword, which can be used to assign a default value to a variable.

```
mysql> DELIMITER //
mysql> CREATE PROCEDURE decl()
    -> BEGIN
    ->    DECLARE count INT DEFAULT 0;
    -> END//
Query OK, 0 rows affected (0.00 sec)
```

Once defined, these variables can be assigned values using either SET or SELECT INTO statements, and can be accessed by name from other statements within the routine. Note that when accessing a local variable defined with DECLARE, there is no need to prefix the variable name with the @ symbol.

```
mysql> DELIMITER //
mysql> CREATE PROCEDURE add_one()
```

```
  -> BEGIN
  ->    DECLARE count INT DEFAULT 99;
  ->    SELECT (count+1);
  -> END//
Query OK, 0 rows affected (0.00 sec)
mysql> DELIMITER ;
mysql> CALL add_one();
+-----------+
| (count+1) |
+-----------+
|       100 |
+-----------+
1 row in set (0.05 sec)
```

Conditional Tests

In addition to storing and retrieving values in variables, MySQL lets programmers evaluate different conditions that occur during routine execution and take decisions based on whether these conditions evaluate to true or false. These conditions can be expressed using two types of conditional constructs: the IF construct and the CASE construct.

The IF Construct

MySQL's IF construct provides a convenient way to alter the control flow within a stored routine. In its simplest form, it tests a condition and executes a block of statements if the condition is true. There are three general forms of this construct, as follows:

```
IF [val 1]
   THEN [result 1];
END IF;

IF [val 1]
   THEN [result 1];
   ELSE [result 2];
END IF;

IF [val 1] THEN [result 1]
   ELSEIF [val 2] THEN [result 2]
   ELSEIF [val 3] THEN [result 3]
   ...
   ELSEIF [val n] THEN [result n]
   ELSE [default result]
END IF;
```

Here's an example, which illustrates the first form:

```
mysql> DELIMITER //
mysql> CREATE FUNCTION what_is_today()
```

```
    -> RETURNS VARCHAR(255)
    -> BEGIN
    ->    DECLARE message VARCHAR(255);
    ->    IF DAYOFWEEK(NOW()) BETWEEN 2 AND 6 THEN
    ->       SET message = 'Today is a weekday';
    ->    END IF;
    ->    RETURN message;
    -> END//
Query OK, 0 rows affected (0.01 sec)
```

In this example, the function will return a message only on weekdays:

```
mysql> SELECT what_is_today();
+--------------------+
| what_is_today()    |
+--------------------+
| Today is a weekday |
+--------------------+
1 row in set (0.00 sec)
```

A slightly more complex version of the IF construct allows you to define an alternative set of actions for when the condition evaluates to false. Consider the next example, which returns different messages on weekdays and weekends:

```
mysql> DELIMITER //
mysql> CREATE FUNCTION what_is_today()
    -> RETURNS VARCHAR(255)
    -> BEGIN
    ->    DECLARE message VARCHAR(255);
    ->    IF DAYOFWEEK(NOW()) BETWEEN 2 AND 6 THEN
    ->       SET message = 'Today is a weekday';
    ->    ELSE
    ->       SET message = 'Today is a Saturday or Sunday';
    ->    END IF;
    ->    RETURN message;
    -> END//
Query OK, 0 rows affected (0.00 sec)
```

The IF construct can come in handy when writing stored procedures that insert or update table data. As an example, consider the next procedure, which only inserts a new aircraft type record if it does not already exist:

```
mysql> DELIMITER //
mysql> CREATE PROCEDURE
    ->    add_aircraft_type(IN aname VARCHAR(255))
    -> BEGIN
    ->    DECLARE count, lastid, retval INT;
    ->    SELECT COUNT(AircraftTypeID) INTO count
    ->    FROM aircrafttype WHERE AircraftName = aname;
```

```
  ->     IF count = 0 THEN
  ->       SELECT MAX(AircraftTypeID) INTO lastid
  ->         FROM aircrafttype;
  ->       INSERT INTO aircrafttype(AircraftTypeID, AircraftName)
  ->         VALUES ((lastid+1), aname);
  ->       SET retval = 1;
  ->     ELSE
  ->       SET retval = 0;
  ->     END IF;
  ->     SELECT retval;
  -> END//
Query OK, 0 rows affected (0.00 sec)
```

In this example, the procedure accepts an aircraft type name as input argument. It then checks the *aircrafttype* table to see if a record with the same data already exists and inserts the new record only if it does not. An IF construct is used to make this decision, and the procedure's return value is set to 0 or 1, depending on whether the INSERT took place.

Here's the output:

```
mysql> CALL add_aircraft_type('Boeing 747');
+--------+
| retval |
+--------+
|      0 |
+--------+
1 row in set (0.16 sec)
mysql> CALL add_aircraft_type('Cessna C60');
+--------+
| retval |
+--------+
|      1 |
+--------+
1 row in set (0.03 sec)
mysql> SELECT AircraftName FROM aircrafttype;
+-----------------+
| AircraftName    |
+-----------------+
| Boeing 747      |
| Boeing 767      |
| Airbus A300/310 |
| Airbus A330     |
| Airbus A340     |
| Airbus A380     |
| Cessna C60      |
+-----------------+
7 rows in set (0.00 sec)
```

As demonstrated already, the IF-ELSE version of the IF construct lets you define actions for two eventualities: a true condition and a false condition. In reality, however, it's likely that you will have more than just two outcomes to contend with. For these situations, MySQL offers a more complex version of the IF construct. Consider the next example, which illustrates by displaying a different message for each day of the week:

```
mysql> DELIMITER //
mysql> CREATE FUNCTION todays_child()
    -> RETURNS VARCHAR(255)
    -> BEGIN
    ->   DECLARE message VARCHAR(255);
    ->   IF DAYOFWEEK(NOW()) = 2 THEN
    ->     SET message = 'Monday\'s child is fair of face.';
    ->   ELSEIF DAYOFWEEK(NOW()) = 3 THEN
    ->     SET message = 'Tuesday\'s child is full of grace.';
    ->   ELSEIF DAYOFWEEK(NOW()) = 4 THEN
    ->     SET message = 'Wednesday\'s child is full of woe.';
    ->   ELSEIF DAYOFWEEK(NOW()) = 5 THEN
    ->     SET message = 'Thursday\'s child has far to go.';
    ->   ELSEIF DAYOFWEEK(NOW()) = 6 THEN
    ->     SET message = 'Friday\'s child is loving and giving.';
    ->   ELSEIF DAYOFWEEK(NOW()) = 7 THEN
    ->     SET message = 'Saturday\'s child works hard for a living.';
    ->   ELSE
    ->     SET message = 'Sunday\'s child is bonny and blithe
    ->       and good and gay.';
    ->   END IF;
    ->   RETURN message;
    -> END
    -> DELIMITER ;
Query OK, 0 rows affected (0.03 sec)
```

In this example, the optional ELSEIF clause to the IF construct is used to define various other values that the condition might have. Depending on what the DAYOFWEEK() function returns, a different message will be set and returned by this function. Here's an example:

```
mysql> SELECT todays_child();
+---------------------------------------------+
| todays_child()                              |
+---------------------------------------------+
| Saturday's child works hard for a living.   |
+---------------------------------------------+
1 row in set (0.00 sec)
```

The CASE Construct

An alternative to the IF-ELSEIF-ELSE version of the IF construct is the CASE construct, which also allows for multiple conditions to be tested. The format of the CASE construct is somewhat complex, and usually looks like this:

```
CASE [expression to be evaluated]
    WHEN [val 1] THEN [result 1];
    WHEN [val 2] THEN [result 2];
    ...
    WHEN [val n] THEN [result n];
    ELSE [default result];
END CASE;
```

Here, the first argument is the value or expression to be evaluated; this is followed by a series of WHEN-THEN blocks, each of which specifies the value against which the first argument is to be compared and the result to be returned if the comparison is true. The entire series of WHEN-THEN blocks is terminated by an ELSE block, which specifies the default result in case none of the preceding blocks match, with an END closing the outer CASE block. In the event no ELSE block is specified and none of the WHEN-THEN comparisons return true, MySQL returns a NULL.

Here's a revision of the previous example using CASE:

```
mysql> DELIMITER //
mysql> CREATE FUNCTION todays_child()
    -> RETURNS VARCHAR(255)
    -> BEGIN
    ->   DECLARE message VARCHAR(255);
    ->   CASE DAYOFWEEK(NOW())
    ->     WHEN 2 THEN
    ->       SET message = 'Monday\'s child is fair of face.';
    ->     WHEN 3 THEN
    ->       SET message = 'Tuesday\'s child is full of grace.';
    ->     WHEN 4 THEN
    ->       SET message = 'Wednesday\'s child is full of woe.';
    ->     WHEN 5 THEN
    ->       SET message = 'Thursday\'s child has far to go.';
    ->     WHEN 6 THEN
    ->       SET message = 'Friday\'s child is loving and giving.';
    ->     WHEN 7 THEN
    ->       SET message = 'Saturday\'s child works hard for a living.';
    ->     ELSE
    ->       SET message = 'Sunday\'s child is bonny and blithe
    ->           and good and gay.';
    ->   END CASE;
    ->   RETURN message;
    -> END//
Query OK, 0 rows affected (0.04 sec)
```

Here's the output:

```
mysql> SELECT todays_child();
+------------------------------------------+
| todays_child()                           |
+------------------------------------------+
| Saturday's child works hard for a living. |
+------------------------------------------+
1 row in set (0.00 sec)
```

And here's a simple example of using the CASE construct in a stored procedure to toggle the status of a route using the UPDATE statement:

```
mysql> DELIMITER //
mysql> CREATE PROCEDURE change_route_status(
    ->          IN rid INT, IN color VARCHAR(10))
    -> BEGIN
    ->   CASE color
    ->     WHEN 'red' THEN
    ->       UPDATE route SET Status = 0 WHERE RouteID = rid;
    ->     WHEN 'green' THEN
    ->       UPDATE route SET Status = 1 WHERE RouteID = rid;
    ->     ELSE
    ->       BEGIN
    ->       END;
    ->   END CASE;
    -> END//
Query OK, 0 rows affected (0.00 sec)
```

In this example, the inputs 'red' and 'green' are used to set a route's status to 0 or 1, respectively. Notice, however, the ELSE clause of the CASE construct, which contains an empty BEGIN. . .END block. This is done to prevent an error being displayed if a nonmatching input is supplied to the procedure. Here's some output explaining how it works:

```
mysql> SELECT RouteID, Status FROM route
    -> WHERE RouteID = 1192;
+---------+--------+
| RouteID | Status |
+---------+--------+
|    1192 |      1 |
+---------+--------+
1 row in set (0.03 sec)
mysql> CALL change_route_status(1192, 'red');
Query OK, 1 row affected (0.05 sec)
mysql> SELECT RouteID, Status FROM route
    -> WHERE RouteID = 1192;
```

```
+----------+--------+
| RouteID  | Status |
+----------+--------+
|    1192  |     0  |
+----------+--------+
1 row in set (0.00 sec)
mysql> CALL change_route_status(1192, 'green');
Query OK, 0 rows affected (0.01 sec)
```

Loops

MySQL also supports loops in stored routines, thus enabling routines that repeat a series of actions until a prespecified condition is fulfilled. Three different loop constructs are currently supported: the LOOP construct, the REPEAT construct, and the WHILE construct. The following sections discuss each of these in greater detail.

The LOOP Construct

The LOOP construct is the simplest type of loop in MySQL, allowing for a set of statements to be repeatedly executed. It looks like this:

```
loop-name: LOOP
  statement 1;
  statement 2;
  ...
  statement n;
END LOOP loop-name;
```

The statements enclosed within the LOOP...END LOOP block are executed repeatedly until interrupted with a LEAVE statement. This, combined with the IF construct, makes it possible to create loops that execute until a specified condition is fulfilled. Consider the next example, which illustrates by building a factorial calculator:

```
mysql> DELIMITER //
mysql> CREATE FUNCTION factorial(num INT UNSIGNED)
    -> RETURNS INT
    -> BEGIN
    ->   DECLARE result INT DEFAULT 1;
    ->   IF num = 0 THEN
    ->     RETURN 0;
    ->   END IF;
    ->   fact: LOOP
    ->     IF num > 0 THEN
    ->       SET result = result * num;
    ->       SET num = num - 1;
    ->     ELSE
    ->       LEAVE fact;
    ->     END IF;
```

```
    ->    END LOOP fact;
    ->    RETURN result;
    -> END//
Query OK, 0 rows affected (0.01 sec)
```

In this function, the number entered by the user is decremented by 1 on each iteration and multiplied by the previously calculated product. This continues until the number entered by the user reaches 0, at which point the LEAVE statement is used to exit the loop. The end result is the factorial of the input number.

```
mysql> SELECT factorial(4);
+--------------+
| factorial(4) |
+--------------+
|           24 |
+--------------+
1 row in set (0.00 sec)
```

Notice the use of the UNSIGNED attribute to the data type, which ensures that only positive numbers are provided to the function as input. MySQL will generate an error if the function receives a negative value as input, as shown:

```
mysql> SELECT factorial(-1);
ERROR 1264 (22003): Out of range value for column 'num' at row 1
```

The WHILE Construct

A WHILE loop repeats continuously while a prespecified condition is true. The typical structure of this loop is as follows:

```
loop-name: WHILE condition DO
   statement 1;
   statement 2;
   ...
   statement n;
END WHILE loop-name;
```

It's possible to revise the previous example in terms of a WHILE loop. Here it is:

```
mysql> DELIMITER //
mysql> CREATE FUNCTION factorial(num INT UNSIGNED)
    -> RETURNS INT
    -> BEGIN
    ->   DECLARE result INT DEFAULT 1;
    ->   IF num = 0 THEN
    ->     RETURN 0;
    ->   END IF;
    ->   fact: WHILE num > 0 DO
    ->     SET result = result * num;
    ->     SET num = num - 1;
```

```
    ->    END WHILE fact;
    ->    RETURN result;
    -> END//
Query OK, 0 rows affected (0.00 sec)
```

Notice the condition specified after the WHILE keyword; so long as this condition evaluates to true, the code within the loop block is executed. As soon as the condition becomes false, the loop stops repeating, and control returns to the lines following the loop.

The REPEAT Construct

A REPEAT loop is slightly different from a WHILE loop: it repeats continuously *until* a prespecified condition becomes true. Here's what it looks like:

```
loop-name: WHILE condition DO
   statement 1;
   statement 2;
   ...
   statement n;
END WHILE loop-name;
```

The difference in structure between WHILE and REPEAT constructs should be apparent: with a REPEAT loop, the condition to be evaluated appears at the bottom of the loop block, rather than the beginning. Here's the factorial calculator again, this time written as a REPEAT loop:

```
mysql> DELIMITER //
mysql> CREATE FUNCTION factorial(num INT UNSIGNED)
    -> RETURNS INT
    -> BEGIN
    ->    DECLARE result INT DEFAULT 1;
    ->    IF num = 0 THEN
    ->      RETURN 0;
    ->    END IF;
    ->    fact: REPEAT
    ->      SET result = result * num;
    ->      SET num = num - 1;
    ->      UNTIL num <= 0
    ->    END REPEAT fact;
    ->    RETURN result;
    -> END//
Query OK, 0 rows affected (0.02 sec)
```

NOTE *There is a subtle difference between a* WHILE *loop and a* DO-WHILE *loop that has one important implication. With a* WHILE *loop, if the conditional expression evaluates to false on the first pass itself, the loop will never be executed. With a* REPEAT *loop, on the other hand, the loop will always be executed once, even if the conditional expression is false, because the condition is evaluated at the end of the loop iteration rather than at the beginning.*

PART I

The LEAVE and ITERATE Statements

MySQL offers two additional statements to assist in loop control: the LEAVE statement, which breaks out of a loop, and the ITERATE statement, which forces the loop to run once again. Here's a trivial example that illustrates the LEAVE statement:

```
mysql> DELIMITER //
mysql> CREATE PROCEDURE f()
    -> BEGIN
    ->    DECLARE i INT DEFAULT 1;
    ->    f: WHILE i <= 5 DO
    ->      IF i = 3 THEN
    ->        LEAVE f;
    ->      END IF;
    ->      SELECT i;
    ->      SET i = i + 1;
    ->    END WHILE f;
    -> END//
Query OK, 0 rows affected (0.01 sec)
```

In this case, the LEAVE statement will force the loop to exit on the third iteration, as illustrated in the output:

```
mysql> CALL f \G
*************************** 1. row ***************************
i: 1
1 row in set (0.00 sec)
*************************** 1. row ***************************
i: 2
1 row in set (0.00 sec)
```

And here's an example that demonstrates the ITERATE statement:

```
mysql> DELIMITER //
mysql> CREATE PROCEDURE g()
    -> BEGIN
    ->    DECLARE i INT DEFAULT 1;
    ->    DECLARE j INT DEFAULT 0;
    ->    f: WHILE i <= 5 AND j < 2 DO
    ->      SELECT i;
    ->      IF i = 3 THEN
    ->        SET j = j + 1;
    ->        ITERATE f;
    ->      END IF;
    ->      SET i = i + 1;
    ->    END WHILE f;
    -> END//
Query OK, 0 rows affected (0.01 sec)
```

In this example, when the loop counter reaches 3, the ITERATE statement will force an additional iteration of the loop:

```
mysql> CALL g \G
*************************** 1. row ***************************
i: 1
1 row in set (0.01 sec)
*************************** 1. row ***************************
i: 2
1 row in set (0.01 sec)
*************************** 1. row ***************************
i: 3
1 row in set (0.01 sec)
*************************** 1. row ***************************
i: 3
1 row in set (0.01 sec)
```

Cursors

Quite often, you'll be using loops closely with SELECT queries to process the collection of records returned by a SELECT. To do this, there's one additional ingredient needed: a cursor.

Wikipedia, at http://en.wikipedia.org/wiki/Cursor_(databases), defines a *cursor* as "a control structure for the successive traversal (and potential processing) of records in a result set…[it] is used for processing individual rows returned by the database system for a query." In simpler terms, if a database result set is analogous to a collection of files in a filing cabinet, a cursor is the equivalent of your finger, flipping through them one after another. At any point in time, your finger is pointing at a specific file; this is the current record. You can trail your finger forward to the next file or backward to the previous one; in database terms, this is accomplished with a loop construct, such as LOOP or REPEAT, which moves the cursor forward to the next record or backward to the previous one.

That said, cursors are a relatively new addition to MySQL and, as such, are still subject to a few important limitations.

- MySQL cursors are forward-only; unlike your finger, they can't be used to go back to a previous record.

- MySQL cursors are read-only; they can only be used to read values from a result set, not write or update existing values.

- When used in transactions, MySQL cursors are automatically closed after a COMMIT.

Cursors are initialized with a DECLARE statement, much like variables (although cursor declarations must come after variable declarations). Each cursor is identified with a unique name and associated with a particular SELECT statement. Here's an example:

```
DECLARE mycur CURSOR FOR SELECT AirportName, NumTerminals FROM airport;
```

Once the cursor has been declared, MySQL offers the OPEN, FETCH, and CLOSE commands to iterate through the result set returned by the cursor's SELECT statement.

- The OPEN command opens the cursor for reading.
- The FETCH command reads the contents of the current record into one or more variables and then advances the cursor to the next record. To process an entire result set, it is necessary to call FETCH as many times as there are records in the result set. This is typically accomplished with a loop.
- The CLOSE command closes the cursor. Cursors are also automatically closed when the stored routine that initialized them ends.

Here's an example of using a cursor in a stored procedure, which iterates through the airport list and marks each airport as 'big' or 'small,' depending on how many terminals it has:

```
mysql> DELIMITER //
mysql> CREATE PROCEDURE get_airport_size()
    -> BEGIN
    ->    DECLARE a VARCHAR(255);
    ->    DECLARE b,x INT;
    ->    DECLARE c CURSOR FOR
    ->      SELECT AirportName, NumTerminals FROM airport;
    ->    OPEN c;
    ->    size: LOOP
    ->      FETCH c INTO a,x;
    ->      IF x > 2
    ->        THEN SELECT a AS Name, 'big' AS Size;
    ->      ELSE
    ->        SELECT a AS Name, 'small' AS Size;
    ->      END IF;
    ->    END LOOP size;
    ->    CLOSE c;
    -> END//
Query OK, 0 rows affected (0.57 sec)
```

This procedure declares a cursor, which operates on the result set returned by the SELECT statement. This cursor is opened for reading with the OPEN command, and a LOOP is then used to iterate over the result set, with the FETCH command returning each record from the collection in a sequential manner. An IF conditional test is then used to check the number of terminals and mark each airport as 'big' or 'small,' respectively. Once the loop ends, the CLOSE command is used to close the cursor.

Here's a snippet of the output:

```
mysql> CALL get_airport_size()\G
*********************** 1. row ****************
Name: Orly Airport
Size: small
1 row in set (0.00 sec)
...
*********************** 1. row *************************
Name: Changi Airport
Size: big
1 row in set (0.04 sec)
ERROR 1329 (02000): No data - zero rows fetched, selected, or processed
```

Handlers

If you're sharp-eyed, you'll have noticed one problem with the output of the previous example: the error message at the end. This error occurs because the loop, as shown, contains no exit condition and, as a result, the cursor reaches the end of the record collection and keeps executing, attempting to access records that don't exist.

One solution to this problem is, of course, to use an additional SELECT COUNT() ... query at the beginning of the procedure, and use that result to force the loop to run only a specified number of times. However, MySQL also offers a somewhat more elegant option, one that doesn't require the overhead of an additional query: an error handler.

There are two steps to defining an error handler for a stored procedure, as explained in the following sections.

Declare the Error Condition to Be Handled

The first step is to decide which error code to trap and assign a unique name to that error condition. This is accomplished by using a DECLARE ... CONDITION FOR statement. Here's an example, which specifies a name for MySQL error code 1050 (table already exists):

```
DECLARE err_table_exists CONDITION FOR 1050;
```

Instead of the MySQL error code, it's possible to trap errors using their SQLSTATE code. Here's an example of this approach:

```
DECLARE err_table_exists CONDITION FOR SQLSTATE '42S01';
```

TIP *A complete list of MySQL error codes and their equivalent SQLSTATE values can be obtained from the MySQL manual at http://dev.mysql.com/doc/refman/5.1/en/error-messages-server.html.*

Declare a Handler for the Named Error Condition

The second step is to define a handler for the error condition. This is accomplished by using a DECLARE ... HANDLER FOR statement, which contains the SQL commands that will be executed when the error occurs. Here's an example, which sets a variable to a new value when the "table already exists" error occurs and then exits the routine:

```
DECLARE EXIT HANDLER FOR err_table_exists
BEGIN
  SET @table=-1;
END;
```

It's also possible to define the error condition to be trapped within the DECLARE ... HANDLER FOR statement itself. To illustrate, consider that the following two sets of statements are equivalent:

```
DECLARE err_table_exists CONDITION FOR 1050;
DECLARE EXIT HANDLER FOR err_table_exists
BEGIN
  SET @table=-1;
END;
```

```
DECLARE EXIT HANDLER FOR 1050
BEGIN
  SET @table=-1;
END;
```

Once the handler code is executed, MySQL will either exit the stored routine or continue processing it, depending on the type of handler used. Within a stored routine, two types of handlers are currently possible: an EXIT handler, which causes the stored routine to stop executing when the error takes place, and a CONTINUE handler, which causes the stored procedure to continue executing after the error takes place. The following sections look at each of these in greater detail.

TIP *When using DECLARE statements in stored routines, MySQL is finicky about the order in which these can appear. To avoid error messages, place variable and condition declarations before cursor and handler declarations.*

The EXIT Handler

An EXIT handler causes MySQL to terminate processing of a stored routine when the specified error condition occurs. Here's a revision of the previous example, which demonstrates by using an exit handler to gracefully terminate processing when the "zero rows" error is triggered:

```
mysql> DELIMITER //
mysql> CREATE PROCEDURE get_airport_size()
    -> BEGIN
    ->   DECLARE a VARCHAR(255);
    ->   DECLARE b,x,e INT;
    ->   DECLARE err_no_more_records CONDITION FOR 1329;
    ->   DECLARE c CURSOR FOR SELECT AirportName, NumTerminals
    ->     FROM airport;
    ->   DECLARE EXIT HANDLER FOR err_no_more_records
    ->   BEGIN
    ->   END;
    ->   OPEN c;
    ->   size: LOOP
    ->     FETCH c INTO a,x;
    ->     IF x > 2
    ->       THEN SELECT a AS Name, 'big' AS Size;
    ->     ELSE
    ->       SELECT a AS Name, 'small' AS Size;
    ->     END IF;
    ->   END LOOP size;
    ->   CLOSE c;
    -> END//
Query OK, 0 rows affected (0.00 sec)
```

In this example, an exit handler is defined for error 1329, which is the error code corresponding to the "zero rows" error. When this handler is triggered, it exits the procedure cleanly without generating an error message.

The CONTINUE Handler

A CONTINUE handler causes MySQL to continue processing a stored routine when the specified error condition occurs. Here's an example, which tries to drop a nonexistent table, intercepts the resulting error, and continues processing the routine:

```
mysql> DELIMITER //
mysql> CREATE PROCEDURE drop_table()
    -> BEGIN
    ->   DECLARE CONTINUE HANDLER FOR 1051
    ->   BEGIN
    ->     SELECT 'ERROR: Attempt to drop a non-existent table'
    ->       AS message;
    ->   END;
    ->   SELECT 'START procedure' AS message;
    ->   DROP TABLE i_dont_exist;
    ->   SELECT 'END procedure' AS message;
    -> END//
Query OK, 0 rows affected (0.00 sec)
```

And here's the output:

```
mysql> CALL drop_table\G
*************************** 1. row ******************
message: START procedure
1 row in set (0.00 sec)
*************************** 1. row ******************
message: ERROR: Attempt to drop a non-existent table
1 row in set (0.00 sec)
*************************** 1. row ******************
message: END procedure
1 row in set (0.00 sec)
```

It's possible to use a CONTINUE handler to replicate the behavior of an EXIT handler by setting a variable in the handler code and then manually exiting the stored procedure if that variable is set. Here's a revision of one of the previous examples, which demonstrates this by using a CONTINUE handler instead of an EXIT handler to avoid the "zero rows" error:

```
mysql> CREATE PROCEDURE get_airport_size()
    -> BEGIN
    ->    DECLARE a VARCHAR(255);
    ->    DECLARE b,x,e INT;
    ->    DECLARE c CURSOR FOR SELECT AirportName, NumTerminals FROM airport;
    ->    DECLARE CONTINUE HANDLER FOR NOT FOUND
    ->    BEGIN
    ->      SET e = 1;
    ->    END;
    ->    OPEN c;
    ->    size: LOOP
    ->      IF e = 1 THEN
    ->        LEAVE size;
    ->      END IF;
    ->      FETCH c INTO a,x;
    ->      IF x > 2
    ->        THEN SELECT a AS Name, 'big' AS Size;
    ->      ELSE
    ->        SELECT a AS Name, 'small' AS Size;
    ->      END IF;
    ->    END LOOP size;
    ->    CLOSE c;
    -> END//
Query OK, 0 rows affected (0.00 sec)
```

In this example, the loop construct checks for an error variable at the beginning of each iteration and executes the cursor FETCH statement only if the error variable remains unset. When the cursor advances past the end of its record set, the CONTINUE handler is triggered; it sets the error variable and then continues executing the stored routine without exiting. On the next loop iteration, because the error variable will be set, the loop will terminate gracefully without executing the FETCH statement.

TIP *The* NOT FOUND *keyword serves as a "catch-all" shortcut that represents all errors occurring due to a cursor reaching the end of its record set.*

And here's another example, this one accepting a weekday number and returning the number of flights on that day, classified by time of day:

```
mysql> DELIMITER //
mysql> CREATE PROCEDURE get_flights_day(IN daynum INT)
    -> BEGIN
    ->   DECLARE morning,afternoon,evening,night,total INT DEFAULT 0;
    ->   DECLARE dt TIME;
    ->   DECLARE c CURSOR FOR SELECT DepTime
    ->     FROM flightdep WHERE DepDay = daynum;
    ->   DECLARE EXIT HANDLER FOR NOT FOUND
    ->   BEGIN
    ->     SET total = morning + afternoon + evening + night;
    ->     SELECT morning, afternoon, evening, night, total;
    ->   END;
    ->   OPEN c;
    ->   seg: LOOP
    ->     FETCH c INTO dt;
    ->     IF dt BETWEEN '00:00:00' AND '05:59:59' THEN
    ->        SET night = night + 1;
    ->     ELSEIF dt BETWEEN '06:00:00' AND '11:59:59' THEN
    ->        SET morning = morning + 1;
    ->     ELSEIF dt BETWEEN '12:00:00' AND '17:59:59' THEN
    ->        SET afternoon = afternoon + 1;
    ->     ELSEIF dt BETWEEN '18:00:00' AND '23:59:59' THEN
    ->        SET evening = evening + 1;
    ->     END IF;
    ->   END LOOP seg;
    ->   CLOSE c;
    -> END//
Query OK, 0 rows affected (0.01 sec)
```

This procedure accepts a day number as input and then retrieves all the flights on that day. A loop-and-cursor combination processes the flight list, with an IF construct taking care of assigning each flight to a specific segment of the day on the basis of its departure time. Once the cursor has reached the end of the result set, the exit handler is triggered and the final count of flights for each day segment is displayed.

Here's an example of the output:

```
mysql> CALL get_flights_day(2);
+---------+-----------+---------+-------+-------+
| morning | afternoon | evening | night | total |
+---------+-----------+---------+-------+-------+
|       2 |         7 |       6 |     2 |    17 |
+---------+-----------+---------+-------+-------+
```

```
1 row in set (0.00 sec)
mysql> CALL get_flights_day(7);
+---------+-----------+---------+-------+-------+
| morning | afternoon | evening | night | total |
+---------+-----------+---------+-------+-------+
|       1 |         4 |       4 |     1 |    10 |
+---------+-----------+---------+-------+-------+
1 row in set (0.01 sec)
```

How Do I Back Up My Stored Routines?

You can export the functions and procedures associated with a given database by passing the *--routines* argument to the *mysqldump* program. Chapter 12 has more information on this program.

Summary

This chapter discussed stored routines, one of the key new features introduced in MySQL 5.0. Stored routines allow developers to transfer some of the application's business logic to the database server, thereby benefitting from greater security and consistency in database-related operations. Support for programming constructs like variables, arguments, return values, conditional statements, loops, and error handlers allow developers to create complex and sophisticated stored routines that can reduce the time spent on application development.

To learn more about the topics discussed in this chapter, consider visiting the following links:

- Stored routines, at http://dev.mysql.com/doc/refman/5.1/en/stored-routines.html

- Handlers, at http://dev.mysql.com/doc/refman/5.1/en/conditions-and-handlers.html

- Frequently asked questions about stored routines, at http://dev.mysql.com/doc/refman/5.1/en/faqs-stored-procs.html

- Limitations on stored routines, at http://dev.mysql.com/doc/refman/5.1/en/stored-program-restrictions.html

- MySQL's internal implementation of stored routines, at http://forge.mysql.com/wiki/MySQL_Internals_Stored_Programs

- A discussion of problems with MySQL's current implementation of stored procedures, at http://www.mysqlperformanceblog.com/2007/06/12/mysql-stored-procedures-problems-and-use-practices

CHAPTER 7

Using Triggers and Scheduled Events

In addition to executing SQL statements and calling stored routines on an ad-hoc basis, MySQL 5.0 introduced database triggers, which allow these actions to be performed automatically by the server. This was not entirely unexpected—triggers and stored routines tend to go hand-in-hand, and both items were in demand from the user community—but it *was* a pleasant surprise to see MySQL 5.1 improve on this even further by introducing a new subsystem for scheduled events.

This event scheduler, together with MySQL's support for triggers, provide a powerful framework for automating database operations, one that can come in handy when constructing complex or lengthy application workflows. This chapter builds on the material in the previous chapter, introducing you to MySQL's implementation of triggers and scheduled events, and providing examples that demonstrate how they can be used in real-world applications.

Understanding Triggers

A *trigger*, as the name suggests, refers to one or more SQL statements that are automatically executed ("triggered") by the database server when a specific event occurs. Triggers can come in handy when automating database operations, and thereby reduce some of the load carried by an application. Common examples of triggers in use include:

- Logging changes in data
- Creating "snapshots" of data prior to a change (for undo functionality)
- Performing automatic calculations
- Changing data in one table in response to a change in another

A trigger is always associated with a particular table, and it can be set to execute either before or after the trigger event takes place. MySQL currently supports three types of trigger events: INSERTs, UPDATEs, and DELETEs.

A Simple Trigger

To understand how triggers work, let's consider a simple example: logging changes to the airline's flight database. Let's suppose that every time an administrator adds a new flight to the database, this action should be automatically logged to a separate table, along with the administrator's MySQL username and the current time. With a trigger, this is easy to do:

```
mysql> CREATE TRIGGER flight_ai
    ->    AFTER INSERT ON flight
    ->    FOR EACH ROW
    ->      INSERT INTO log (ByUser, Note, EventTime)
    ->      VALUES (CURRENT_USER(), 'Record added: flight', NOW());
Query OK, 0 rows affected (0.04 sec)
```

To define a trigger, MySQL offers the CREATE TRIGGER command. This command must be followed by the trigger name and the four key trigger components, namely:

- The trigger *event,* which can be any one of INSERT, UPDATE, or DELETE
- The trigger *activation time,* which can be either AFTER the event or BEFORE it
- The trigger's *subject table,* which is the table the trigger should be attached to
- The trigger *body,* which contains the SQL statements to be executed

NOTE *To create a trigger, a user must have the* TRIGGER *privilege (in MySQL 5.1.6+) or the* SUPER *privilege (in MySQL 5.0.x). Privileges are discussed in greater detail in Chapter 11.*

These components are illustrated in the previous example, which creates a trigger named *flight_ai.* The FOR EACH ROW clause in the trigger ensures that it is activated after every operation that adds a new record to the *flight* table and it, in turn, adds a record to the *log* table recording the operation. To see this trigger in action, try adding a new record to the *flight* table, as shown:

```
mysql> INSERT INTO flight (FlightID, RouteID, AircraftID)
    -> VALUES (900, 1141, 3452);
Query OK, 1 row affected (0.08 sec)
mysql> SELECT * FROM log\G
*********************** 1. row ******************
 RecordID: 2
   ByUser: root@localhost
     Note: Record added: flight
EventTime: 2009-01-09 15:40:46
1 row in set (0.00 sec)
```

It's easy to add another trigger, this one to log record deletions. Here's an example:

```
mysql> CREATE TRIGGER flight_ad
    ->     AFTER DELETE ON flight
    ->     FOR EACH ROW
    ->        INSERT INTO log (ByUser, Note, EventTime)
    ->        VALUES (CURRENT_USER(), 'Record deleted: flight', NOW());
Query OK, 0 rows affected (0.08 sec)
```

And now, when you delete a record, that operation should also be recorded in the log table:

```
mysql> DELETE FROM flight
    -> WHERE flightid = 900;
Query OK, 1 row affected (0.01 sec)
mysql> SELECT * FROM log\G
*********************** 1. row **************
 RecordID: 3
   ByUser: root@localhost
     Note: Record deleted: flight
EventTime: 2009-01-09 15:42:42
*********************** 2. row **************
 RecordID: 2
```

```
  ByUser: root@localhost
    Note: Record added: flight
EventTime: 2009-01-09 15:40:46
2 rows in set (0.00 sec)
```

How Do I Name My Triggers?

Peter Gulutzan has suggested an easy-to-understand and consistent naming scheme for triggers in his article at http://dev.mysql.com/tech-resources/articles/mysql-triggers.pdf, which is also followed in this chapter: Name each trigger with the name of the table to which it is linked, with an additional suffix consisting of the letters *a* (for "after") or *b* (for "before"), and *i* (for "insert"), *u* (for "update") and *d* (for "delete"). So, for example, an AFTER INSERT trigger on the *pax* table would be named *pax_ai*.

The main body of the trigger is not limited only to single SQL statements; it can contain any of MySQL's programming constructs, including variable definitions, conditional tests, loops, and error handlers. BEGIN and END blocks are mandatory when the procedure body contains these complex control structures. In all other cases (such as the previous example, which contains only a single INSERT), they are optional.

NOTE *To avoid ambiguity, MySQL does not allow more than one trigger with the same trigger event and trigger time per table. This means that, for example, a table cannot have two AFTER INSERT triggers (although it can have separate BEFORE INSERT and AFTER INSERT triggers). Or, to put it another way, a table can have, at most, six possible triggers.*

To remove a trigger, use the DROP TRIGGER command with the trigger name as argument:

```
mysql> DROP TRIGGER flight_ad;
Query OK, 0 rows affected (0.03 sec)
```

TIP *Dropping a table automatically removes all triggers associated with it.*

To view the body of a specific trigger, use the SHOW CREATE TRIGGER command with the trigger name as argument. Here's an example:

```
mysql> SHOW CREATE TRIGGER flight_ad\G
*************************** 1. row ***************************
               Trigger: flight_ad
              sql_mode: STRICT_TRANS_TABLES
SQL Original Statement: CREATE DEFINER=`root`@`localhost`
  TRIGGER flight_ad
  AFTER DELETE ON flight
  FOR EACH ROW
```

```
          INSERT INTO log (ByUser, Note, EventTime)
          VALUES (CURRENT_USER(), 'Record deleted: flight', NOW());
   character_set_client: latin1
 collation_connection: latin1_swedish_ci
    Database Collation: latin1_swedish_ci
1 row in set (0.00 sec)
```

To view a list of all triggers on the server, use the SHOW TRIGGERS command. You can filter the output of this command with a WHERE clause, as shown:

```
mysql> SHOW TRIGGERS FROM db1 WHERE `Table` = 'flight'\G
*************************** 1. row ***************************
              Trigger: flight_ai
                Event: INSERT
                Table: flight
            Statement: INSERT INTO log (ByUser, Note, EventTime)
   VALUES (CURRENT_USER(), 'Record added: flight', NOW());
               Timing: AFTER
              Created: NULL
             sql_mode: STRICT_TRANS_TABLES
              Definer: root@localhost
 character_set_client: latin1
 collation_connection: latin1_swedish_ci
   Database Collation: latin1_swedish_ci
*************************** 2. row ***************************
              Trigger: flight_ad
                Event: DELETE
                Table: flight
            Statement: INSERT INTO log (ByUser, Note, EventTime)
   VALUES (CURRENT_USER(), 'Record deleted: flight', NOW());
               Timing: AFTER
              Created: NULL
             sql_mode: STRICT_TRANS_TABLES
              Definer: root@localhost
 character_set_client: latin1
 collation_connection: latin1_swedish_ci
   Database Collation: latin1_swedish_ci
2 rows in set (0.00 sec)
```

Trigger Security

The CREATE TRIGGER command supports an additional DEFINER clause, which specifies the user account whose privileges should be considered when executing the trigger. For the trigger to execute successfully, this user should have all the privileges necessary to perform the statements listed in the trigger body. By default, MySQL sets the DEFINER value to the user who created the trigger.

Here's an example:

```
mysql> CREATE DEFINER = 'jack@example.com'
    -> TRIGGER flight_ad
```

```
     ->    AFTER DELETE ON flight
     ->    FOR EACH ROW
     ->       INSERT INTO log (ByUser, Note, EventTime)
     ->       VALUES (USER(), 'Record deleted: flight', NOW());
Query OK, 0 rows affected (0.08 sec)
```

Which Is Better: a BEFORE Trigger or an AFTER Trigger?

There's no hard-and-fast rule as to which trigger is "better"—it's like asking which flavor of ice cream is best. But if you're stuck trying to decide whether your code should run before or after a DML operation, the following rule of thumb (posted by Scott White in the online MySQL manual, at http://dev.mysql.com/doc/refman/5.0/en/create-trigger.html) might help: "Use BEFORE triggers primarily for constraints or rules, not transactions. Stick with AFTER triggers for most other operations, such as inserting into a history table or updating a denormalization."

Triggers and Old/New Values

Within the body of a trigger, it's possible to reference field values from both before and after the trigger event by prefixing the field name with the OLD and NEW keywords. This means that, for example, if you have an UPDATE trigger on a table, the SQL statements within the trigger body can access both the existing field values (OLD) and the new, incoming field values (NEW).

To illustrate this, consider the next example, which logs changes to the *flight* table and specifies the changed values as part of the log message:

```
mysql> DELIMITER //
mysql> CREATE TRIGGER flight_au
    -> AFTER UPDATE ON flight
    -> FOR EACH ROW
    ->   BEGIN
    ->     DECLARE str VARCHAR(255) DEFAULT '';
    ->     IF OLD.FlightID != NEW.FlightID THEN
    ->       SET str = CONCAT(str, 'FlightID ',
    ->         OLD.FlightID, ' -> ', NEW.FlightID, ' ');
    ->     END IF;
    ->     IF OLD.RouteID != NEW.RouteID THEN
    ->       SET str = CONCAT(str, 'RouteID ',
    ->         OLD.RouteID, ' -> ', NEW.RouteID, ' ');
    ->     END IF;
    ->     IF OLD.AircraftID != NEW.AircraftID THEN
    ->       SET str = CONCAT(str, 'AircraftID ',
    ->         OLD.AircraftID, ' -> ', NEW.AircraftID);
    ->     END IF;
    ->     INSERT INTO log (ByUser, Note, EventTime)
```

```
  ->       VALUES (USER(),
  ->          CONCAT('Record updated: flight: ', str),
  ->          NOW());
  ->    END//
Query OK, 0 rows affected (0.00 sec)
```

In this example, the prefix OLD returns the pre-update value of the corresponding field, while the prefix NEW returns the post-update value of the field. Within the trigger body, IF conditional tests are used to check if the old and new values are the same; if not, the field is flagged and its old and new values are inserted as part of the log string.

OLD and NEW values typically appear together only in UPDATE triggers. This is only logical: OLD values are neither relevant nor supported in the case of INSERT triggers, while the same applies to NEW values for DELETE triggers.

Triggers and More Complex Applications

Let's look at another, more complex example. Consider that an airline has a limited inventory of seats per flight and flight class, and the seat inventory for each flight needs to be updated on a continual basis as passengers book their flights. Consider also that the airline would like to automatically increase the price of tickets as the flight begins to fill up in order to increase its profit margin.

Figure 7-1 explains how this information is stored in the example database.

- Passenger records for each flight and class combination are recorded in the *pax* table.

- The live seat inventory for a particular flight-and-class combination can be found in the *stats* table.

- The *pax* and *stats* tables are linked to each other by means of the common *FlightID*, *FlightDate*, and *ClassID* fields.

- The maximum number of seats possible in each class of a particular flight, together with the base (starting) ticket price, is recorded in the *flightclass* table.

So, for example, flight #652 which operates on the Orly-Budapest route, has a maximum of 10 seats available in Gold class at a base price of $200 and 20 seats available in Silver class at a base price of $100.

```
mysql> SELECT FlightID, ClassID, MaxSeats, BasePrice
    -> FROM flightclass WHERE FlightID=652;
+----------+---------+----------+-----------+
| FlightID | ClassID | MaxSeats | BasePrice |
+----------+---------+----------+-----------+
|      652 | 2       |       10 |       200 |
|      652 | 3       |       20 |        50 |
+----------+---------+----------+-----------+
2 rows in set (0.00 sec)
```

ClassID	ClassName
1	Platinum
2	Gold
3	Silver

FlightID	ClassID	MaxSeats	BasePrice
535	2	50	200
535	3	150	50
652	2	10	200
652	3	20	50
876	2	85	250
876	3	100	35
876	1	10	300

FlightID	FlightDate	ClassID	CurrSeats	CurrPrice
652	1/20/2009	2	9	200
652	1/20/2009	3	18	50

RecordID	FlightID	FlightDate	ClassID	PaxName	PaxRef
197	652	1/20/2009	2	Henry Rabbit	TG75850303
198	652	1/20/2009	3	Harry Hippo	TG75847493
199	652	1/20/2009	3	Henrietta Hippo	TG75847493

FIGURE 7-1   Passenger, flight, and seat information

Looking into the *stats* table for this flight on January 20, 2009, we see that there are currently 9 seats available in Gold class and 18 seats available in Silver class—that is, three passengers are currently scheduled to fly on that day.

```
mysql> SELECT ClassID, CurrSeats, CurrPrice
    -> FROM stats WHERE FlightID=652
    -> AND FlightDate = '2009-01-20';
+---------+-----------+-----------+
| ClassID | CurrSeats | CurrPrice |
+---------+-----------+-----------+
|       2 |         9 |       200 |
|       3 |        18 |        50 |
+---------+-----------+-----------+
2 rows in set (0.00 sec)
```

With this information at hand, it becomes possible to construct a trigger that automatically handles updating the live seat inventory in the *stats* table. Every time a passenger books a flight, a new record is inserted into the *pax* table. So an AFTER INSERT trigger on this table can be used to automatically reduce the seat inventory in the *stats* table by 1 on every record insertion.

Here's the code:

```
mysql> DELIMITER //
mysql> CREATE TRIGGER pax_ai
    -> AFTER INSERT ON pax
    -> FOR EACH ROW
    ->   BEGIN
    ->     UPDATE stats AS s
    ->       SET s.CurrSeats = s.CurrSeats - 1
    ->       WHERE s.FlightID = NEW.FlightID
    ->       AND s.FlightDate = NEW.FlightDate
    ->       AND s.ClassID = NEW.ClassID;
    ->   END//
Query OK, 0 rows affected (0.03 sec)
```

Similarly, every time a cancellation occurs, the corresponding record will be deleted from the passenger manifest, and an AFTER DELETE trigger can be used to simultaneously increase the seat inventory by 1:

```
mysql> DELIMITER //
mysql> CREATE TRIGGER pax_ad
    -> AFTER DELETE ON pax
    -> FOR EACH ROW
    ->   BEGIN
    ->     UPDATE stats AS s
    ->       SET s.CurrSeats = s.CurrSeats + 1
    ->       WHERE s.FlightID = OLD.FlightID
    ->       AND s.FlightDate = OLD.FlightDate
    ->       AND s.ClassID = OLD.ClassID;
    ->   END//
Query OK, 0 rows affected (0.01 sec)
```

See this in action by inserting a new passenger record into the *pax* table and then reviewing the *stats* table:

```
mysql> INSERT INTO pax
    -> (FlightID, FlightDate, ClassID, PaxName, PaxRef)
    -> VALUES (652, '2009-01-20', 3,
    -> 'Igor Iguana', 'TR58304888');
Query OK, 1 row affected (0.01 sec)
mysql> SELECT ClassID, CurrSeats, CurrPrice
    -> FROM stats WHERE FlightID=652
    -> AND FlightDate = '2009-01-20';
+---------+-----------+-----------+
| ClassID | CurrSeats | CurrPrice |
+---------+-----------+-----------+
|       2 |         9 |       200 |
|       3 |        17 |        50 |
+---------+-----------+-----------+
2 rows in set (0.00 sec)
```

And if you remove a passenger record, the seat inventory should tick upwards by one.

Automatically increasing (or decreasing) the ticket price as the seat count reduces (or increases) can be accomplished by defining different "slabs" of seat utilization and adjusting the current price upwards or downwards by a fixed percentage depending on the current slab. So, for example, the airline might decide that once 25 percent of the seats in a class are sold, the price should automatically increase by 50 percent. Similarly, once 75 percent of the seats are sold, the price should once again increase by 50 percent.

Adding this logic entails modifying the previously defined triggers, as shown:

```
mysql> DELIMITER //
mysql> CREATE TRIGGER pax_ai
    -> AFTER INSERT ON pax
    -> FOR EACH ROW
    ->    BEGIN
    ->       DECLARE u FLOAT DEFAULT 0;
    ->       DECLARE cs, ms, bp, cp INT DEFAULT 0;
    ->       UPDATE stats AS s
    ->         SET s.CurrSeats = s.CurrSeats - 1
    ->         WHERE s.FlightID = NEW.FlightID
    ->         AND s.FlightDate = NEW.FlightDate
    ->         AND s.ClassID = NEW.ClassID;
    ->       SELECT s.CurrSeats, s.CurrPrice INTO cs, cp
    ->         FROM stats AS s
    ->         WHERE s.FlightID = NEW.FlightID
    ->         AND s.FlightDate = NEW.FlightDate
    ->         AND s.ClassID = NEW.ClassID;
    ->       SELECT fc.MaxSeats, fc.BasePrice INTO ms, bp
    ->         FROM flightclass AS fc
    ->         WHERE fc.FlightID = NEW.FlightID
    ->         AND fc.ClassID = NEW.ClassID;
    ->       SET u = 1 - (cs/ms);
    ->       IF (u >= 0.25 AND u < 0.75 AND cp != ROUND(bp * 1.5)) THEN
    ->          UPDATE stats AS s
    ->            SET s.CurrPrice = ROUND(bp * 1.5)
    ->            WHERE s.FlightID = NEW.FlightID
    ->            AND s.FlightDate = NEW.FlightDate
    ->            AND s.ClassID = NEW.ClassID;
    ->       END IF;
    ->       IF (u >= 0.75 AND cp != ROUND(bp * 2.25)) THEN
    ->          UPDATE stats AS s
    ->            SET s.CurrPrice = ROUND(bp * 2.25)
    ->            WHERE s.FlightID = NEW.FlightID
    ->            AND s.FlightDate = NEW.FlightDate
    ->            AND s.ClassID = NEW.ClassID;
    ->       END IF;
    ->    END//
Query OK, 0 rows affected (0.00 sec)
```

This looks complicated, but it really isn't! The trigger begins by first updating the seat inventory and then retrieving the current seat availability, the maximum seats possible, the current price, and the base price for that particular flight/class combination. It then calculates the seat utilization ratio and updates the current price, depending on whether this ratio is between 25 and 75 percent or greater than 75 percent.

It's also necessary to update the price if passengers cancel their reservation. Here's the revised AFTER DELETE trigger:

```
mysql> DELIMITER //
mysql> CREATE TRIGGER pax_ad
    -> AFTER DELETE ON pax
    -> FOR EACH ROW
    ->   BEGIN
    ->     DECLARE u FLOAT DEFAULT 0;
    ->     DECLARE cs, ms, bp, cp INT DEFAULT 0;
    ->     UPDATE stats AS s
    ->       SET s.CurrSeats = s.CurrSeats + 1
    ->       WHERE s.FlightID = OLD.FlightID
    ->       AND s.FlightDate = OLD.FlightDate
    ->       AND s.ClassID = OLD.ClassID;
    ->     SELECT s.CurrSeats, s.CurrPrice INTO cs, cp
    ->       FROM stats AS s
    ->       WHERE s.FlightID = OLD.FlightID
    ->       AND s.FlightDate = OLD.FlightDate
    ->       AND s.ClassID = OLD.ClassID;
    ->     SELECT fc.MaxSeats, fc.BasePrice INTO ms, bp
    ->       FROM flightclass AS fc
    ->       WHERE fc.FlightID = OLD.FlightID
    ->       AND fc.ClassID = OLD.ClassID;
    ->     SET u = 1 - (cs/ms);
    ->     IF (u < 0.25 AND cp != bp) THEN
    ->       UPDATE stats AS s
    ->         SET s.CurrPrice = bp
    ->         WHERE s.FlightID = OLD.FlightID
    ->         AND s.FlightDate = OLD.FlightDate
    ->         AND s.ClassID = OLD.ClassID;
    ->     END IF;
    ->     IF (u >= 0.25 AND u < 0.75 AND cp != ROUND(bp * 1.5)) THEN
    ->       UPDATE stats AS s
    ->         SET s.CurrPrice = ROUND(bp * 1.5)
    ->         WHERE s.FlightID = OLD.FlightID
    ->         AND s.FlightDate = OLD.FlightDate
    ->         AND s.ClassID = OLD.ClassID;
    ->     END IF;
    ->     IF (u >= 0.75 AND cp != ROUND(bp * 2.25)) THEN
    ->       UPDATE stats AS s
    ->         SET s.CurrPrice = ROUND(bp * 2.25)
    ->         WHERE s.FlightID = OLD.FlightID
```

```
    ->              AND s.FlightDate = OLD.FlightDate
    ->              AND s.ClassID = OLD.ClassID;
    ->        END IF;
    ->    END//
Query OK, 0 rows affected (0.00 sec)
```

Let's try it by booking two passengers in Gold class on that flight:

```
mysql> INSERT INTO pax
    -> (FlightID, FlightDate, ClassID, PaxName, PaxRef)
    -> VALUES (652, '2009-01-20', 2,
    -> 'Gerry Giraffe', 'TR75950888');
Query OK, 1 row affected (0.01 sec)
mysql> INSERT INTO pax
    -> (FlightID, FlightDate, ClassID, PaxName, PaxRef)
    -> VALUES (652, '2009-01-20', 2,
    -> 'Adam Anteater', 'TR88404015');
Query OK, 1 row affected (0.00 sec)
```

Since 7 of the 10 available seats are now booked, the 25 percent threshold has been crossed and a price rise should automatically occur. Look in the *stats* table, and you'll see that the ticket price for the flight in Gold class has risen by 50 percent, from $200 to $300.

```
mysql> SELECT ClassID, CurrSeats, CurrPrice
    -> FROM stats WHERE FlightID=652
    -> AND FlightDate = '2009-01-20';
+---------+-----------+-----------+
| ClassID | CurrSeats | CurrPrice |
+---------+-----------+-----------+
|       2 |         7 |       300 |
|       3 |        17 |        50 |
+---------+-----------+-----------+
2 rows in set (0.01 sec)
```

Triggers and Constraints

Now, if you're sharp-eyed, you'll have noticed that there's a glaring problem in the previous example: It's possible to keep adding passengers until the seat inventory falls below zero. While this is theoretically possible in one sense (a negative seat inventory might well be considered overbooking, a fairly common airline practice these days), let's assume that, for our airline at least, showing a negative value for seats available on a flight is a Bad Thing.

This occurs, quite naturally, because while the trigger in the previous example is pretty good at increasing and decreasing the seat inventory in response to passenger bookings and cancellations, it doesn't include any checks that prevent the available seat count falling below zero or rising above the maximum number of seats specified for that class. To make things even more…ahem, airtight, the trigger should be updated to check for these upper and lower limits, and allow the INSERT into the *pax* table only if these range constraints are not violated.

And therein lies the problem. Unlike Oracle, which allows you to abort a trigger with the RAISE APPLICATION ERROR statement, MySQL does not currently offer any mechanism to abort a trigger or to raise an error in the event that a user-specified constraint is not met. This is a key limitation of MySQL's current implementation of triggers, and has generated a large amount of discussion in the MySQL user forums… as well as a creative workaround!

The fundamental principle of this workaround is simple: Deliberately generate a MySQL error by performing an illegal operation, thereby forcing MySQL to abort execution of the trigger. There are various ways in which this can be done, including:

- Inserting a value into a nonexistent field
- Inserting a NULL value into a field with the NOT NULL constraint
- Calling a nonexistent stored routine

The end result of all these operations is the same: a fatal error, which will cause MySQL to terminate execution of the statement causing the error. If this statement is enclosed within a BEFORE trigger, the resulting error will force MySQL to abort trigger execution, as well as the INSERT, UPDATE, or DELETE statement that is supposed to follow it.

To illustrate this in action, consider the following trivial example: a trigger that only allows new airports to be registered in the *airport* table if they have at least three runways:

```
mysql> DELIMITER //
mysql> CREATE TRIGGER airport_bi
    -> BEFORE INSERT ON airport
    -> FOR EACH ROW
    -> BEGIN
    ->   IF NEW.NumRunways < 3 THEN
    ->     CALL i_dont_exist;
    ->   END IF;
    -> END//
Query OK, 0 rows affected (0.06 sec)
```

Now, try it out:

```
mysql> INSERT INTO airport
    -> (AirportID, AirportCode, AirportName,
    -> CityName, CountryCode, NumRunways,
    -> NumTerminals) VALUES (207, 'LTN',
    -> 'Luton Airport', 'London', 'GB',
    -> 2,1);
ERROR 1305 (42000): PROCEDURE db1.i_dont_exist does not exist
```

In this case, because the specified constraint in the BEFORE INSERT trigger isn't met, a deliberate error is generated, which causes the failure of the INSERT altogether. On the other hand, if you were to try the same query specifying three or more runways, the INSERT statement would execute successfully.

Now, let's use a couple of BEFORE triggers on the *pax* table to enforce the constraints discussed at the beginning of this section:

```
mysql> DELIMITER //
mysql> CREATE TRIGGER pax_bi
    -> BEFORE INSERT ON pax
    -> FOR EACH ROW
    -> BEGIN
    ->   DECLARE cs INT DEFAULT 0;
    ->   SELECT s.CurrSeats INTO cs
    ->     FROM stats AS s
    ->     WHERE s.FlightID = NEW.FlightID
    ->     AND s.FlightDate = NEW.FlightDate
    ->     AND s.ClassID = NEW.ClassID;
    ->   IF cs <= 0 THEN
    ->     SET @trigger_error = 'No seats available';
    ->     CALL i_dont_exist();
    ->   END IF;
    -> END//
Query OK, 0 rows affected (0.01 sec)
mysql> CREATE TRIGGER pax_bd
    -> BEFORE DELETE ON pax
    -> FOR EACH ROW
    -> BEGIN
    ->   DECLARE cs, ms INT DEFAULT 0;
    ->   SELECT s.CurrSeats INTO cs
    ->     FROM stats AS s
    ->     WHERE s.FlightID = OLD.FlightID
    ->     AND s.FlightDate = OLD.FlightDate
    ->     AND s.ClassID = OLD.ClassID;
    ->   SELECT fc.MaxSeats INTO ms
    ->     FROM flightclass AS fc
    ->     WHERE fc.FlightID = OLD.FlightID
    ->     AND fc.ClassID = OLD.ClassID;
    ->   IF cs >= ms THEN
    ->     SET @trigger_error = 'Cannot increase seat count';
    ->     CALL i_dont_exist();
    ->   END IF;
    -> END//
Query OK, 0 rows affected (0.01 sec)
```

In this case, whenever one of the range constraints is violated and the trigger aborts, a message indicating the cause of the error will be placed in the @trigger_error session variable. This suggestion (which must be again credited to the MySQL forum, which developed the workaround in the first place) allows applications to access a human-readable error message and display it to the user.

Understanding Scheduled Events

The triggers discussed in the previous section are written for, and activated by, a particular type of event, such as a new record insertion or modification. However, MySQL 5.1 also supports a slightly different approach to database automation in the form of scheduled events.

Scheduled events, as the name suggests, are triggered at particular times. They provide a framework to perform one or more SQL operations on a time-based schedule. Scheduled events, like triggers, are always associated with a particular table, and can be set to execute either once or repeatedly at predefined intervals. This can come in handy for tasks that need to take place periodically, such as log rotation, statistics generation, or counter updates.

A Simple Scheduled Event

To understand how scheduled events work, let's consider a simple example: archiving old passenger data. Let's suppose that a database administrator wishes to automatically move all passenger records for flights that are 30 days old out of the *pax* table and into a different archive table. A scheduled event makes this easy to do:

```
mysql> CREATE TABLE paxarchive LIKE pax;
Query OK, 0 rows affected (0.03 sec)
mysql> ALTER TABLE paxarchive ENGINE=ARCHIVE;
Query OK, 0 rows affected (0.12 sec)
Records: 0  Duplicates: 0  Warnings: 0

mysql> DELIMITER //
mysql> CREATE EVENT pax_day
    -> ON SCHEDULE EVERY 1 DAY
    -> STARTS '2009-01-14 22:45:00' ENABLE
    -> DO
    ->   BEGIN
    ->     INSERT INTO paxarchive
    ->       SELECT * FROM pax
    ->       WHERE FlightDate <=
    ->       DATE_SUB(CURRENT_DATE(), INTERVAL 30 DAY);
    ->     DELETE FROM pax
    ->       WHERE FlightDate <=
    ->       DATE_SUB(CURRENT_DATE(), INTERVAL 30 DAY);
    ->   END//
Query OK, 0 rows affected (0.01 sec)
```

To define a scheduled event, MySQL offers the CREATE EVENT command. This command must be followed by the event name, the event schedule, an active/inactive flag, and the main body, which contains the SQL statements to be executed when the event fires.

These components are illustrated in the previous example, which creates a scheduled event named *paxarchive*. The ON SCHEDULE EVERY 1 DAY clause in the event definition ensures that it is activated daily, while the STARTS clause specifies the event's start date and time. The ENABLE keyword tells the system that this is an active event, while the DO clause contains the main body of the trigger; this can contain either a single SQL statement or (as in the previous example) multiple SQL statements enclosed within a BEGIN...END block.

Defining an event is not, however, sufficient to have it fire automatically. By default, MySQL's event scheduling engine is deactivated and must be activated with the following command:

```
mysql> SET GLOBAL event_scheduler = ON;
Query OK, 0 rows affected (0.38 sec)
```

This command starts the global event scheduling daemon, which periodically checks for scheduled events and runs them at the appropriate time.

As a result of these actions, MySQL will, on a daily basis, copy all passenger records that relate to flights 30 days in the past to the *paxarchive* table and then delete the same records from the *pax* table.

NOTE *To create a scheduled event, a user must have the* EVENT *privilege. To turn the global event scheduler on or off, a user must have the* SUPER *privilege. Privileges are discussed in greater detail in Chapter 11.*

To modify a scheduled event, use the ALTER EVENT command and provide new parameters for the event. Here's an example, which alters the previous event to run every two hours instead:

```
mysql> DELIMITER //
mysql> ALTER EVENT pax_day
    -> ON SCHEDULE EVERY 2 HOUR
    -> STARTS '2009-01-14 22:45:00' ENABLE
    -> DO
    ->   BEGIN
    ->     INSERT INTO paxarchive
    ->       SELECT * FROM pax
    ->       WHERE FlightDate <=
    ->       DATE_SUB(CURRENT_DATE(), INTERVAL 30 DAY);
    ->     DELETE FROM pax
    ->       WHERE FlightDate <=
    ->       DATE_SUB(CURRENT_DATE(), INTERVAL 30 DAY);
    ->   END//
Query OK, 0 rows affected (0.24 sec)
```

Here's another example, which disables a specified event (disabled events will not fire at all):

```
mysql> ALTER EVENT pax_day DISABLE;
Query OK, 0 rows affected (0.00 sec)
```

By default, once an event has completed, it is automatically removed from the event queue by the event scheduler. However, you can manually remove it at any time; use the DROP EVENT command with the event name as argument:

```
mysql> DROP EVENT pax_day;
Query OK, 0 rows affected (0.03 sec)
```

TIP *To prevent an event from being automatically removed from the event queue once it is completed (for audit or other reasons), attach an* ON COMPLETION PRESERVE *clause to the* CREATE EVENT *command.*

Alternatively, to turn off all scheduled events, turn off the global scheduler, as shown:

```
mysql> SET GLOBAL event_scheduler = OFF;
Query OK, 0 rows affected (0.38 sec)
```

To view the body of a specific event, use the SHOW CREATE EVENT command with the event name as argument. Here's an example:

```
mysql> SHOW CREATE EVENT pax_day\G
*************************** 1. row ***************************
               Event: pax_day
            sql_mode: STRICT_TRANS_TABLES
           time_zone: SYSTEM
        Create Event: CREATE EVENT `pax_day`
ON SCHEDULE EVERY 1 DAY
STARTS '2009-01-14 22:45:00' ON COMPLETION NOT PRESERVE
ENABLE DO
  BEGIN
    INSERT INTO paxarchive
      SELECT * FROM pax
      WHERE FlightDate <=
      DATE_SUB(CURRENT_DATE(), INTERVAL 30 DAY);
    DELETE FROM pax
      WHERE FlightDate <=
      DATE_SUB(CURRENT_DATE(), INTERVAL 30 DAY);
  END
character_set_client: latin1
collation_connection: latin1_swedish_ci
  Database Collation: latin1_swedish_ci
1 row in set (0.00 sec)
```

To view a list of all events scheduled on the server, use the SHOW EVENTS command, as shown:

```
mysql> SHOW EVENTS\G
*************************** 1. row ***************************
                  Db: db1
                Name: pax_day
             Definer: root@localhost
           Time zone: SYSTEM
                Type: RECURRING
          Execute at: NULL
      Interval value: 1
      Interval field: DAY
              Starts: 2009-01-14 22:45:00
                Ends: NULL
              Status: ENABLED
          Originator: 0
character_set_client: latin1
collation_connection: latin1_swedish_ci
   Database Collation: latin1_swedish_ci
1 row in set (0.00 sec)
```

Event Security

The CREATE EVENT command supports a DEFINER clause, which specifies the user account whose privileges should be considered when executing the event code. For the event to execute successfully, this user should have all the privileges necessary to perform the statements listed in the event body. By default, MySQL sets the DEFINER value to the user who created the trigger.

Here's an example:

```
mysql> DELIMITER //
mysql> CREATE DEFINER = 'jack@example.com'
    -> EVENT pax_day
    -> ON SCHEDULE EVERY 1 DAY
    -> STARTS '2009-01-14 22:45:00' ENABLE
    -> DO
    ->    BEGIN
    ->      INSERT INTO paxarchive
    ->        SELECT * FROM pax
    ->        WHERE FlightDate <=
    ->        DATE_SUB(CURRENT_DATE(), INTERVAL 30 DAY);
    ->      DELETE FROM pax
    ->        WHERE FlightDate <=
    ->        DATE_SUB(CURRENT_DATE(), INTERVAL 30 DAY);
    ->    END//
Query OK, 0 rows affected (0.01 sec)
```

Recurring Events

Let's take a closer look at recurring events. As the previous section illustrated, a recurring event contains the EVERY clause in the event definition; this clause tells MySQL that the event is one that repeats "every XX time units." The EVERY clause also contains the *repeat interval*—typically, this consists of a number and a keyword representing the time unit. Valid time units include YEAR, QUARTER, MONTH, DAY, HOUR, MINUTE, WEEK, and SECOND.

Here's an example, which checks the percentage of seats that have been booked for each flight every hour and logs flights that are more than 80 percent full:

```
mysql> DELIMITER //
mysql> CREATE EVENT util_hour
    -> ON SCHEDULE EVERY 1 HOUR ENABLE
    -> DO
    -> BEGIN
    ->  DECLARE fid INT;
    ->  DECLARE fdate DATE;
    ->  DECLARE str TEXT DEFAULT '';
    ->  DECLARE util FLOAT;
    ->  DECLARE c CURSOR FOR
    ->   SELECT s.FlightID, s.FlightDate, 1-(SUM(s.CurrSeats) /
    ->     (SELECT SUM(fc.MaxSeats)
    ->     FROM flightclass AS fc
    ->     WHERE fc.FlightID = s.FlightID
    ->     GROUP BY FlightID))
    ->   AS u FROM stats AS s
    ->   GROUP BY s.FlightID, s.FlightDate
    ->   HAVING u > 0.80;
    ->  OPEN c;
    ->  1: LOOP
    ->    FETCH c INTO fid,fdate,util;
    ->    SET str = CONCAT('Flight # ', fid, ' on ',
    ->      fdate, ": ", ROUND(util*100), '%');
    ->    INSERT INTO log (ByUser, Note, EventTime)
    ->      VALUES (CURRENT_USER(), str, NOW());
    ->  END LOOP 1;
    ->  CLOSE c;
    -> END//
Query OK, 0 rows affected (0.00 sec)
```

CAUTION *Open-ended recurring events that write new data to a table and have no defined end time (like the previous example) are dangerous, because they could cause the target table to grow in size quite quickly, with no end in sight. Avoid using these as much as possible (the previous example is only illustrative and should not be used in a production environment), and if you must do so, always specify an end time and as many additional constraints as possible to limit the event's action.*

You can also configure the event to fire only within a certain time period by specifying optional STARTS and ENDS clauses, which contain the starting and ending times for the event. Here's a revision of the previous example, which configures the event to fire only during a particular month:

```
mysql> DELIMITER //
mysql> CREATE EVENT util_hour
    -> ON SCHEDULE EVERY 1 HOUR
    -> STARTS '2009-04-01 00:00:01'
    -> ENDS '2009-04-30 23:59:01'
    -> ENABLE
    -> DO
    -> BEGIN
    ->   DECLARE fid INT;
    ->   DECLARE fdate DATE;
    ->   DECLARE str TEXT DEFAULT '';
    ->   DECLARE util FLOAT;
    ->   DECLARE c CURSOR FOR
    ->     SELECT s.FlightID, s.FlightDate, 1-(SUM(s.CurrSeats) /
    ->        (SELECT SUM(fc.MaxSeats)
    ->         FROM flightclass AS fc
    ->         WHERE fc.FlightID = s.FlightID
    ->         GROUP BY FlightID))
    ->       AS u FROM stats AS s
    ->       GROUP BY s.FlightID, s.FlightDate
    ->       HAVING u > 0.80;
    ->    OPEN c;
    ->    1: LOOP
    ->      FETCH c INTO fid,fdate,util;
    ->      SET str = CONCAT('Flight # ', fid, ' on ',
    ->        fdate, ": ", ROUND(util*100), '%');
    ->      INSERT INTO log (ByUser, Note, EventTime)
    ->        VALUES (CURRENT_USER(), str, NOW());
    ->    END LOOP 1;
    ->    CLOSE c;
    -> END//
Query OK, 0 rows affected (0.01 sec)
```

One-Off Events

Although MySQL's event scheduler is great for setting up recurring events, it also supports events that only fire once, at a predefined time and date. To set up such an event, replace the EVERY clause in the CREATE EVENT statement with an AT clause that contains the date and time at which the event should fire. Here's an example, which sets up an event to fire at 1:25 A.M. on April 1, 2009:

```
mysql> CREATE EVENT log_onetime
    -> ON SCHEDULE AT '2009-04-01 01:25' ENABLE
    -> DO
    -> INSERT INTO log (ByUser, Note, EventTime)
    -> VALUES (CURRENT_USER(), 'Updating all accounts', NOW());
Query OK, 0 rows affected (0.50 sec)
```

TIP *To force an event to fire at the instant it is created, use the NOW() function in the AT clause instead of a timestamp.*

Summary

This chapter focused on database automation, explaining how database triggers and scheduled events can be used to easily perform operations that would otherwise need separate application-level workflows and/or integration with scheduling agents such as *cron*. Utilizing simple applications, it showed you how to construct various types of triggers, schedule events for either one-time or repeated execution, and build in complex programming logic using the conditional tests, loops, and cursors discussed in the previous chapter.

To learn more about the topics discussed in this chapter, consider visiting the following links:

- Triggers, at http://dev.mysql.com/doc/refman/5.1/en/create-trigger.html and http://forge.mysql.com/wiki/Triggers

- Scheduled events, at http://dev.mysql.com/doc/refman/5.1/en/events-overview .html

- Key limitations on triggers and scheduled events, at http://dev.mysql.com/ doc/refman/5.1/en/stored-program-restrictions.html

- A MySQL forum discussion of raising errors inside triggers, at http://forums .mysql.com/read.php?99,55108,55108#msg-55108 and http://rpbouman .blogspot.com/2005/11/using-udf-to-raise-errors-from-inside.html

CHAPTER 8

Working with Data in Different Formats

So far, all of the examples in this book have had you entering records into tables using INSERT statements. However, in the real world, data comes in all shapes and sizes, and entering records one by one is not a feasible technique, especially when migrating data sets containing hundreds of thousands of records.

To assist developers in tackling this issue, MySQL has, for many years, shipped with various tools that significantly aid the process of importing and exporting data in different formats, such as comma- or tab-delimited formats. And, keeping in mind the near-ubiquity of XML-encoded data, MySQL 5.1 adds a bunch of new functions and statements designed specifically for working with XML documents. This chapter discusses these tools and functions in greater detail.

Importing Records

The INSERT statement isn't the only way to insert data into a table. MySQL also permits insertion of multiple records in one fell swoop with the LOAD DATA INFILE statement. This statement can be used to read raw data from a text file (located on either the server or the client end of the connection), parse it on the basis of column and row delimiters, and automatically generate INSERT statements to write the data to a table.

This approach comes in handy when you need to enter a large volume of information into a database but the data, though structured, is not available in the form of SQL statements. Manually creating INSERT statements for every single record would be tedious and time-consuming; LOAD DATA INFILE offers a faster and more reliable alternative.

The best way to understand LOAD DATA INFILE is with an example. Consider the following text file containing passenger information, separated with commas, in the temporary area on the server:

```
"201","652","2009-01-20","3","Rich Rabbit","HH83282949",""
"202","652","2009-01-27","2","Zoe Zebra","JY64940400",""
"203","652","2009-01-27","2","Zane Zebra","JY64940401",""
"204","652","2009-01-20","2","Barbara Bear","JD74391994",""
"205","652","2009-01-27","3","Harriet Horse","JG74860994",""
```

Now, this comma-separated data could be imported into a table, as illustrated here:

```
mysql> CREATE TABLE p LIKE pax;
Query OK, 0 rows affected (0.08 sec)
mysql> LOAD DATA INFILE '/tmp/in.txt'
    -> INTO TABLE p
    -> FIELDS TERMINATED BY ','
    -> ENCLOSED BY '"'
    -> LINES TERMINATED BY '\r\n';
Query OK, 5 rows affected (0.00 sec)
Records: 5  Deleted: 0  Skipped: 0  Warnings: 0
```

Your data should now have been inserted correctly into the table, as a quick SELECT verifies:

```
mysql> SELECT ClassID, PaxName
    -> FROM p WHERE RecordID > 200;
+---------+---------------+
| ClassID | PaxName       |
+---------+---------------+
|       3 | Harriet Horse |
|       2 | Barbara Bear  |
|       3 | Rich Rabbit   |
|       2 | Zoe Zebra     |
|       2 | Zane Zebra    |
+---------+---------------+
5 rows in set (0.03 sec)
```

By default, MySQL assumes the data file is on the server in the location specified in the LOAD DATA INFILE statement. If, instead, you want to use a data file on the client, you can add the keyword LOCAL to the statement to tell MySQL to look for the file on the client's file system. The following example demonstrates this by loading data from a file on the client machine:

```
mysql> TRUNCATE TABLE p;
Query OK, 0 rows affected (0.01 sec)
mysql> LOAD DATA LOCAL INFILE '/tmp/in.txt'
    -> INTO TABLE p
    -> FIELDS TERMINATED BY ','
    -> ENCLOSED BY '"'
    -> LINES TERMINATED BY '\r\n';
Query OK, 5 rows affected (0.00 sec)
Records: 5  Deleted: 0  Skipped: 0  Warnings: 0
```

NOTE *When using data files on the server, if no file path is specified in the call to* LOAD DATA INFILE *(or if a relative path is specified), MySQL looks in the corresponding database directory on the server for the file (or uses it as the relative path root). Absolute paths, however, will be used as is.*

If fewer fields are in the data file than in the table, or if the values in the file are not ordered in the same sequence as the fields in the table, you can tell MySQL how to map the data in the file to the fields of the table by specifying a list of field names after the LOAD DATA INFILE statement. For example, if the input file looked like this:

```
"Rich Rabbit","652","2009-01-20","3"
"Zoe Zebra","652","2009-01-27","2"
"Zane Zebra","652","2009-01-27","2"
"Barbara Bear","652","2009-01-20","2"
"Harriet Horse","652","2009-01-27","3"
```

you could have MySQL import only these fields into the table with the following statement:

```
mysql> TRUNCATE TABLE p;
Query OK, 0 rows affected (0.01 sec)
mysql> LOAD DATA LOCAL INFILE '/tmp/in.txt'
    -> INTO TABLE p
    -> FIELDS TERMINATED BY ','
    -> ENCLOSED BY '"'
    -> LINES TERMINATED BY '\r\n'
    -> (PaxName, FlightID, FlightDate, ClassID, PaxRef);
Query OK, 5 rows affected (1.02 sec)
Records: 5  Deleted: 0  Skipped: 0  Warnings: 0
```

Here's how the result would look:

```
mysql> SELECT FlightID, ClassID, PaxName,
    -> PaxRef, Note FROM p;
+----------+---------+---------------+----------+------+
| FlightID | ClassID | PaxName       | PaxRef   | Note |
+----------+---------+---------------+----------+------+
|      652 |       3 | Rich Rabbit   | NULL     | NULL |
|      652 |       2 | Zoe Zebra     | NULL     | NULL |
|      652 |       2 | Zane Zebra    | NULL     | NULL |
|      652 |       2 | Barbara Bear  | NULL     | NULL |
|      652 |       3 | Harriet Horse | NULL     | NULL |
+----------+---------+---------------+----------+------+
5 rows in set (0.00 sec)
```

It should be clear that MySQL inserts NULL values (if permitted to do so by the table and field constraints) when it encounters missing field values.

A number of keywords can be used to modify the behavior of the LOAD DATA INFILE statement.

- The LOW_PRIORITY keyword causes the server to wait until no other threads are using the table before beginning the import process. The CONCURRENT keyword, on the other hand, permits clients to read data from the table while the import is in process (although this keyword applies only to MyISAM tables).

- The IGNORE keyword ensures that if any of the new records has a key that duplicates an existing record, MySQL will simply step over it to the next one (instead of aborting the entire operation, which is the default action in such a situation). Or, you can choose to replace existing records with new records from the data file. This can be accomplished by using the keyword REPLACE instead of IGNORE.

- The LINES TERMINATED BY clause specifies the end-of-record delimiter (by default, the newline character \n).

- The FIELDS clause specifies field delimiters, and must be followed by one or more of the keywords TERMINATED BY, ESCAPED BY, or ENCLOSED BY. These specify the end-of-field delimiter (default is the tab character \t), the sequence used to escape special characters when reading and writing values (default is a backslash), and the character used to enclose field values (no default), respectively.

- The IGNORE LINES clause tells MySQL to skip the specified number of lines at the beginning of the file. This is useful if your data file contains field metadata in its first few lines.

Exporting Records

Just as you can import data into a table from a file with the LOAD DATA INFILE statement, you can extract records from a table into a file with the SELECT ... INTO OUTFILE construct. This construct lets you do everything you would do with the regular SELECT statement and then send the resulting record collection to a file.

To illustrate, consider the following statement, which would extract all records from the *airport* table to a text file:

```
mysql> SELECT AirportID, AirportName
    -> FROM airport
    -> INTO OUTFILE '/tmp/airport.txt'
    -> FIELDS TERMINATED BY ','
    -> LINES TERMINATED BY '\r\n';
Query OK, 15 rows affected (0.02 sec)
```

Here's what the result looks like:

```
34,Orly Airport
48,Gatwick Airport
56,Heathrow Airport
59,Rome Ciampino Airport
62,Schiphol Airport
72,Barcelona International Airport
74,Franz Josef Strauss Airport
83,Lisbon Airport
87,Budapest Ferihegy International Airport
92,Zurich Airport
126,Chhatrapati Shivaji International Airport
129,Bristol International Airport
132,Barajas Airport
165,Nice Côte d'Azur Airport
201,Changi Airport
```

Obviously, you can use a WHERE clause (and any other clause or keyword usable in a normal SELECT statement) to further constrain the output. The following example demonstrates by only writing records for those airports with at least three runways to the file */tmp/airport.txt*:

```
mysql> SELECT AirportID, AirportName
    -> FROM airport
    -> WHERE NumRunways >= 3
    -> INTO OUTFILE '/tmp/airport.txt'
    -> FIELDS TERMINATED BY ','
    -> LINES TERMINATED BY '\r\n';
Query OK, 8 rows affected (0.01 sec)
```

Here's the result:

```
34,Orly Airport
48,Gatwick Airport
62,Schiphol Airport
72,Barcelona International Airport
74,Franz Josef Strauss Airport
92,Zurich Airport
132,Barajas Airport
201,Changi Airport
```

To retrieve binary data, such as the contents of BLOB fields, from the database into a file, replace the INTO OUTFILE clause with the INTO DUMPFILE clause. This causes MySQL to write the data to the file as a single line (without field or record termination characters), thereby avoiding corruption of the binary data.

The file specified in the INTO OUTFILE and INTO DUMPFILE clauses will be written to the server's file system and must not already exist there. Because this file will be written by the user the MySQL server process runs as, that user must have appropriate permissions to write files to the specified location. For security reasons, MySQL does not allow the target file to be written to the client file system using this method. The client application, therefore, needs to retrieve it from the server using external methods.

NOTE *To use either the* SELECT ... INTO OUTFILE *or* LOAD DATA INFILE *statements, a user must have the* FILE *privilege. Privileges are discussed in greater detail in Chapter 11.*

As with the LOAD DATA INFILE statement, you can specify field and record delimiters for the data being dumped. The following example demonstrates how to create a tab-delimited output file:

```
mysql> SELECT AirportID, AirportName
    -> FROM airport
    -> INTO OUTFILE '/tmp/airport.txt'
    -> FIELDS TERMINATED BY '\t'
    -> LINES TERMINATED BY '\r\n';
Query OK, 15 rows affected (0.10 sec)
```

Here's a sample of the output:

```
34      Orly Airport
48      Gatwick Airport
56      Heathrow Airport
59      Rome Ciampino Airport
. . .
```

This next one demonstrates how to create a file using custom delimiters:

```
mysql> SELECT AirportID, AirportName
    -> FROM airport
    -> INTO OUTFILE '/tmp/airport.txt'
    -> FIELDS TERMINATED BY '|'
    -> LINES TERMINATED BY '\n';
Query OK, 15 rows affected (0.00 sec)
```

Here's a sample of the output:

```
34|Orly Airport
48|Gatwick Airport
56|Heathrow Airport
59|Rome Ciampino Airport
. . .
```

TIP *You can also use the* mysqldump *utility to extract the contents of a database or table into a file. Chapter 12 has more information on how to use this utility to back up and restore your MySQL databases.*

MySQL also supports combining the INSERT and SELECT statements to export records from one table into another. Here's an example, which copies passenger names from the *pax* table to a separate *user* table:

```
mysql> CREATE TABLE user (
    -> FirstName VARCHAR(255),
    -> LastName VARCHAR(255)
    -> );
Query OK, 0 rows affected (0.25 sec)
mysql> INSERT INTO user (FirstName, LastName)
    -> SELECT SUBSTRING_INDEX(PaxName, ' ', 1),
    -> SUBSTRING_INDEX(PaxName, ' ', -1)
    -> FROM pax;
Query OK, 8 rows affected (0.47 sec)
Records: 8  Duplicates: 0  Warnings: 0
```

The field list specified in the INSERT statement must obviously match the columns returned by the SELECT clause. A mismatch can cause MySQL to produce an error like the following one:

```
mysql> INSERT INTO tbl1 (fld1, fld2) SELECT fld1, fld2, fld3 FROM tbl2;
ERROR 1136 (21S01): Column count doesn't match value count at row 1
```

Naturally, you can also attach a WHERE clause to the SELECT statement to copy only a subset of the original table's records into the new table:

```
mysql> INSERT INTO user (FirstName, LastName)
    -> SELECT SUBSTRING_INDEX(PaxName, ' ', 1),
    -> SUBSTRING_INDEX(PaxName, ' ', -1)
    -> FROM pax WHERE ClassID = 2;
Query OK, 4 rows affected (0.49 sec)
Records: 4  Duplicates: 0  Warnings: 0
```

Working with XML Data

XML is a powerful tool for the management and effective exploitation of information, and is widely used today as a way to describe almost any kind of data. MySQL 5.1 includes limited support for XML, providing various functions that can be used to import and search XML fragments, while MySQL 6.0 (in alpha at the time of this writing) provides a new statement, the LOAD XML statement, which allows easier conversion of XML-encoded records into MySQL tables.

Obtaining Results in XML

The easiest way to get started with XML in MySQL is to exit and restart the MySQL command-line client, this time passing it the --*xml* option, as shown:

```
[user@host]# mysql --xml -u root -p
Password: ******
```

This option puts the command-line client in "XML mode," forcing its output to be formatted as well-formed XML. To illustrate, try running a SELECT query:

```
mysql> SELECT AirportName, AirportID, AirportCode
    -> FROM airport
    -> LIMIT 0,3;
<?xml version="1.0"?>
<resultset statement="SELECT AirportName, AirportID, AirportCode
FROM airport LIMIT 0,3" xmlns:xsi="http://www.w3.org/2001/XMLSchema-
instance">
  <row>
        <field name="AirportName">Orly Airport</field>
        <field name="AirportID">34</field>
        <field name="AirportCode">ORY</field>
  </row>
```

```
<row>
        <field name="AirportName">Gatwick Airport</field>
        <field name="AirportID">48</field>
        <field name="AirportCode">LGW</field>
</row>

<row>
        <field name="AirportName">Heathrow Airport</field>
        <field name="AirportID">56</field>
        <field name="AirportCode">LHR</field>
</row>
</resultset>
3 rows in set (0.03 sec)
```

Using XML Functions

MySQL 5.1 introduced two new built-in functions that make it easier to handle data encoded in XML. These functions, which make use of XPath expressions to access and update node values, are a significant addition to the MySQL toolkit. The following sections introduce the basics of XPath and how it can be used in the context of MySQL's XML-handling functions.

XPath

If you've worked with XML data, you already know that the XML specification defines certain rules that a document must adhere to in order to be well formed. One of the most important rules is that every XML document must have a single outermost element, called the "root element," which, in turn, may contain other elements, nested in a hierarchical manner.

Now, it seems logical to assume that if an XML document is laid out in this structured, hierarchical tree, it's possible to move at will from any node on the tree to any other node on the tree. And that's where XPath comes in—it provides a standard addressing mechanism for an XML document that makes it possible to access and manipulate any element, attribute, or text node on the tree.

XPath is an important component of both XML stylesheet transformations (XSLT) and the XPointer linking language. By providing XML developers with a standard method of addressing any part of an XML document, XPath is a small, yet important piece of the whole XML jigsaw. XSLT uses it extensively to match nodes in an XML source tree, while XPointer uses it in combination with XLink to identify specific locations in an XML document.

Location Paths   XPath represents an XML document as a tree containing a number of different node types. In order to illustrate this, consider the following XML document:

```
<?xml version="1.0"?>
<recipe>
    <name source="India">Chicken Tikka</name>
    <author>Anonymous</author>
    <date>1 June 1999</date>
```

```
    <ingredients>
        <item>Boneless chicken breasts</item>
        <item>Chopped onions</item>
        <item>Ginger</item>
        <item>Garlic</item>
        <item>Red chili powder</item>
        <item>Butter</item>
    </ingredients>
    <process>
        <step num="1">Cut chicken into cubes, wash and apply lime juice and
salt</step>
        <step num="2">Add ginger, garlic, chili, coriander and lime juice in
a separate bowl</step>
        <step num="3">Mix well, and add chicken to marinate for 3-4 hours</step>
        <step num="4">Place chicken pieces on skewers and barbeque</step>
        <step num="5">Remove, apply butter, and barbeque again until meat is
tender</step>
        <step num="6">Garnish with lemon and chopped onions</step>
    </process>
</recipe>
```

XPath makes it possible to locate a node, or set of nodes, at any level of this tree, using a location path. A *location path* may be either an absolute path, which expresses a location with reference to the root node, or a relative path, which expresses a location with reference to the current node (also known as the *context node*). Location paths are made up of a series of *location steps,* each identifying one level in the XPath tree and separated from each other by a forward slash (/).

A location step is expressed as the sum of three components in the format *axis::node-test[predicates]*. The *axis* defines the relationship to use when selecting nodes, a *node-test* specifies the types of nodes to select, and optional *predicates* filter out unwanted nodes from the resulting collection.

Axes, Node Tests, and Predicates   An axis defines the relationship between the current node and the nodes to be selected—whether, for example, they are children of the current node, siblings of the current node, or the parent of the current node.

The XPath specification defines a number of axes; the most important ones are listed in Table 8-1.

CAUTION *The "following" and "preceding" axes are not supported in MySQL at the time of this writing.*

Once the relationship to be established has been defined and an appropriate node collection obtained, a node test can be used to further filter the items in the collection. This node test is connected to the axis by a double colon (::) symbol. A node test can be specified either on the basis of node name or node type; XPath offers various predefined node tests, such as the text() function to select text nodes, the comment() function to select comments, and so on.

Axis	Description
self	The context node
parent	The parent of the context node
child	The children of the context node
attribute	The attributes of the context node
ancestor	All ancestors of the context node
descendant	All descendants (children) of the context node
following	All nodes that follow (are placed after) the context node
preceding	All nodes that precede (are placed before) the context node
namespace	All nodes in the same namespace as the context node

TABLE 8-1   XPath Axes

Finally, in case the resulting collection needs to be broken down further, XPath allows you to add optional predicates to each location step, enclosed within square brackets.

Retrieving Records and Fields

With the basic theory out of the way, let's see how this works in the MySQL context. MySQL 5.1 and later provides an ExtractValue() function, which can be used to retrieve a specific value from an XML document using location paths. This ExtractValue() function accepts two arguments: the source XML document and the location path to the value.

To illustrate how this works in practice, let's first load the example XML file shown earlier into a MySQL session variable using the LOAD_FILE() function. This function can be used to read the contents of a file (which must already exist on the server) into either a variable or a table field.

```
mysql> SET @xml = LOAD_FILE('/tmp/in.xml');
Query OK, 0 rows affected (0.18 sec)
```

Now, consider that the location path */child::recipe/child::author/child::text()* references the name of the recipe author. Calling the MySQL ExtractValue() function with this location path produces the necessary result, as shown:

```
mysql> SELECT ExtractValue(@xml,
    -> '/child::recipe/child::author/child::text()'
    -> ) AS value;
+-----------+
| value     |
+-----------+
| Anonymous |
+-----------+
1 row in set (0.02 sec)
```

This location path can also be more simply written as */recipe/author,* because XPath assumes a default axis of 'child' if none is specified.

```
mysql> SELECT ExtractValue(@xml, '/recipe/author')
    -> AS value;
+-----------+
| value     |
+-----------+
| Anonymous |
+-----------+
1 row in set (0.00 sec)
```

In a similar vein, the location path */recipe/ingredients/item[3]* would reference the third ingredient, 'Ginger', while the location path */recipe/process/step[1]* would reference the first step of the cooking process. Notice also that the square brackets represent a predicate—in this case, the *<item>* in position 3. The following output demonstrates:

```
mysql> SELECT ExtractValue(@xml,
    -> '/recipe/ingredients/item[3]/text()'
    -> ) AS value;
+--------+
| value  |
+--------+
| Ginger |
+--------+
1 row in set (0.00 sec)
mysql> SELECT ExtractValue(@xml,
    -> '/recipe/process/step[1]/text()'
    -> ) AS value;
+-------------------------------------------------------------+
| value                                                       |
+-------------------------------------------------------------+
| Cut chicken into cubes, wash and apply lime juice and salt  |
+-------------------------------------------------------------+
1 row in set (0.01 sec)
```

CAUTION *When dealing with a collection of nodes generated by a location path, remember that indexing starts at 1, not 0.*

The // shortcut is equivalent to the "descendant-or-self" axis and selects elements matching the supplied node test anywhere below the current context node. So, the path *//item* would reference all *<item>* elements within the document, while the path *//item[6]* would be a quick shortcut to the sixth *<item>* element, 'Butter'.

```
mysql> SELECT ExtractValue(@xml,
    -> '//item[6]'
    -> ) AS value;
```

```
+---------+
| value   |
+---------+
| Butter  |
+---------+
1 row in set (0.00 sec)
```

NOTE *Notice that although the location path //ingredients should actually return a collection of <item> nodes, the* ExtractValue() *function will instead return the character data of these nodes.*

```
mysql> SELECT ExtractValue(@xml, '//item');
+---------------------------------------------------------------------+
| ExtractValue(@xml, '//item')                                        |
+---------------------------------------------------------------------+
| Boneless chicken breasts Ginger Garlic Red chili powder Butter      |
+---------------------------------------------------------------------+
1 row in set (0.00 sec)
```

This is a limitation of the ExtractValue() function, as currently implemented in MySQL, and it also explains why the call to text() in the location paths of previous example is unnecessary ... although MySQL will not return an error if you use it.

The @ prefix indicates that attributes, rather than elements, are to be matched. So, for example, the location path */recipe/name/@source* would represent the value 'India', while the location path *//step[@num=3]* contains a predicate that references the *<step>* element with the attribute value 'num=3':

```
mysql> SELECT ExtractValue(@xml,
    -> '/recipe/name/@source'
    -> ) AS value;
+--------+
| value  |
+--------+
| India  |
+--------+
1 row in set (0.00 sec)
mysql> SELECT ExtractValue(@xml,
    -> '//step[@num=3]'
    -> ) AS value;
+-----------------------------------------------------+
| value                                               |
+-----------------------------------------------------+
| Mix well, and add chicken to marinate for 3-4 hours |
+-----------------------------------------------------+
1 row in set (0.01 sec)
```

Finally, XPath supports a number of different functions to work with nodes and node collections. While it's not possible to discuss them all here, it's worthwhile mentioning the count() function, which counts the number of nodes in a node collection returned by a location path. Here's an example, which counts the number of ingredients in the recipe:

```
mysql> SELECT ExtractValue(@xml,
    -> 'count(//ingredients/item)'
    -> ) AS value;
+-------+
| value |
+-------+
| 6     |
+-------+
1 row in set (0.01 sec)
```

NOTE *Other XPath functions, such as* name() *and* id()*, are not currently supported by MySQL.*

Updating Records and Fields

To update values in an XML document, MySQL offers the UpdateXML() function. This function accepts three arguments: the source XML document, the location path to the node to be updated, and the replacement XML. To illustrate, consider the next example, which updates the author name:

```
mysql> SET @xml = UpdateXML(@xml,
    -> '//author', '<author>John Doe</author>');
Query OK, 0 rows affected (0.00 sec)
mysql> SELECT ExtractValue(@xml, '//author');
+------------------------------+
| ExtractValue(@xml, '//author') |
+------------------------------+
| John Doe                     |
+------------------------------+
1 row in set (0.03 sec)
```

Here's another example, which updates the second ingredient:

```
mysql> SET @xml = UpdateXML(@xml,
    -> '//item[2]', '<item>Coriander</item>');
Query OK, 0 rows affected (0.01 sec)
mysql> SELECT ExtractValue(@xml, '//item[2]');
```

```
+----------------------------------+
| ExtractValue(@xml, '//item[2]') |
+----------------------------------+
| Coriander                        |
+----------------------------------+
1 row in set (0.00 sec)
```

And here's one that removes the final step from the recipe:

```
mysql> SET @xml = UpdateXML(@xml, '//step[@num=6]', '');
Query OK, 0 rows affected (0.00 sec)
mysql> SELECT ExtractValue(@xml, '//step[num=6]');
+------------------------------------+
| ExtractValue(@xml, '//step[num=6]') |
+------------------------------------+
|                                    |
+------------------------------------+
1 row in set (0.01 sec)
```

Importing XML

When it comes to importing XML data into a MySQL database, MySQL 5.1 is fairly limited. It does not offer any easy way to convert structured XML data into table records and fields, and only allows XML fragments to be imported "as is." To illustrate, consider the following simple XML document, which contains passenger records:

```xml
<?xml version='1.0'?>
<doc>
  <pax>
    <paxname>Rich Rabbit</paxname>
    <flightid>652</flightid>
    <flightdate>2009-01-20</flightdate>
    <classid>3</classid>
  </pax>
  <pax>
    <paxname>Zoe Zebra</paxname>
    <flightid>652</flightid>
    <flightdate>2009-01-27</flightdate>
    <classid>2</classid>
  </pax>
  <pax>
    <paxname>Zane Zebra</paxname>
    <flightid>652</flightid>
    <flightdate>2009-01-27</flightdate>
    <classid>2</classid>
  </pax>
```

```
  <pax>
    <paxname>Barbara Bear</paxname>
    <flightid>652</flightid>
    <flightdate>2009-01-20</flightdate>
    <classid>2</classid>
  </pax>
  <pax>
    <paxname>Harriet Horse</paxname>
    <flightid>652</flightid>
    <flightdate>2009-01-27</flightdate>
    <classid>3</classid>
  </pax>
</doc>
```

The LOAD_FILE() function, discussed in the previous section, can be used to import the contents of a file into a table field, as follows:

```
mysql> CREATE TABLE p_tmp(
    -> xmldata TEXT);
Query OK, 0 rows affected (0.46 sec)
mysql> INSERT INTO p_tmp (xmldata)
    -> VALUES(LOAD_FILE('/tmp/in.xml'));
Query OK, 1 row affected (0.27 sec)
```

Look in the table, and you'll see the imported XML document:

```
mysql> SELECT xmldata FROM p_tmp\G
*************************** 1. row ***************************
xmldata: <?xml version='1.0'?>
<doc>
  <pax>
    <paxname>Rich Rabbit</paxname>
    <flightid>652</flightid>
    <flightdate>2009-01-20</flightdate>
    <classid>3</classid>
  </pax>
  <pax>
    <paxname>Zoe Zebra</paxname>
    <flightid>652</flightid>
    <flightdate>2009-01-27</flightdate>
    <classid>2</classid>
  </pax>
  <pax>
    <paxname>Zane Zebra</paxname>
    <flightid>652</flightid>
    <flightdate>2009-01-27</flightdate>
    <classid>2</classid>
  </pax>
```

```
  <pax>
    <paxname>Barbara Bear</paxname>
    <flightid>652</flightid>
    <flightdate>2009-01-20</flightdate>
    <classid>2</classid>
  </pax>
  <pax>
    <paxname>Harriet Horse</paxname>
    <flightid>652</flightid>
    <flightdate>2009-01-27</flightdate>
    <classid>3</classid>
  </pax>
</doc>
1 row in set (0.00 sec)
```

The downside of this, of course, is that while the LOAD_FILE() function provides a way to get XML data into MySQL, you can't easily generate result sets from that data using normal SELECT statements. MySQL 5.1 does include some support for XPath (as discussed earlier in this chapter), and this can make your task easier … but this approach is still far from perfect!

Other approaches to import structured XML documents into MySQL, such as that shown in the previous example, involve using XSLT to reformat the XML data into INSERT statements, which can then be executed through the MySQL client, or writing a customized stored routine that parses the XML and inserts the values found into a table. Here's an example of the latter approach, which uses the ExtractValue() function discussed earlier:

```
mysql> TRUNCATE TABLE p;
Query OK, 0 rows affected (0.01 sec)
mysql> DELIMITER //
mysql> CREATE PROCEDURE import_xml_pax(
    ->    IN xml TEXT
    -> )
    -> BEGIN
    ->   DECLARE i INT DEFAULT 1;
    ->   DECLARE c INT DEFAULT 0;
    ->   SET c = ExtractValue(xml, 'count(//pax)');
    ->   WHILE (i <= c) DO
    ->     INSERT INTO p (FlightID, FlightDate,
    ->       ClassID, PaxName, Note)
    ->       VALUES (
    ->         ExtractValue(xml, '//pax[$i]/flightid'),
    ->         ExtractValue(xml, '//pax[$i]/flightdate'),
    ->         ExtractValue(xml, '//pax[$i]/classid'),
    ->         ExtractValue(xml, '//pax[$i]/paxname'),
    ->         'XML import via stored routine'
```

```
   ->          );
   ->        SET i = i + 1;
   ->      END WHILE;
   -> END//
Query OK, 0 rows affected (0.01 sec)
```

You can now call this stored routine and pass it the source XML file:

```
mysql> CALL import_xml_pax(
    ->    LOAD_FILE('/tmp/in.xml')
    -> );
```

A quick SELECT will verify that the records have been imported:

```
mysql> SELECT RecordID, FlightDate, ClassID, PaxName
    -> FROM p;
+----------+------------+---------+---------------+
| RecordID | FlightDate | ClassID | PaxName       |
+----------+------------+---------+---------------+
|      234 | 2009-01-27 |       2 | Zoe Zebra     |
|      233 | 2009-01-20 |       3 | Rich Rabbit   |
|      235 | 2009-01-27 |       2 | Zane Zebra    |
|      236 | 2009-01-20 |       2 | Barbara Bear  |
|      237 | 2009-01-27 |       3 | Harriet Horse |
+----------+------------+---------+---------------+
5 rows in set (0.00 sec)
```

Needless to say, this is a somewhat tedious approach, because you need to rewrite the stored routine for different XML documents and tables (although you can certainly make it more generic than the previous example).

If you're using MySQL 6.0, things are much cheerier. This is because MySQL 6.0 includes a new statement, the LOAD XML statement, which can directly import structured XML data as table records. This function, which is analogous to the LOAD DATA INFILE statement discussed in the previous section, can read XML data that is formatted using any of the following three conventions:

- Element attributes correspond to field names, with attribute values representing field values:

```
<?xml version='1.0?>
<resultset>
   <row PaxName='Zoe Zebra' FlightID='652' FlightDate='2009-01-27'
ClassID='2' />
   ...
</resultset>
```

- Elements correspond to field names, with the enclosed content representing field values:

```xml
<?xml version='1.0'?>
<resultset>
  <row>
    <PaxName>Rich Rabbit</PaxName>
    <FlightID>652</FlightID>
    <FlightDate>2009-01-20</FlightDate>
    <ClassID>3</ClassID>
  </row>
  ...
</resultset>
```

- Element 'name' attributes specify field names, with element content representing field values:

```xml
<?xml version='1.0'?>
<resultset>
  <row>
    <field name='PaxName'>Rich Rabbit</field>
    <field name='FlightID'>652</field>
    <field name='FlightDate'>2009-01-20</field>
    <field name='ClassID'>3</field>
  </row>
  ...
</resultset>
```

To illustrate, consider the following XML file, which is formatted according to the second convention listed previously:

```xml
<?xml version='1.0'?>
<resultset>
  <row>
    <RecordID>201</RecordID>
    <PaxName>Rich Rabbit</PaxName>
    <FlightID>652</FlightID>
    <FlightDate>2009-01-20</FlightDate>
    <ClassID>3</ClassID>
    <PaxRef>HH83282949</PaxRef>
  </row>
  <row>
    <RecordID>202</RecordID>
    <PaxName>Zoe Zebra</PaxName>
    <FlightID>652</FlightID>
    <FlightDate>2009-01-27</FlightDate>
    <ClassID>2</ClassID>
    <PaxRef>JY64940400</PaxRef>
  </row>
```

```xml
<row>
   <RecordID>203</RecordID>
   <PaxName>Zane Zebra</PaxName>
   <FlightID>652</FlightID>
   <FlightDate>2009-01-27</FlightDate>
   <ClassID>2</ClassID>
   <PaxRef>JY64940401</PaxRef>
</row>
<row>
   <RecordID>204</RecordID>
   <PaxName>Barbara Bear</PaxName>
   <FlightID>652</FlightID>
   <FlightDate>2009-01-20</FlightDate>
   <ClassID>2</ClassID>
   <PaxRef>JD74391994</PaxRef>
</row>
<row>
   <RecordID>205</RecordID>
   <PaxName>Harriet Horse</PaxName>
   <FlightID>652</FlightID>
   <FlightDate>2009-01-27</FlightDate>
   <ClassID>3</ClassID>
   <PaxRef>JG74860994</PaxRef>
</row>
</resultset>
```

Here's an example of how it could be loaded into a table:

```
mysql> TRUNCATE TABLE p;
Query OK, 0 rows affected (0.00 sec)
mysql> LOAD XML LOCAL INFILE '/tmp/in.xml'
    -> INTO TABLE p;
Query OK, 5 rows affected (0.00 sec)
Records: 5  Deleted: 0  Skipped: 0  Warnings: 0
mysql> SELECT RecordID, PaxName, PaxRef FROM p;
+----------+---------------+------------+
| RecordID | PaxName       | PaxRef     |
+----------+---------------+------------+
|      201 | Rich Rabbit   | HH83282949 |
|      202 | Zoe Zebra     | JY64940400 |
|      203 | Zane Zebra    | JY64940401 |
|      204 | Barbara Bear  | JD74391994 |
|      205 | Harriet Horse | JG74860994 |
+----------+---------------+------------+
5 rows in set (0.03 sec)
```

Needless to say, the LOAD XML function can save you a great deal of custom programming!

The LOAD XML statement supports an additional ROWS IDENTIFIED BY clause, which specifies the XML element that marks the beginning and end of a single record in the XML file, and comes in handy when working with XML data in different formats. For example, if the input file looked like this:

```
<?xml version='1.0'?>
<resultset>
  <paxdata>
    <PaxName>Rich Rabbit</PaxName>
    <FlightID>652</FlightID>
    <FlightDate>2009-01-20</FlightDate>
    <ClassID>3</ClassID>
    <PaxRef>HH83282949</PaxRef>
  </paxdata>
  <paxdata>
    <PaxName>Zoe Zebra</PaxName>
    <FlightID>652</FlightID>
    <FlightDate>2009-01-27</FlightDate>
    <ClassID>2</ClassID>
    <PaxRef>JY64940400</PaxRef>
  </paxdata>
  <paxdata>
    <PaxName>Zane Zebra</PaxName>
    <FlightID>652</FlightID>
    <FlightDate>2009-01-27</FlightDate>
    <ClassID>2</ClassID>
    <PaxRef>JY64940401</PaxRef>
  </paxdata>
  <paxdata>
    <PaxName>Barbara Bear</PaxName>
    <FlightID>652</FlightID>
    <FlightDate>2009-01-20</FlightDate>
    <ClassID>2</ClassID>
    <PaxRef>JD74391994</PaxRef>
    <Note>Special meal</Note>
  </paxdata>
  <paxdata>
    <PaxName>Harriet Horse</PaxName>
    <FlightID>652</FlightID>
    <FlightDate>2009-01-27</FlightDate>
    <ClassID>3</ClassID>
    <PaxRef>JG74860994</PaxRef>
    <Note>Special service</Note>
  </paxdata>
</resultset>
```

you could still import it using the following command:

```
mysql> LOAD XML LOCAL INFILE '/tmp/in.xml'
    -> INTO TABLE p
    -> ROWS IDENTIFIED BY '<paxdata>';
Query OK, 5 rows affected (0.01 sec)
Records: 5  Deleted: 0  Skipped: 0  Warnings: 0
```

Like the LOAD DATA INFILE statement, the LOAD XML statement also supports the LOW_PRIORITY, CONCURRENT, REPLACE, and IGNORE keywords for greater control over how XML data is imported.

Exporting XML

When it comes to exporting XML, MySQL currently lacks an equivalent to the SELECT ... INTO OUTFILE statement, so XML-based export can only be accomplished using either the *mysql* or *mysqldump* command-line tools.

To export the contents of a table using *mysqldump*, pass it the *--xml* command-line option, together with other connection-specific parameters. Here's an example, which generates an XML file containing airport records:

```
[user@host] mysqldump --xml -u root  -p db1 airport > /tmp/airport.xml
Password: ******
```

Here's an example of the output:

```
<?xml version="1.0"?>
<mysqldump xmlns:xsi="http://www.w3.org/2001/XMLSchema-instance">
<database name="db1">
  <table_data name="airport">
    <row>
      <field name="AirportID">34</field>
      <field name="AirportCode">ORY</field>
      <field name="AirportName">Orly Airport</field>
      <field name="CityName">Paris</field>
      <field name="CountryCode">FR</field>
      <field name="NumRunways">3</field>
      <field name="NumTerminals">2</field>
    </row>
    <row>
      <field name="AirportID">48</field>
      <field name="AirportCode">LGW</field>
      <field name="AirportName">Gatwick Airport</field>
      <field name="CityName">London</field>
      <field name="CountryCode">GB</field>
      <field name="NumRunways">3</field>
      <field name="NumTerminals">1</field>
    </row>
```

```
   . . .
  </table_data>
 </database>
</mysqldump>
```

If you're trying to generate custom output using a SELECT query and WHERE clause, you'd be better off using the MySQL command-line client, which also supports the --*xml* argument. Here's an example, which generates an XML file listing only those airports with three or more runways:

```
[user@host] mysql --xml -u root -p --execute="SELECT AirportID,
AirportName FROM airport WHERE NumRunways >= 3" db1 > /tmp/airport.xml
Enter password: ******
```

And here's a sample of the output:

```
<?xml version="1.0"?>
<resultset statement="SELECT AirportID, AirportName
  FROM airport WHERE NumRunways &gt;= 3"
  xmlns:xsi="http://www.w3.org/2001/XMLSchema-instance">
  <row>
       <field name="AirportID">34</field>
       <field name="AirportName">Orly Airport</field>
  </row>
  <row>
       <field name="AirportID">48</field>
       <field name="AirportName">Gatwick Airport</field>
  </row>
  <row>
       <field name="AirportID">62</field>
       <field name="AirportName">Schiphol Airport</field>
  </row>
  <row>
       <field name="AirportID">72</field>
       <field name="AirportName">Barcelona International Airport</field>
  </row>
  . . .
</resultset>
```

Summary

This chapter discussed the many ways of getting data into, and out of, MySQL. While MySQL offers fairly sophisticated tools for importing and exporting data in standard comma-separated or tab-delimited formats, its support for XML-encoded data is still fairly primitive. MySQL 5.1 provides some XML-handling functions that are useful when accessing and changing values in an XML document, while MySQL 6.0 offers a new LOAD XML function that significantly simplifies the task of importing structured XML data into a MySQL table.

In summary, however, while it is fairly easy to store an entire XML document "as is" in a MySQL table, separating and storing XML data sets as individual records is still a hard task—expect improvements to this aspect of the RDBMS in future releases.

To read more about the topics discussed in this chapter, consider visiting the following links:

- Importing records using the LOAD DATA INFILE statement, at http://dev.mysql .com/doc/refman/5.1/en/load-data.html

- Exporting records using the SELECT ... INTO OUTFILE statement, at http:// dev.mysql.com/doc/refman/5.1/en/select.html

- Importing structured XML data using the LOAD XML statement, at http:// dev.mysql.com/doc/refman/6.0/en/load-xml.html

- XML functions in MySQL, at http://dev.mysql.com/doc/refman/5.1/en/ xml-functions.html

CHAPTER 9

Optimizing Performance

As your databases grow, you'll find yourself constantly looking for ways to extract better performance from them. While processor speed, bigger and faster disks, and additional memory certainly have something to do with performance, they're outside the scope of this discussion. Instead, the intent of this chapter is to teach you some techniques to improve server and query performance using the tools available within MySQL to ensure that you're getting the best possible performance from your MySQL setup.

Newer MySQL features, such as stored routines and subqueries, can significantly simplify complex database operations, but because of their relative new-ness, are not yet completely optimized and so always incur some performance cost. This chapter considers each of these features and offers some tips to help you improve their performance.

Database design is another aspect to consider when discussing performance. Various strategies for optimizing a table for better performance are, therefore, also a part of this chapter. Most of the optimization you should do, however, first involves refining your queries, adding indexes, and so forth. Accordingly, query optimization is considered first in this chapter.

Optimizing Queries

One of the first places to look to improve performance is queries, particularly the ones that run often. Big gains can be achieved by analyzing a query and rewriting it more efficiently. You can use MySQL's slow query log (described in Chapter 12) to get an idea of which queries might be fine-tuned, and then try applying some of the techniques in the following sections to improve their performance.

Indexing

A surprising number of people in online forums request information about slow queries without having tried to add an index to a frequently accessed field. As you know from Chapter 3, tables with fields that are accessed frequently can be ordered by creating an index. An index points to the place on a database where specific data is located, and creating an index on a field sorts the information in that field. When the server needs to access that information to execute a query, it knows where to look because the index points to the relevant location.

Indexing is even more important on multitable queries. If it takes a while to do a full table scan on one table, imagine how much longer it would take if you have several tables to check. If optimization of your queries is a goal, the first thing to do is to try implementing an index.

Deciding which fields should be indexed involves several considerations. If you have a field involved in searching, grouping, or sorting, indexing it will likely result in a performance gain. These include fields that are part of join operations or fields that appear with clauses such as WHERE, GROUP BY, or ORDER BY.

Consider the following example:

```
SELECT a.AircraftID, at.AircraftName FROM
  aircraft AS a JOIN aircrafttype AS at
  ON a.AircraftTypeID = at.AircraftTypeID;
```

The fields that should be indexed here are *aircraft.AircraftTypeID* and *aircrafttype.AircraftTypeID* because they're part of a join. If this query is commonly repeated with the same WHERE or HAVING clause, then the fields used in those clauses would also be a good choice for indexing.

Another factor to consider here is that indexes on fields with many duplicate values won't produce good results. A table column that contains only "yes" or "no" values won't be improved by indexing. On the other hand, a field where the values are unique (for example, employee Social Security numbers) can benefit greatly from indexing.

You can associate multiple nonunique indexes with a table to improve performance. No limit exists to the number of nonunique indexes that can be created.

Taking this to its logical extreme, then, you might think the more indexes, the merrier. This is a fallacy: Adding an index doesn't necessarily improve performance. Small tables, for example, don't need indexing. In addition, every index takes up additional space on the disk—each indexed field requires MySQL to store information for every record in that field and its location within the database. As your indexes build, these tables begin to take up more room. Furthermore, indexing speeds up searches, but slows down write operations, such as INSERT, DELETE, or UPDATE. Until you work with indexing on your database, your first few attempts might not achieve much performance gain.

Certain administrative counters can help you monitor your indexes or come up with candidates for adding an index. Both the SHOW STATUS or *mysqladmin extended-status* commands display values to consider in terms of indexes.

- If your indexes are working, the value of *Handler_read_key* should be high. This value represents the number of times a record was read by an index value. A low value indicates that not much performance improvement has been achieved by the added indexing because the index isn't being used frequently.

- A high value for *Handler_read_rnd_next* means your queries are running inefficiently and indexing should be considered as a remedy. This value indicates the number of requests to read the next row in sequence. This occurs when a table is scanned sequentially from the first record to the last to execute the query. For frequent queries, this is a wasteful use of resources. An associated index points directly to the record(s), so this full table scan doesn't need to occur. Poorly functioning indexes could also result in a high number here.

To view these counters, run a command like the one shown here:

```
mysql> SHOW STATUS LIKE 'handler_read%';
+-----------------------+-------+
| Variable_name         | Value |
+-----------------------+-------+
| Handler_read_first    | 0     |
| Handler_read_key      | 23    |
| Handler_read_next     | 0     |
| Handler_read_prev     | 0     |
| Handler_read_rnd      | 0     |
| Handler_read_rnd_next | 41    |
+-----------------------+-------+
6 rows in set (0.01 sec)
```

TIP If your SELECT statements frequently end up sorting results by a particular field, use the ALTER TABLE statement with an ORDER BY clause to re-sort the contents of the table by that field. Your SELECT statements will then no longer need an ORDER BY clause, resulting in faster and more efficient reads.

Once you've got your tables loaded with data and indexed the way you want them, you should run the ANALYZE TABLE command on them. This command analyzes the data in the table and creates table statistics on the average number of rows that share the same value. This information is used by the MySQL optimizer when deciding which index to use in table joins.

```
mysql> ANALYZE TABLE airport, aircraft, flight;
+--------------+---------+----------+------------------------------+
| Table        | Op      | Msg_type | Msg_text                     |
+--------------+---------+----------+------------------------------+
| db1.airport  | analyze | status   | OK                           |
| db1.aircraft | analyze | status   | Table is already up to date  |
| db1.flight   | analyze | status   | OK                           |
+--------------+---------+----------+------------------------------+
3 rows in set (0.00 sec)
```

It's a good idea to run the ANALYZE TABLE command frequently, especially after you've added a significant amount of data to your table, to ensure that the optimizer is always using the most efficient index.

Query Caching

When you run a SELECT query, MySQL "remembers" both the query and the results it returns. This is accomplished by storing the result set in a special cache (called the *query cache*) each time a SELECT query is executed. Then, the next time you ask the server for the same query, MySQL will retrieve the results from the cache instead of running the query again. As you can imagine, this speeds up the process considerably.

Although enabled by default, you must always verify that query caching is turned on, which can be done by checking the server variables. The following example illustrates:

```
mysql> SHOW VARIABLES LIKE '%query_cache%';
+-------------------------------+----------+
| Variable_name                 | Value    |
+-------------------------------+----------+
| have_query_cache              | YES      |
| query_cache_limit             | 1048576  |
| query_cache_min_res_unit      | 4096     |
| query_cache_size              | 0        |
| query_cache_type              | ON       |
| query_cache_wlock_invalidate  | OFF      |
+-------------------------------+----------+
6 rows in set (0.00 sec)
```

- The first variable, *have_query_cache,* indicates the server was configured for query caching when it was installed (the default).

- The *query_cache_size* variable indicates the amount of memory allotted for the cache in bytes. If this value is 0, query caching will be off.

- The values for the *query_cache_type* variable range from 0 to 2. A value of 0 or OFF indicates that query caching is turned off. ON or 1 means that query caching is turned on, with the exception of SELECT statements using the SQL_NO_CACHE option. DEMAND or 2 provides query caching on demand for SELECT statements running with the SQL_CACHE option.

- The *query_cache_limit* variable specifies the maximum result set size that should be cached. Result sets larger than this value will not be cached.

You can alter any of these variables using the SET GLOBAL or SET SESSION statements, as shown:

```
mysql> SET GLOBAL query_cache_size = 16777216;
Query OK, 0 rows affected (0.00 sec)
```

To see for yourself what impact the query cache is having on performance, run the same query with and without query caching to compare the performance difference. Here's the version without using the query cache:

```
mysql> SELECT SQL_NO_CACHE r.RouteID, a1.AirportCode, a2.AirportCode,
    -> r.Distance, r.Duration, r.Status FROM route AS r,
    -> airport AS a1, airport AS a2
    -> WHERE r.From LIKE a1.AirportID
    -> AND r.To LIKE a2.AirportID
    -> AND r.RouteID IN
    ->    (SELECT f.RouteID
    ->    FROM flight AS f, flightdep AS fd
    ->    WHERE f.FlightID = fd.FlightID
```

```
    ->    AND f.RouteID = r.RouteID
    ->    AND fd.DepTime BETWEEN '00:00' AND '04:00');
+---------+-------------+-------------+----------+----------+--------+
| RouteID | AirportCode | AirportCode | Distance | Duration | Status |
+---------+-------------+-------------+----------+----------+--------+
|    1133 | MUC         | BOM         |     6336 |      470 |      1 |
|    1141 | BOM         | SIN         |     3913 |      320 |      1 |
+---------+-------------+-------------+----------+----------+--------+
2 rows in set (0.21 sec)
```

Now perform the same query with the cache:

```
mysql> SELECT SQL_CACHE r.RouteID, a1.AirportCode,
    -> a2.AirportCode, r.Distance, r.Duration, r.Status FROM
    -> route AS r, airport AS a1, airport AS a2
    -> WHERE r.From LIKE a1.AirportID
    -> AND r.To LIKE a2.AirportID
    -> AND r.RouteID IN
    ->   (SELECT f.RouteID
    ->   FROM flight AS f, flightdep AS fd
    ->   WHERE f.FlightID = fd.FlightID
    ->   AND f.RouteID = r.RouteID
    ->   AND fd.DepTime BETWEEN '00:00' AND '04:00');
+---------+-------------+-------------+----------+----------+--------+
| RouteID | AirportCode | AirportCode | Distance | Duration | Status |
+---------+-------------+-------------+----------+----------+--------+
|    1133 | MUC         | BOM         |     6336 |      470 |      1 |
|    1141 | BOM         | SIN         |     3913 |      320 |      1 |
+---------+-------------+-------------+----------+----------+--------+
2 rows in set (0.02 sec)
```

Dramatic improvements in performance aren't unusual if query caching is enabled on frequent queries.

CAUTION *Once a table is changed, the cached queries that use this table become invalid and are removed from the cache. This prevents a query from returning inaccurate data from the old table. While this makes query caching much more useful, a constantly changing table won't benefit from caching. In this situation, you might want to consider eliminating query caching. This can be done by adding the SQL_NO_CACHE option, as previously shown, to a SELECT statement.*

Query Analysis

Attaching the EXPLAIN keyword to the beginning of a SELECT query tells MySQL to return a chart describing how this query will be processed. Included within this chart is information on which tables the query will access and the number of rows the query is expected to return. This information comes in handy to see which tables should be indexed to speed up performance and to analyze where the bottlenecks are.

***

CAUTION *Only queries that are textually exact will match what's in the query cache; any difference will be treated as a new query. For example,* SELECT * FROM airport *won't return the result from* select * FROM airport *in the cache.*

As an example, consider the following query:

```
SELECT p.PaxName, f.FlightID
  FROM pax AS p,
  flight AS f, route AS r
  WHERE p.FlightID = f.FlightID
  AND p.ClassID = 2 AND r.Duration = 85;
```

Now, by adding the EXPLAIN keyword to the beginning of the query, one can obtain some information on how MySQL processes it:

```
mysql> EXPLAIN SELECT p.PaxName, f.FlightID
    -> FROM pax AS p,
    -> flight AS f, route AS r
    -> WHERE p.FlightID = f.FlightID
    -> AND p.ClassID = 2 AND r.Duration = 85\G
*************************** 1. row ***************************
           id: 1
  select_type: SIMPLE
        table: p
         type: ALL
possible_keys: NULL
          key: NULL
      key_len: NULL
          ref: NULL
         rows: 30
        Extra: Using where
*************************** 2. row ***************************
           id: 1
  select_type: SIMPLE
        table: r
         type: ALL
possible_keys: NULL
          key: NULL
      key_len: NULL
          ref: NULL
         rows: 290
        Extra: Using where; Using join buffer
*************************** 3. row ***************************
           id: 1
  select_type: SIMPLE
        table: f
         type: eq_ref
```

```
possible_keys: PRIMARY
          key: PRIMARY
      key_len: 2
          ref: db1.p.FlightID
         rows: 1
        Extra: Using where
3 rows in set (0.00 sec)
```

This might all seem a little intimidating, so an explanation is in order. The result of EXPLAIN SELECT is a table listing all the SELECTs in the query, together with how MySQL plans to process them.

- The *id* field indicates the position of the SELECT within the complete query, while the *table* field holds the name of the table being queried.

- The *select_type* field indicates the type of query: a simple query without subqueries, a UNION, a subquery, an outer query, a subquery within an outer query, or a subquery in a FROM clause.

- The *type* field indicates how the join will be performed. A number of values are possible here, ranging from *const* (the best kind of join, since it means the table contains a single matching record only) to *all* (the worst kind, because it means that MySQL has to scan every single record to find a match to records in the other joined tables).

- The *possible_keys* field indicates the indexes available for MySQL to use in order to speed up the search.

- The *key* field indicates the key it will actually use, with the key length displayed in the *key_len* field.

- The *rows* field indicates the number of rows MySQL needs to examine in the corresponding table to successfully execute the query. To obtain the total number of rows MySQL must scan to process the complete query, multiply the *rows* value for each table together.

- The *Extra* field contains additional information on how MySQL will process the query—say, by using the WHERE clause, by using an index, with a temporary table, and so on.

Now, from the previous output, it's clear that in order to execute the query, MySQL will need to examine all the rows in two of the named tables. The total number of rows MySQL needs to scan, then, is approximately 290 × 30 = 8,700 rows—an extremely large number!

However, by reviewing the output of the EXPLAIN SELECT command output, it's clear that there is room for improvement. For example, the *possible_keys* field for some of the tables is NULL, indicating that MySQL couldn't find any indexes to use. This can quickly be rectified by reviewing the tables and adding indexes wherever possible:

```
mysql> ALTER TABLE pax ADD INDEX (ClassID);
Query OK, 30 rows affected (0.06 sec)
Records: 30  Duplicates: 0  Warnings: 0
```

```
mysql> ALTER TABLE route ADD INDEX (Duration);
Query OK, 290 rows affected (0.06 sec)
Records: 290  Duplicates: 0  Warnings: 0
```

Now, try running the query again with EXPLAIN:

```
mysql> EXPLAIN SELECT p.PaxName, f.FlightID
    -> FROM pax AS p,
    -> flight AS f, route AS r
    -> WHERE p.FlightID = f.FlightID
    -> AND p.ClassID = 2 AND r.Duration = 85\G;
*************************** 1. row ***************************
           id: 1
  select_type: SIMPLE
        table: p
         type: ref
possible_keys: ClassID
          key: ClassID
      key_len: 4
          ref: const
         rows: 1
        Extra:
*************************** 2. row ***************************
           id: 1
  select_type: SIMPLE
        table: r
         type: ref
possible_keys: Duration
          key: Duration
      key_len: 2
          ref: const
         rows: 1
        Extra: Using index
*************************** 3. row ***************************
           id: 1
  select_type: SIMPLE
        table: f
         type: eq_ref
possible_keys: PRIMARY
          key: PRIMARY
      key_len: 2
          ref: db1.p.FlightID
         rows: 1
        Extra: Using where; Using index
3 rows in set (0.00 sec)
```

As you can see, MySQL is now using the newly added indexes to cut down on the number of rows that need to be examined. Looking at the *rows* field for each table, we now see that MySQL only needs to scan one row in each table to process the query—a significant improvement over the earlier, nonindexed approach.

Optimizing Joins and Subqueries

A *join* is a multitable query performed across tables that are connected to each other by means of one or more common fields. It is commonly used to exploit relationships between the normalized tables of an RDBMS, and it gives SQL programmers the ability to link records from separate tables to create different views of the same data.

A *subquery* is a SELECT statement nested inside another SELECT statement. A subquery is often used to break down a complicated query into a series of logical steps or to answer a query with the results of another query. As a result, instead of executing two (or more) separate queries, you execute a single query containing one (or more) subqueries.

Although MySQL comes with built-in intelligence to automatically optimize joins and subqueries, this optimization is far from perfect. An experienced database architect can often improve query performance by orders of magnitude through simple tweaks to the way queries are written. With this in mind, the following section outlines some common tips and tricks to help you maximize the performance of your joins and subqueries.

Use Joins Instead of Subqueries

MySQL is better at optimizing joins than subqueries, so if you find the load averages on your MySQL server hitting unacceptably high levels, examine your application code and try rewriting your subqueries as joins or sequences of joins. For example, while the following subquery is certainly legal:

```
SELECT r.RouteID, f.FlightID FROM route AS r, flight AS f
   WHERE r.RouteID = f.RouteID AND r.Status = 1 AND f.AircraftID IN
   (SELECT AircraftID FROM aircraft
   WHERE AircraftTypeID = 616);
```

the following equivalent join would run faster due to MySQL's optimization algorithms:

```
SELECT r.RouteID, f.FlightID FROM route AS r, flight AS f, aircraft AS a
   WHERE r.RouteID = f.RouteID AND f.AircraftID = a.AircraftID
   AND r.Status = 1 AND a.AircraftTypeID = 616;
```

It's a good idea to match the fields being joined in terms of both type and length. MySQL tends to be a little inefficient when using indexes on joined fields that are of different lengths and/or types.

You can also turn inefficient queries into more efficient ones through creative use of MySQL's ORDER BY and LIMIT clauses. Consider the following subquery:

```
SELECT RouteID, Duration FROM route
   WHERE Duration =
   (SELECT MAX(duration) FROM route);
```

This works better as the following query, which is simpler to read and also runs much faster:

```
SELECT RouteID, Duration FROM route
  ORDER BY duration DESC
  LIMIT 0,1;
```

Use Session Variables and Temporary Tables for Transient Data and Calculations

Session-based server variables can also come in handy if you want to avoid nesting queries within each other. Therefore, while the following query will list all flights where the current price is above average:

```
SELECT FlightID FROM stats
  WHERE CurrPrice >
  (SELECT AVG(CurrPrice) FROM stats);
```

you can accomplish the same thing by splitting the task into two queries and using a server-side MySQL variable to connect them:

```
SELECT @avg:=AVG(CurrPrice) FROM stats;
SELECT FlightID FROM stats WHERE CurrPrice > @avg;
```

These two queries combined will run faster than the first subquery.

MySQL also lets you create temporary tables with the CREATE TEMPORARY TABLE command. These tables are so-called because they remain in existence only for the duration of a single MySQL session and are automatically deleted when the client that instantiates them closes its connection with the MySQL server. These tables come in handy for transient, session-based data or calculations, or for the temporary storage of data. And because they're session-dependent, two different sessions can use the same table name without conflicting.

Since temporary tables are stored in memory, they are significantly faster than disk-based tables. Consequently, they can be effectively used as intermediate storage areas, to speed up query execution by helping to break up complex queries into simpler components, or as a substitute for subquery and join support.

MySQL's INSERT...SELECT syntax, together with its IGNORE keyword and its support for temporary tables, provides numerous opportunities for creative rewriting of SELECT queries to have them execute faster. For example, say you have a complex query that involves selecting a set of distinct values from a particular field and the MySQL engine is unable to optimize your query because of its complexity. Creative SQL programmers can improve performance by breaking down the single complex query into numerous simple queries (which lend themselves better to optimization) and then using the INSERT IGNORE...SELECT command to save the results generated to a temporary table, after first creating the temporary table with a UNIQUE key on the appropriate field. The result: a set of distinct values for that field and possibly faster query execution.

Here's another example: Assume you have a table containing information on a month's worth of transactions, say about 300,000 records. At the end of each day, your application needs to generate a report summarizing that day's transactions. In such a situation it's not a good idea, performance-wise, to run SUM() and AVG() functions on the entire set of 300,000 records on a daily basis. A more efficient solution here would be to extract only the transactions for the day into a temporary table using INSERT... SELECT, run summary functions on the temporary table to generate the required reports, and then delete the temporary table. Since the temporary table would contain a much smaller subset of records, performance would be better and the server load would also be lower.

```
CREATE TEMPORARY TABLE t_stats
   SELECT CurrPrice FROM stats WHERE FlightDate = '2009-04-01';
SELECT @avg:=AVG(CurrPrice) FROM t_stats;
DROP TABLE t_stats
```

Explicitly Name Output Fields

It's common to see queries like these:

```
SELECT (*) FROM airport;
SELECT COUNT(*) FROM airport;
```

These queries use the asterisk (*) wildcard for convenience. However, this convenience comes at a price: The * wildcard forces MySQL to read every field or record in the table, adding to the overall query processing time. To avoid this, explicitly name the output fields you wish to see in the result set, as shown:

```
SELECT AirportID FROM airport;
SELECT COUNT(AirportID) FROM airport;
```

In a similar vein, when using subqueries with a WHERE or HAVING clause, it's also a good idea to be as specific as possible in the WHERE or HAVING clause to reduce the size of the result set that needs to be processed by the outer query. If you're using MySQL from a client application over TCP/IP, following these simple rules will also reduce the size of the result set that is transmitted to the client by the server, reducing bandwidth consumption and improving performance.

Index Join Fields

Fields that are accessed frequently should be indexed. As a general rule, if you have a field involved in searching, grouping, or sorting, indexing it will likely result in a performance gain. Indexing should include fields that are part of join operations or fields that appear with clauses such as WHERE, GROUP BY, or ORDER BY. In addition, joining tables on integer fields, rather than on character fields, will produce better performance.

Rewrite Correlated Subqueries as Joins

When MySQL encounters a correlated subquery, it has to reevaluate the subquery once for every record generated by the outer query. This is obviously expensive in terms of performance, and so correlated subqueries should be avoided unless absolutely necessary. Thus, you are far better off using joins, unions, multitable updates or deletes, and temporary tables instead of correlated subqueries. As an example, consider the following correlated subquery:

```
SELECT r.RouteID, r.From, r.To
  FROM route AS r WHERE EXISTS
    (SELECT 1 FROM flight AS f,
    flightdep AS fd
    WHERE f.FlightID = fd.FlightID
    AND f.RouteID = r.RouteID
    AND fd.DepTime BETWEEN '00:00' AND '04:00');
```

This would execute faster if rewritten as a join, as shown:

```
SELECT DISTINCT r.RouteID, r.From, r.To
  FROM route AS r, flight AS f, flightdep AS fd
  WHERE f.FlightID = fd.FlightID
  AND r.RouteID = f.RouteID
  AND fd.DepTime BETWEEN '00:00' AND '04:00';
```

Replace Materialized Subqueries with Temporary Tables

When subqueries are used in the FROM clause, MySQL materializes them by storing the results in a temporary table. This temporary table is not automatically indexed, which often results in MySQL having to perform a full table scan in order to satisfy the outer query. Here's an example:

```
SELECT x.DepDay FROM
  (SELECT fd.DepDay, COUNT(fd.FlightID) AS c
  FROM flightdep AS fd
  GROUP BY fd.DepDay)
AS x
WHERE x.c >
  (SELECT COUNT(fd.FlightID)/7 FROM flightdep AS fd);
```

An easy way to improve performance in these cases is to manually create (and index) your own temporary table containing the result set of the inner query, and rewrite the outer query to reference this temporary table. Here's how you'd apply this principle to the previous query:

```
CREATE TEMPORARY TABLE x (
  INDEX (DepDay),
  INDEX (c)) ENGINE=MEMORY
```

```
SELECT fd.DepDay, COUNT(fd.FlightID) AS c
FROM flightdep AS fd
GROUP BY fd.DepDay;
SELECT DepDay FROM x WHERE x.c >
  (SELECT COUNT(fd.FlightID)/7 FROM flightdep AS fd);
```

Optimizing Transactional Performance

Because a database that supports transactions has to work a lot harder than a nontransactional database at keeping different user sessions isolated from each other, it's natural for this to be reflected in the system's performance. Compliance with the other ACID rules, specifically the ones related to maintaining the integrity of the database in the event of a system failure through the use of a transaction log, adds additional overhead to such transactional systems. MySQL is no exception to this rule—other things remaining the same, nontransactional MyISAM tables are much faster than the transactional InnoDB and BDB table types.

That said, if you have no choice but to use a transactional table type, you can still do a few things to ensure that your transactions don't add undue overhead to the system.

Use Small Transactions

Clichéd though it might be, the KISS (Keep It Simple, Stupid!) principle is particularly applicable in the complex world of transactions. This is because MySQL uses a row-level locking mechanism to prevent simultaneous transactions from editing the same record in the database and possibly corrupting it. The row-level locking mechanism prevents more than one transaction from accessing a row at the same time—this safeguards the data, but has the disadvantage of causing other transactions to wait until the transaction initiating the locks has completed its work. So long as the transaction is small, this wait time is not very noticeable. When dealing with a large database and many complex transactions, however, the long wait time while the various transactions wait for each other to release locks can significantly affect performance.

For this reason, it is generally considered a good idea to keep the size of your transactions small and to have them make their changes quickly and exit so that other transactions queued behind them do not get unduly delayed. At the application level, two common strategies exist for accomplishing this.

- Ensure that all user input required for the transaction is available before issuing a START TRANSACTION command. Often, novice application designers initiate a transaction before the complete set of values needed by it is available. Other transactions initiated at the same time now have to wait while the user inputs the required data and the application processes it, and then asks for more data, and so on. In a single-user environment, these delays will not matter as much because no other transactions are trying to access the database. In a multiuser scenario, however, a delay caused by a single transaction can have a ripple effect on all other transactions queued in the system, resulting in severe performance degradation.

- Try breaking down large transactions into smaller subtransactions and executing them independently. This will ensure that each subtransaction executes quickly, freeing up valuable system resources that would otherwise be used to maintain the state of the system.

Select an Appropriate Isolation Level

As you move from the carefree READ UNCOMMITTED isolation level to the more secure SERIALIZABLE level, the performance of the RDBMS is affected as well. The reason for this is fairly simple: The greater the data integrity you demand from the system, the more work it has to do and the slower it runs. Therefore, as a database administrator or a system analyst, you will usually have to walk a tightrope between the RDBMS's isolation requirements and its performance.

At the SERIALIZABLE level of isolation, the RDBMS executes transactions sequentially and, thereby, offers the highest level of protection against data corruption. However, because this often involves waiting for locks set by other transactions to be released, it can significantly reduce the speed of your application. At the other end of the spectrum, the READ UNCOMMITTED isolation level allows parallel transactions to see the unsaved changes made by each other, providing much improved performance at a greater risk of inconsistent data. Figure 9-1 illustrates the inverse relationship between transaction security and performance.

MySQL defaults to the REPEATABLE READ isolation level. This isolation level is suitable for most applications, and you would usually only need to alter it if your application has specific need of a higher or lower level. There is no standard formula

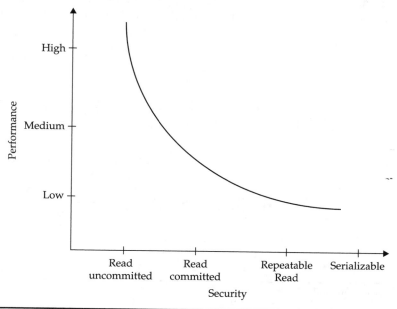

FIGURE 9-1   The relationship between transaction isolation levels and performance

for deciding what isolation level is right for your application—most often, it is a subjective decision reached on the basis of the application's tolerance for errors and of the application developer's judgment of the impact of potentially incorrect data. This selection of isolation level need not even be standard across an application. It's quite likely, for example, that different transactions within the same application might require different isolation levels based on the tasks each is performing.

Avoid Deadlocks

No discussion of transactional performance is complete without a brief look at deadlocks. If you're familiar with OS programming, you might already know what a *deadlock* is—a situation wherein two processes are locked in limbo while accessing the same resource, each waiting for the other to finish.

In a transactional context, a deadlock occurs when two or more clients try to update the same data simultaneously, but in a different sequence. To illustrate, consider Figure 9-2, in which two different transactions are working with the same set of tables, but in a different sequence.

The first transaction is attempting to remove 400 shares from a portfolio account, while the second is trying to add 1,000. Both transactions are initiated at the same time, but the first proceeds by (1) reducing the portfolio account by 400 shares and (2) updating the portfolio net worth table, while the second tries to (1) update the portfolio net worth table to reflect the lower value and (2) deduct 1,000 shares from the portfolio account.

As is clearly visible from the previous example, the result is a deadlock wherein each transaction waits for the other one to finish working with the table it needs to access. If left unresolved, a deadlock such as this would result in each transaction waiting indefinitely for the other one to release its lock on the data. Fortunately, MySQL's InnoDB table handler comes with built-in intelligence to detect deadlock situations.

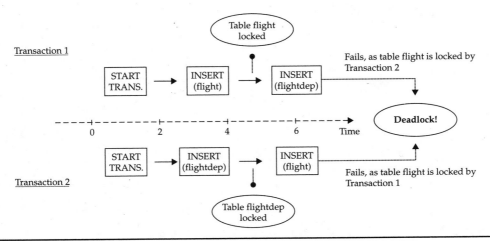

FIGURE 9-2   A transactional deadlock

If it notices one, the InnoDB table handler immediately resolves the deadlock situation by rolling back one of the transactions and releasing its locks, thereby permitting the other one to proceed to its logical end. As in the previous sample output, the client owning the cancelled transaction is notified of the rollback via an error message.

NOTE *A postmortem of the previous deadlock example would reveal that, more than a database issue, it was a result of poor application design. The order in which the tables were manipulated by the two clients was completely different, resulting in the creation of a deadlock. Most often, deadlocks can be avoided through careful planning and design at the application level. This can ensure that resources are shared gracefully between competing processes and that circular chains (such as the one previously demonstrated) are detected and resolved at the earliest possible opportunity.*

A developer can do a number of fundamental things at the application level to avoid deadlocks: obtain all needed locks at the beginning of a session, always process tables in the same order, or include built-in recovery routines to try the transaction again in case it is cancelled by the RDBMS to resolve a deadlock situation.

Optimizing Stored Routines

Stored routines are one of the newer additions to MySQL and, as such, are significantly less optimized than other components of the server. As a result, it's generally not advisable for your application to rely entirely on stored routines, as doing so will likely degrade performance significantly. That said, stored routines do have a role to play in application development and cannot be ignored completely. The following section provides some tips that should help in developing stored routines that don't add undue overhead to an application.

Follow the KISS Principle

MySQL compiles and stores execution plans for stored routines per connection thread. As a result, as the number of clients accessing a stored routine increases, so does the CPU and memory usage required by the stored routine parser. In addition, because there currently exists no mechanism to track cache hits per client or per routine, the server cannot dynamically optimize its caching plan for stored routines. This too results in memory being consumed without necessarily being reclaimed in an optimal fashion.

Keeping these limitations in mind, it's important that stored procedures and functions in MySQL be as simple as possible. Not only do complex stored routines consume more memory, but they take longer to process, straining both the CPU and your application user's patience. In a similar vein, recursive or deeply nested stored routines and stored routines that perform large transactions or use long prepared statements can quickly gobble up server memory and CPU cycles, slowing down other threads accessing the server and affecting overall performance.

Optimize SQL Statements Within Routines

In the final analysis, stored routines are simply containers for blocks of SQL statements. Therefore, it follows that optimizing those SQL statements is the best way to improve stored routine performance. Stored routines that contain loops are the ideal targets for this kind of optimization; keeping in mind that statements within a loop are repeatedly executed, it's often possible to improve performance by "cutting loop flab" and moving out unnecessary statements from the loop. Consider the following simple example, which illustrates:

```
seg: LOOP
  SET @total = @total + 1;
  IF dt BETWEEN '00:00:00' AND '05:59:59' THEN
     UPDATE summary SET night = night + 1;
  ELSEIF dt BETWEEN '06:00:00' AND '11:59:59' THEN
     UPDATE summary SET morning = morning + 1;
  ELSEIF dt BETWEEN '12:00:00' AND '17:59:59' THEN
     UPDATE summary SET afternoon = afternoon + 1;
  ELSEIF dt BETWEEN '18:00:00' AND '23:59:59' THEN
     UPDATE summary SET evening = evening + 1;
  END IF;
END LOOP seg;
```

A better way to do this might be to store the separate counts in individual variables and write them to the summary table after the loop has completed. Similarly, it makes more sense to calculate the total after the loop has completed executing, instead of on each iteration. Here's the revised loop:

```
seg: LOOP
  IF dt BETWEEN '00:00:00' AND '05:59:59' THEN
     SET n = n + 1;
  ELSEIF dt BETWEEN '06:00:00' AND '11:59:59' THEN
     SET m = m + 1;
  ELSEIF dt BETWEEN '12:00:00' AND '17:59:59' THEN
     SET a = a + 1;
  ELSEIF dt BETWEEN '18:00:00' AND '23:59:59' THEN
     SET e = e + 1;
  END IF;
END LOOP seg;
INSERT INTO summary (morning, afternoon, evening, night)
  VALUES (m, a, e, n);
SET @total = morning + afternoon + evening + night;
```

TIP *For an example of improving performance by rewriting MySQL cursors as joins, read Roland Bouman's blog post on the topic, at http://rpbouman.blogspot.com/2006/09/ refactoring-mysql-cursors.html.*

Don't Mix Stored Procedures and Triggers

Triggers with the FOR EACH ROW clause are executed for each record in a table. If these triggers are, in turn, linked to a stored procedure, MySQL will execute the stored procedure as many times as there are records in the table. Needless to say, this is expensive and usually unnecessary. A better approach is to make the trigger as specific as possible, making use of session variables or temporary tables for interim data storage or conditional testing, such that the stored procedure is called only when needed.

Optimizing Table Design

In the context of keeping your queries lean and mean, you need to consider several things in terms of table design. First, if a frequently queried table also gets a lot of changes, the way to improve performance is to stay with fixed-length fields, rather than variable-length ones. The trade-off is this: By definition, fixed-length fields take up a certain amount of space, regardless of the content, whereas variable-length fields adjust themselves depending on the data entered. Thus, you're bound to waste more disk space using fixed-length fields. If it's speed you're after, however, MySQL will perform better with fixed- rather than variable-length fields.

If one field in a frequently changed table cannot be formatted to a fixed length, consider moving that field to a separate table and converting the rest of the fields in the original table to fixed-length fields. Although this might not be workable in all circumstances, it is a viable way to achieve the performance gain of using fixed-length fields rather than variable-length fields.

NOTE *InnoDB tables handle row storage differently from MyISAM or ISAM tables. Using fixed-length fields instead of variable-length ones won't result in a performance boost with these table types.*

This being said, if you *are* going to use fixed-length fields, make sure the field size is kept to a minimum. For example, when designing a table, creating a CHAR(255) field is often easier than worrying about exactly how big you need to make it. In practice, you might find that a field half that size can adequately take care of your needs. Paring the field size not only takes up less disk space, it also means less I/O when processing—and deleting unnecessary fields entirely can also increase performance.

Another technique to improve performance is to use the OPTIMIZE TABLE command frequently on tables that are modified often (discussed more fully in Chapter 12). Frequent modification results in fragmentation, which, in turn, leads to extra time spent reading unused blocks of space to get at the desired data.

When considering ways of improving performance, check to see if you need all the tables you have set up. Again, when originally designing a table, dividing your data might have seemed like a good idea, but extra tables mean your performance will suffer. Look at the tables you join frequently. Is it possible to combine the data into one table instead? If you find you cannot, for whatever reason, try to match the fields you join. Queries will run more efficiently if joined fields are of the same data type and length.

Optimizing Server Settings

If you want your server to perform optimally, the best solution is to get tons of memory and big, fast drives. However, in most situations, these brute-force techniques won't be an option. Given that we operate under less-than-ideal conditions, getting a handle on some subtler techniques for optimizing server performance makes more sense. Accordingly, this section gives a brief overview of some of the major things you can do to fine-tune your server.

As Chapter 10 discusses in detail, MySQL exposes a large number of variables whose values can be modified to meet custom requirements. Some of these variables can be set at the time of starting the MySQL server, and others can be set while the server is running.

When it comes to tuning server variables for maximum performance, the MySQL manual recommends that you first look at the *key_buffer_size* and *table_cache* variables.

- The *key_buffer_size* variable controls the amount of memory available for the MySQL index buffer. The higher this value, the more memory available for indexes and the better the performance. Typically, you would want to keep this value near 25 to 30 percent of the total available memory on the server.

- The *table_cache* variable controls the amount of memory available for the table cache, and thus the total number of tables MySQL can hold open at any given time. For busy servers with many databases and tables, this value should be increased so that MySQL can serve all requests reliably. Also relevant here is the *max_connections* variable, because the MySQL manual recommends setting the *table_cache* value using the formula *(table_cache = max_connections x N)*, where *N* is the number of tables in a typical join.

As noted in Chapter 10, these values can be changed using the SET command, as in the example shown:

```
mysql> SET GLOBAL table_cache=200;
Query OK, 0 rows affected (0.00 sec)
mysql> SELECT @@table_cache;
+---------------+
| @@table_cache |
+---------------+
|           200 |
+---------------+
1 row in set (0.01 sec)
```

Note that once you change a global server variable, it remains in effect until the server is shut down. This means if you find a beneficial setting, you need to reset it on startup every time. Because this is cumbersome, it's useful to know a way of making your changes permanent. This can be accomplished by setting a variable in an option file (discussed in Chapter 10).

Once you've got your table cache and index buffer set up the way you want them, you can turn your attention to the various other memory buffers MySQL uses.

- You can speed up queries that use the ORDER BY or GROUP BY clause to sort the result set by increasing the value of MySQL's sort buffer, controlled via the *sort_buffer* variable. Also consider increasing the *read_rnd_buffer_size* variable to speed up reading of the sorted rows.

- You can speed up SELECT queries that scan the table sequentially by increasing the size of MySQL's read buffer via the *read_buffer_size* variable.

- When performing a transaction, MySQL stores the statements that make up the transaction in a cache until it receives instructions to write them to the binary log and commit them to the database. For long or complex transactions, the size of this cache should be increased to obtain better performance via the *binlog_cache_size* variable.

- If you're planning on so-called "bulk inserts" (that is, inserting multiple records using a single INSERT command), you can speed things up by increasing the value of the *bulk_insert_buffer_size* variable. However, this only works with the MyISAM table type.

- If you're anticipating a lot of new connections to the server, it's a good idea to increase the value of the `thread_cache_size` variable. This variable controls the size of the cache where server threads go when the client they're servicing disconnects. Threads from this cache are then reused to service new connections. The higher this value, the more threads can be cached, and the better the response time to new connection requests.

Benchmarking

Altering the server configuration and optimizing your queries is all very well, but how do you measure the results of your changes and test if there is any appreciable change in performance? Well, the folks at MySQL have got you covered on that one, too. Every MySQL source distribution includes a benchmarking suite called (what else?) the MySQL Benchmark Suite, which does exactly what its name says: It stresses a database server to detect weaknesses, verify compliance with SQL standards, and measure performance.

TIP *The MySQL Benchmark Suite isn't the only game in town. Alternatives exist in the form of SuperSmack, available from http://vegan.net/tony/supersmack, and the Open Source Database Benchmark, available from http://osdb.sourceforge.net.*

In order to run the MySQL Benchmark Suite, you must have Perl installed on your system, together with the Perl DBI package and a MySQL database driver (DBD).

Script name	Test case description
copy-db	Measures copy speed between two servers
crash-me	Tests capabilities of the SQL server by executing different queries
Innotest	Stress test for concurrent inserts, updates, and commits in both transactional (InnoDB) and nontransactional (MyISAM) contexts
test-alter-table	Measures performance of the ALTER TABLE command
test-big-tables	Measures performance with extremely large tables
test-connect	Measures server connection speed
test-create	Measures speed of creating and dropping tables
test-insert	Measures speed of inserting records into a table and then running SELECT queries on it
test-select	Measures SELECT speed with multipart field indexes
test-transactions	Measures speed of transaction rollback
test-wisconsin	Performs the Wisconsin benchmark test
test-ATIS	Performs the ATIS benchmark test

TABLE 9-1 Test Cases in the MySQL Benchmark Suite

If you're using a stock UNIX system, it's quite likely that these packages are already installed. A simple way to test for their presence is to run the following command at your shell prompt:

```
[user@host]$ perl -e "use DBI"
```

If Perl doesn't exit with an error, it's a good bet that the module is installed. If the module isn't installed, you'll have to download it from http://www.cpan.org and install it according to the installation instructions for your platform.

The MySQL Benchmark Suite is located in the *sql-bench/* directory of your MySQL installation. It consists of a number of scripts, together with the raw data for the various benchmark tests. Table 9-1 has a list of these scripts, together with a brief description of what each one does.

The MySQL Benchmark Suite includes support for the Wisconsin benchmark, a widely accepted benchmark for relational database systems. A controlled single-user experiment that uses so-called "synthetic" data instead of "real" data, this benchmark is primarily designed to measure query performance using the metric of elapsed time per query. Test cases include selection, inserts, updates, table joins, and data aggregation.

The simplest way to get started with the MySQL Benchmark Suite is to change to the *sql-bench/* directory and run all the tests using the *run-all-tests* script, like this:

```
[user@host]# /usr/local/mysql/sql-bench/run-all-tests --server=mysql
```

Figure 9-3 illustrates what the output of this might look like.

```
[root@production sql-bench]# ./run-all-tests --server=mysql

Benchmark DBD suite: 2.15
Date of test:        2009-02-20 16:58:31
Running tests on:    Linux 2.6.9-42.ELsmp i686
Arguments:
Comments:
Limits from:
Server version:      MySQL 5.0.37 community log
Optimization:        None
Hardware:

alter-table: Total time: 33 wallclock secs ( 0.03 usr  0.02 sys +  0.00 cusr  0.
00 csys =  0.05 CPU)
ATIS: Total time:  8 wallclock secs ( 5.60 usr  0.25 sys +  0.00 cusr  0.00 csys
 =  5.85 CPU)
big-tables: Total time:  9 wallclock secs ( 4.35 usr  0.41 sys +  0.00 cusr  0.0
0 csys =  4.76 CPU)
connect: Total time: 113 wallclock secs (29.96 usr 11.33 sys +  0.00 cusr  0.00
csys = 41.29 CPU)
create: Total time: 116 wallclock secs ( 2.46 usr  0.76 sys +  0.00 cusr  0.00 c
sys =  3.22 CPU)
insert: ▮
```

FIGURE 9-3 The output of the *run-all-tests* script

As you can see, this script runs each of the test cases listed in Table 9-1, returning the time taken by each. More information on the details of each test case can be obtained by invoking the corresponding script without any parameters. Most of the scripts print a brief description of their purpose before starting.

If you'd like to run a specific test only, you can do that, too, simply by invoking the appropriate script. Consider the following example, which runs the *test-connect* script to benchmark the time taken to connect to the server and send data to it:

```
[user@host]# /usr/local/mysql/sql-bench/test-connect
```

Figure 9-4 illustrates what this might look like.

Notable among the various test scripts included in the MySQL Benchmark Suite is *crash-me,* a utility designed specifically for the purpose of evaluating a SQL server's capabilities by pushing it up to (and beyond) its limits. *Crash-me* works by sending a variety of legal SQL queries to the server and, from its response, determining the feature set, capabilities, and limitations of the server.

CAUTION *In order to test server functionality,* crash-me *pushes the database server to its limits. It will almost certainly affect system performance while it is running and may even cause the server to crash. Therefore, it should be used with care, and never on a production server.*

Figure 9-5 illustrates the output of a *crash-me* run.

```
[root@production sql-bench]#
[root@production sql-bench]# ./test-connect
Testing server 'MySQL 5.0.37 community log' at 2009-02-20 17:04:50

Testing the speed of connecting to the server and sending of data
Connect tests are done 10000 times and other tests 100000 times

Testing connection/disconnect
Time to connect (10000):  6 wallclock secs ( 3.96 usr  0.73 sys +  0.00 cusr  0.
00 csys =  4.69 CPU)

Test connect/simple select/disconnect
Time for connect+select_simple (10000):  8 wallclock secs ( 4.36 usr  0.83 sys +
  0.00 cusr  0.00 csys =  5.19 CPU)

Test simple select
Time for select_simple (100000):  9 wallclock secs ( 2.45 usr  1.36 sys +  0.00
cusr  0.00 csys =  3.81 CPU)

Test simple select
Time for select_simple_cache (100000):  9 wallclock secs ( 2.04 usr  1.44 sys +
 0.00 cusr  0.00 csys =  3.48 CPU)

Testing connect/select 1 row from table/disconnect
```

FIGURE 9-4 The output of the *test-connect* script

```
Group function COUNT (*): yes
Group function COUNT column name: yes
Group function COUNT(DISTINCT expr): yes
Group function MAX on numbers: yes
Group function MAX on strings: yes
Group function MIN on numbers: yes
Group function MIN on strings: yes
Group function SUM: yes
Group function ANY: no
Group function EVERY: no
Group function SOME: no

Supported extra group functions
Group function BIT_AND: yes
Group function BIT_OR: yes
Group function COUNT(DISTINCT expr,expr,...): yes
Group function STD: yes
Group function STDDEV: yes
Group function VARIANCE: yes

mixing of integer and float in expression: yes
No need to cast from integer to float: yes
Is 1+NULL = NULL: yes
Is concat('a',NULL) = NULL: yes
```

FIGURE 9-5 An example *crash-me* run

Summary

This chapter explored the important topic of MySQL performance optimization, discussing some of the techniques and options available to help you squeeze a little more speed out of your MySQL installation. Various strategies for query optimization were covered, including:

- Using indexes to speed up access to frequently used fields
- Using the MySQL query cache to improve query response time
- Analyzing queries with the EXPLAIN SELECT command to understand and then improve the query plan
- Rewriting subqueries as joins to take advantage of MySQL's optimization algorithms
- Using server variables, aggregate functions, and sorting to make multitable queries more efficient
- Selecting an isolation level appropriate to your needs
- Avoiding deadlocks by keeping the internal flow of database transactions consistent
- Using session variables for transient data within stored routines
- Creating data subsets with the INSERT. . .SELECT command and one or more temporary tables to simplify the processing of complex queries
- Choosing field sizes appropriately, and removing unnecessary tables from your database design
- Tuning the server's cache and memory buffers to obtain better performance
- Benchmarking server performance with the MySQL Benchmark Suite to evaluate the results of your changes

Query optimization is almost a science unto itself, and impossible to cover in the limited space available in this chapter. However, these techniques (as well as the additional following links) are essential reading for the efficient operation of your database, and they should be part of every administrator's tool box.

Here are some links for further reading:

- An overview of optimization issues, at http://dev.mysql.com/doc/refman/5.1/en/optimize-overview.html
- Extensive information, tips, and techniques to speed up your MySQL queries and make them run more efficiently, at http://dev.mysql.com/doc/refman/5.1/en/query-speed.html
- Information on optimizing server performance, at http://dev.mysql.com/doc/refman/5.1/en/optimizing-the-server.html
- The MySQL Benchmark Suite, at http://dev.mysql.com/doc/refman/5.1/en/mysql-benchmarks.html
- The MySQL Performance blog, at http://www.mysqlperformanceblog.com

PART II
Administration

CHAPTER 10

Performing Basic Server Administration

Previous chapters of this book have focused more on using MySQL for day-to-day work—creating databases and running queries, defining triggers and events, building stored routines—than on the administrative end of things—managing security, assigning user privileges, and backing up data. More and more often, however, and especially where open-source products are concerned, users are also administrators, responsible for all aspects of system performance, reliability, and data security.

In these cases, merely understanding the intricacies of SQL queries is not sufficient. Users also need to know how to administer a MySQL RDBMS and take over responsibility for ensuring that MySQL services are always available to users of the system. This role involves a number of different facets: securing the MySQL server against unauthorized usage or mischief, assigning users privileges appropriate to their intended use of the system, performing regular checks and backups of the MySQL databases to avoid data corruption or loss, and optimizing the server to ensure that it always delivers the best performance possible.

The next few chapters will explore the different aspects of MySQL server administration, showing you how to accomplish common tasks quickly and efficiently. This chapter serves as a brief introduction to the topic, covering common tasks like starting and stopping the server, obtaining server status, altering server configuration, and using the MySQL log files. It also discusses one of the major new features in MySQL 5.*x*, the *information_schema* database, which provides run-time access to information about database objects.

Database Administration and MySQL

A database administrator holds an important position in an organization's management information system (MIS) team. As the person tasked with the responsibility of ensuring smooth and efficient access to network databases, the job description involves ensuring 24/7/365 database uptime for users and applications, performing regular backups to avoid data corruption or loss in the event of a system crash, tuning server parameters for maximum performance, and securing the database against malicious mischief and unauthorized access. Even individually, none of these tasks can be called simple; taken together, they constitute one of the most demanding—and challenging—positions in the industry.

Luckily, MySQL comes with sophisticated tools to help the beleaguered database administrator in his or her daily chores.

Uptime

Intelligent design decisions by the developers of MySQL have meant that, so far as uptime is concerned, there's almost nothing a database administrator need worry about. MySQL is designed to offer maximum reliability and uptime, and has been tested and certified for use in high-volume, mission-critical applications by companies like SAP, Motorola, Sony, Yahoo!, NASA, and HP (just to name a few).

A common cause of system crashes involves glitches, or "bugs," in the application code. MySQL's open-source history makes this less of a problem than with its more commercial counterparts. Since MySQL development occurs in full view of the public, a final release has the unique benefit of being exhaustively tested by users all over the world, on a variety of different platforms and in a range of different environments, before it is certified for use in production environments. This approach has resulted in an RDBMS that is both exceedingly stable and virtually bug-free.

Data Backup

While MySQL is certainly extremely stable and reliable, and quite capable of running itself without any special care required, basic maintenance and an established backup and restoration process is required from the administrator in any production environment. A backup regimen, in particular, is critical to ensuring that the data stored in an organization's databases does not get corrupted or lost in the event of a disk failure or system crash.

With this in mind, MySQL comes with a number of tools designed to speed up this process and make it more efficient. The most important of these is the *mysqldump* utility, discussed in Chapter 12, which makes it possible to write MySQL table structures, table data, or both to backup files in a variety of different formats. The output of *mysqldump* can be used to easily and quickly restore one or more MySQL databases, either from the command-line with the *mysqlimport* utility or via the LOAD DATA INFILE command, discussed in Chapter 8. In the event of table corruption, MySQL improves the chances of data recovery through a suite of recovery utilities, which are extremely good at delving into the innards of a corrupted table and either fixing it completely or repairing the damage to a point where most of its data can be recovered.

MySQL also comes with built-in replication, which makes it possible to mirror the changes made on one database server to other servers using predefined master-slave relationships. Earlier versions of MySQL only supported one-way replication; newer versions now support two-way replication as well, for more sophisticated mirroring and load-balancing.

Security and Access Control

MySQL comes with a sophisticated access control and privilege system to prevent unauthorized users from accessing the system. This system, implemented as a five-tiered privilege hierarchy, makes it possible to create comprehensive access rules that MySQL uses when deciding how to handle a particular user request.

- Connections to the server are allowed only if they match the access rules laid down in the MySQL privilege system. These access rules can be specified on the basis of user and/or host, and can be used to restrict access from hosts outside a specific subnetwork or IP address range. Further, such connections to the server are permitted only after the user provides a valid password.

- Once a connection has been established, MySQL checks every action performed by a user to verify whether he or she has sufficient privileges to perform it. Users can be restricted to performing operations only on specified databases or fields, and MySQL even makes it possible to control which types of queries a user can run: at database, table, or field level.

The security of the system is further enhanced through the use of a one-way encryption scheme for user passwords. Newer versions of MySQL also support Secure Sockets Layer (SSL), which can be used to encrypt the data sent out over the MySQL client-server connection (such as query results) for greater security.

Performance Optimization

Once the routine matters—backing up data and securing the system—have been taken care of, a database administrator must usually focus on squeezing the maximum performance out of the RDBMS. MySQL's multithreaded engine and numerous optimization algorithms make this activity less critical than it usually is. An out-of-the-box MySQL installation is usually blazingly fast and requires very little alteration.

That said, it is certainly possible to tune MySQL to specific needs. MySQL exposes a fair number of its internal parameters via system variables, and allows developers and administrators to easily modify them to meet custom requirements. Many of the features that degrade performance—transactions, referential integrity, and stored procedures—can be enabled or disabled at the user's choice, thereby making it possible to select the optimal mix of features and performance on a per-application basis. Commands like ANALYZE TABLE and EXPLAIN SELECT assist SQL developers in benchmarking queries and identifying performance bottlenecks, while new features like the query cache (which works by caching the results of common queries and returning this cached data to the caller without having to reexecute the query every time) help in improving performance without too much extra programming. Many of these features have already been discussed in detail in Chapter 9.

An important issue when discussing performance is scalability. Too many database systems work exceedingly well when dealing with a few thousands of records, but display a significant drop in performance when the numbers jump into the millions. No such problems with MySQL, though. The RDBMS is built to be extremely scalable, and can handle extremely large and complex databases (tables of several gigabytes containing hundreds of thousands of records) without breaking a sweat. This makes MySQL suitable for everything ranging from simple content-based websites to extremely large and diversified data networks, such as the ones used in e-tailing, data warehousing, or business knowledge management.

Understanding Basic Server Administration

The MySQL distribution ships with a command-line tool designed specifically to help administrators perform common tasks, such as changing the MySQL administrator password or reloading MySQL privileges. This tool, called *mysqladmin,* can be found in the *bin/* directory of your MySQL installation, and it is usually invoked with one or more commands, as shown:

```
[root@host]# /usr/local/mysql/bin/mysqladmin shutdown
```

Table 10-1 lists the more useful commands supported by *mysqladmin.*

Command	What It Does
status	Returns information on server state
password	Changes a user password
shutdown	Shuts down the MySQL server
reload	Reloads the MySQL grant tables
refresh	Resets all caches and logs
variables	Returns values of all server variables
version	Returns the server version
processlist	Returns a list of all processes active on the server
kill	Kills an active server process
ping	Tests if the server is alive

TABLE 10-1   Commands Supported by *mysqladmin*

You can obtain a complete list of available commands by running *mysqladmin --help*.

TIP   *If you don't like command-line administration, there are two graphical alternatives to the* mysqladmin *tool:* phpMyAdmin, *a browser-based interface to MySQL administration, and* MySQL Administrator, *a visual tool for user administration, database backup and restore, log analysis, and server fine-tuning.*

Starting and Stopping the Server

On UNIX, MySQL comes with a startup/shutdown script, which is the recommended way of starting and stopping the MySQL database server. This script, named *mysql.server*, is available in the *support-files/* subdirectory of your MySQL installation, and it can be invoked as follows to start the MySQL server:

```
[root@host]# /usr/local/mysql/support-files/mysql.server start
```

An alternative approach is to invoke the server directly by calling the *mysqld_safe* wrapper, as shown:

```
[root@host]# /usr/local/mysql/bin/mysqld_safe --user=mysql &
```

While you can certainly invoke MySQL by directly executing the *mysqld* binary from your installation's *bin/* directory, this is not a recommended approach. Using the *mysqld_safe* wrapper is considered a safe approach, as this wrapper takes care of automatically logging errors and runtime information to a file and of restarting the MySQL daemon in case of an unexpected shutdown.

NOTE *In older versions of MySQL,* mysqld_safe *is called* safe_mysqld.

On Windows, the easiest way to start the MySQL server is by diving into the *bin/* subdirectory of your MySQL installation and launching the *mysqld.exe* program. Alternatively, you can install MySQL as a Windows service, such that it starts and stops automatically with Windows, by changing to the *bin/* subdirectory of your MySQL installation directory and launching the *mysqld.exe* program with the special *--install* argument, as shown:

```
C:\mysql\bin> mysqld.exe --install
```

You can verify that the server is running by using the *mysqladmin ping* command, as shown; this returns a status message indicating whether the server is active:

```
[root@host]# /usr/local/mysql/bin/mysqladmin ping
mysqld is alive
```

The *mysqladmin* utility can also be used to reload the server's grant tables, as shown (this example is for UNIX; simply replace the path with the correct path to your MySQL installation for Windows):

```
[root@host]# /usr/local/mysql/bin/mysqladmin reload
```

Once the server is running, you can shut it down at any time with the *mysqladmin shutdown* command. On UNIX, it looks like this:

```
[root@host]# /usr/local/mysql/bin/mysqladmin shutdown
mysqld is alive
```

On UNIX, you can also use the provided *mysql.server* startup/shutdown script to shut down the server, as shown:

```
[root@host]# /usr/local/mysql/support-files/mysql.server stop
```

On Windows, you will usually need to open a new Command Prompt window, or use the Start | Run dialog box to execute these commands, as shown:

```
C:\> c:\mysql\bin\mysqladmin shutdown
```

CAUTION *Resist the urge to shut down MySQL by abruptly killing the* mysqld *process with the* kill *command (UNIX) or the Task Manager (Windows), as such premature termination can cause data loss or corruption if the server is in the process of writing data to the disk when it receives the termination signal.*

Checking MySQL Server Status

You can find out the current state of the server (server uptime, queries per second, number of currently open tables, and so on) via the *mysqladmin status* command. Here's an example:

```
[root@host]# /usr/local/mysql/bin/mysqladmin status
Uptime: 10208  Threads: 1  Questions: 540  Slow queries: 0  Opens: 49
Flush tables: 1   Open tables: 0  Queries per second avg: 0.52
```

The *mysqladmin version* command offers a more concise summary, together with information on the MySQL server version:

```
[root@host]# /usr/local/mysql/bin/mysqladmin version
Server version          5.1.30-community
Protocol version        10
Connection              localhost via TCP/IP
TCP port                3306
Uptime:                 3 hours 23 min 38 sec

Threads: 1  Questions: 541  Slow queries: 0  Opens: 49
Flush tables: 1  Open tables: 0  Queries per second avg: 0.44
```

An equivalent approach is to use the VERSION() built-in function, as shown:

```
mysql> SELECT VERSION();
+------------------+
| VERSION()        |
+------------------+
| 5.1.30-community |
+------------------+
1 row in set (0.02 sec)
```

Extended status information is also available via the *mysqladmin extended-status* command, or with the SHOW STATUS command:

```
mysql> SHOW STATUS;
+-----------------------------------+----------+
| Variable_name                     | Value    |
+-----------------------------------+----------+
| Aborted_clients                   | 0        |
| Aborted_connects                  | 0        |
| Binlog_cache_disk_use             | 0        |
| Binlog_cache_use                  | 0        |
| Bytes_received                    | 116      |
| Bytes_sent                        | 255      |
...
```

```
| Threads_cached                  | 1       |
| Threads_connected               | 1       |
| Threads_created                 | 2       |
| Threads_running                 | 1       |
| Uptime                          | 12300   |
| Uptime_since_flush_status       | 12300   |
+---------------------------------+---------+
290 rows in set (0.11 sec)
```

As you can see, this extended status message provides a great deal of real-time status information. The report contains the amount of traffic the server has received since it was last started, including the number of bytes sent and received and the client connections, together with a breakdown of how many succeeded, how many failed, and how many were aborted. It also contains statistics on the total number of queries processed by the server since startup, together with information on the number of queries in each type (SELECT, DELETE, INSERT, ...), the number of threads active, the number of current client connections, the number of running queries, and the number of open tables.

Managing MySQL Client Processes

It's also possible to obtain a complete list of all client processes connected to the server with the SHOW PROCESSLIST command, as shown:

```
mysql> SHOW PROCESSLIST\G
*************************** 1. row ***************************
     Id: 57
   User: root
   Host: localhost:3390
     db: NULL
Command: Query
   Time: 0
  State: NULL
   Info: SHOW PROCESSLIST
*************************** 2. row ***************************
     Id: 64
   User: propertysg
   Host: localhost:3399
     db: NULL
Command: Sleep
   Time: 128
  State:
   Info: NULL
*************************** 3. row ***************************
     Id: 65
   User: gwl
   Host: localhost:3400
     db: gwl
```

```
Command: Sleep
   Time: 18
  State:
   Info: NULL
3 rows in set (0.00 sec)
```

A "regular" user will only be able to see his or her own threads in the output of SHOW PROCESSLIST. Users with the PROCESS privilege will, however, be able to see all running threads, and users with the all-powerful SUPER privilege will even be able to kill running threads with the KILL command. Here's an example:

```
mysql> KILL 64;
Query OK, 0 rows affected (0.01 sec)
```

The *mysqladmin* tool offers equivalent *processlist* and *kill* commands as well.

NOTE *It's important to note that a thread does not die immediately on receiving a kill signal. Rather, MySQL sets a kill flag for that particular thread, which is checked by the thread once it has completed whatever operation it is currently performing. This approach is considered safer than an immediate kill, since it allows the thread to complete whatever it's doing and release any locks it's created before terminating. Threads typically check for a kill flag after every significant read or write operation.*

More information on the MySQL privilege system, together with instructions on how to assign privileges to users, is available in Chapter 11.

Altering the Server Configuration

Most of the time, you won't need to alter MySQL's default configuration—the software comes preconfigured to meet most common needs. However, in case the default configuration doesn't work for you, MySQL exposes a large number of variables whose values can be modified to meet custom requirements. Some of these variables can be set at the time of starting the MySQL server; others can be set while the server is running.

Using an Option File

The recommended method of setting MySQL options is through an *option file*— essentially, an ASCII configuration file containing variable-value pairs that the MySQL server reads when it starts up. MySQL looks for this option file in some standard places when it starts up.

- On Windows, MySQL will look for option files named *my.ini* or *my.cnf* in the MySQL installation directory, the Windows installation directory, or the drive root directory.

- On UNIX, MySQL will look for an option file named *my.cnf* in /etc, /etc/mysql, the MySQL installation directory, and the user home directory.

You can tell MySQL client programs, such as *mysql* and *mysqladmin,* to look for startup options in a different place by invoking these programs with the *--defaults-file* option and the file path.

The format of an option file is fairly simple, and resembles a Windows INI file; it is broken up into groups, each containing variable-value pairs. Any option that can be given on the command line can be placed in this file, without the leading double dash. Here's an example:

```
[mysqld]
port=3306
skip-locking
log-bin
skip-bdb
```

TIP *A number of sample configuration files ship with the MySQL distribution. Take a look inside* my-large.cnf, my-huge.cnf, my-medium.cnf, *and* my-small.cnf *to get a better idea of how these files can be used.*

Typically, MySQL looks in the groups [mysql] and [mysqld] for configuration options. On UNIX, if you're using the *mysqld_safe* wrapper script to start MySQL, you can also use the [mysqld_safe] group to pass options to MySQL.

All the binary programs that ship with MySQL can read options from an options file. Simply specify the program name as a group (by enclosing it within square brackets) in the option file and follow it with the variables you want to set. MySQL client programs can also make use of a special [client] group, which is typically used to store user and password connection parameters. Here's a simple example of how this works:

```
[client]
user=timothy
password=greenpeas
```

In this case, whenever any MySQL client program attempts a connection to a MySQL server, it will default to connecting as "timothy" with the password "greenpeas."

Table 10-2 lists the more common and useful options available to configure the MySQL server (refer to the MySQL manual for the complete list).

It's important to note that all of these options can be specified on the MySQL command line as well, simply by prefixing the option name with a double dash. The following example illustrates:

```
[root@host]# /usr/local/mysql/bin/mysqld_safe --socket=/usr/tmp/mysql.socket
--user=mysql --skip-networking &
```

In case multiple option files exist, or the same option is specified multiple times with different values, MySQL uses the last found value. Since MySQL reads option files before command-line arguments, this means that options specified on the command line take precedence over options in an option file.

Option	What It Means
ansi	Uses stricter ANSI SQL-99 syntax
basedir	Sets location of MySQL installation directory
datadir	Sets location of MySQL data directory
debug	Creates a debug file
default-character-set	Sets default character set
default-table-type	Sets default table type for new tables
init-file	Sets a file containing SQL commands to be executed at startup
language	Sets the language for error messages
log	Writes MySQL messages (connections and queries) to log
log-error	Writes critical error messages to log
log-warnings	Writes warning messages to log
port	Sets port to accept client connections
safe-show-database	Only shows databases to which user has access
skip-innodb	Disables the InnoDB table handler
skip-grant-tables	Bypasses grant tables when performing access control
skip-networking	Only allows local requests; stops listening for TCP/IP requests
socket	Sets name of socket/named pipe to use for local connections
transaction-isolation	Sets default transaction isolation level
user	Specifies the user the server should run as
tmpdir	Sets location for temporary files

TABLE 10-2   MySQL Server Command-Line Options

TIP *If your application is on the same physical machine as the MySQL server and you don't anticipate MySQL client connections from other hosts, using the --skip-networking option to turn off TCP/IP listening can significantly enhance the security of your MySQL installation.*

Using the SET Command

MySQL also allows you to modify server variables while the server is running, using the SET command. Here's an example, in which the SET command is used to set the default table type for new tables:

```
mysql> SET table_type = innodb;
Query OK, 0 rows affected (0.00 sec)
```

Variables set using the SET command can be set globally for all sessions, or only for the current session, by following the SET keyword with either the GLOBAL or SESSION keyword. The default, when no keyword is specified, is to assume the SESSION keyword. The following example limits the server to 10 client connections at any time and sets the size of the read buffer to 250KB:

```
mysql> SET GLOBAL max_user_connections=10, SESSION read_buffer_size=250000;
Query OK, 0 rows affected (0.08 sec)
```

Note that the SUPER privilege is required for setting GLOBAL variables. You can read more about the MySQL privilege system in Chapter 11.

Table 10-3 lists some important variables that can be set using the SET command (refer to the MySQL manual for the complete list).

Variable	What It Does
autocommit	Toggles autocommit mode on/off
key_buffer_size	Sets the size of the buffer used for indexes
table_cache	Sets the total number of tables MySQL can hold open at any given time
table_type	Sets the default table type
concurrent_inserts	Permits concurrent INSERTs and SELECTs on MyISAM tables
interactive_timeout	Sets the timeout for interactive client connections
language	Sets the language used for error messages
lower_case_table_names	Automatically lowercases table names
sort_buffer_size	Sets the maximum size of the buffer used for sorting results
read_buffer_size	Sets the size of the buffer used for table reads
max_binlog_size	Sets the maximum size of the binary log
max_connections	Sets the maximum number of client connections allowed at any given time
max_user_connections	Sets the maximum number of connections a single user can have active at any given time
max_tmp_tables	Sets the maximum number of temporary tables a client can keep open at any given time
query_cache_type	Toggles the query cache on/off
query_cache_size	Sets the maximum size of the query cache
sql_mode	Sets the server's SQL mode
tmpdir	Sets the location of the temporary file area
tx_isolation	Sets the transaction isolation level

TABLE 10-3 MySQL Server Variables

Retrieving Variable Values

Once a variable has been set, either via SET or through a startup option, its value can be
retrieved using the SHOW VARIABLES command or by invoking the *mysqladmin variables*
command. Since the output of SHOW VARIABLES is somewhat prodigious, MySQL
allows you to filter it down to just the variable you want through the addition of a
LIKE clause, as shown:

```
mysql> SHOW VARIABLES LIKE 'table_type';
+---------------+--------+
| Variable_name | Value  |
+---------------+--------+
| table_type    | InnoDB |
+---------------+--------+
1 row in set (0.08 sec)

mysql> SHOW VARIABLES LIKE '%innodb%';
+--------------------------------+-----------------------+
| Variable_name                  | Value                 |
+--------------------------------+-----------------------+
| have_innodb                    | YES                   |
| innodb_adaptive_hash_index     | ON                    |
| innodb_additional_mem_pool_size | 2097152              |
| innodb_autoextend_increment    | 8                     |
| innodb_autoinc_lock_mode       | 1                     |
| innodb_buffer_pool_size        | 48234496              |
| innodb_checksums               | ON                    |
| innodb_commit_concurrency      | 0                     |
| innodb_concurrency_tickets     | 500                   |
| innodb_data_file_path          | ibdata1:10M:autoextend |
| innodb_data_home_dir           |                       |
| innodb_doublewrite             | ON                    |
| innodb_fast_shutdown           | 1                     |
| innodb_file_io_threads         | 4                     |
| innodb_file_per_table          | OFF                   |
| innodb_flush_log_at_trx_commit | 1                     |
| innodb_flush_method            |                       |
| innodb_force_recovery          | 0                     |
| innodb_lock_wait_timeout       | 50                    |
| innodb_locks_unsafe_for_binlog | OFF                   |
| innodb_log_buffer_size         | 1048576               |
| innodb_log_file_size           | 24117248              |
| innodb_log_files_in_group      | 2                     |
| innodb_log_group_home_dir      | .\                    |
| innodb_max_dirty_pages_pct     | 90                    |
| innodb_max_purge_lag           | 0                     |
| innodb_mirrored_log_groups     | 1                     |
| innodb_open_files              | 300                   |
| innodb_rollback_on_timeout     | OFF                   |
| innodb_support_xa              | ON                    |
| innodb_sync_spin_loops         | 20                    |
```

```
| innodb_table_locks            | ON                        |
| innodb_thread_concurrency     | 8                         |
| innodb_thread_sleep_delay     | 10000                     |
+-------------------------------+---------------------------+
```

You can also obtain the value of a system variable using the SELECT @@GLOBAL
.*variable* or SELECT @@LOCAL.*variable* syntax, as shown:

```
mysql> SELECT @@GLOBAL.tx_isolation;
+-----------------------+
| @@GLOBAL.tx_isolation |
+-----------------------+
| REPEATABLE-READ       |
+-----------------------+
1 row in set (0.00 sec)
```

Setting the Server's SQL Mode

With newer versions of MySQL, it is possible to alter the server's default behavior in
certain situations by changing its *SQL mode*. Think of the SQL mode as a modifier for
how the server reacts in certain situations—for example, when an invalid date value is
entered or when a division-by-zero error occurs. MySQL comes with a number of SQL
modes, some of which are listed in Table 10-4.

SQL Mode	Description
ANSI	Operate as per ANSI SQL conventions
STRICT_ALL_TABLES	Abort operations containing invalid values
STRICT_TRANS_TABLES	Abort operations containing invalid values on transactional tables
ONLY_FULL_GROUP_BY	Reject SELECT statements containing fields other than those specified in the GROUP BY clause
NO_ENGINE_SUBSTITUTION	Disable automatic substitution of one storage engine by another
NO_BACKSLASH_ESCAPES	Disable use of the backslash (\) character to escape strings
NO_AUTO_CREATE_USER	Disable automatic creation of MySQL user accounts unless a password is provided
ERROR_FOR_DIVISION_BY_ZERO	Reject INSERT/UPDATE statements containing a division-by-zero operation (only in STRICT_ALL_TABLES or STRICT_TRANS_TABLES modes)
NO_ZERO_DATE	Reject date values containing zeroes (only in STRICT_ALL_TABLES or STRICT_TRANS_TABLES modes)
ALLOW_INVALID_DATES	Allow invalid date values (only in STRICT_ALL_TABLES or STRICT_TRANS_TABLES modes)

TABLE 10-4 MySQL SQL Modes

These SQL modes can be set independently of each other. They are controlled by the *sql_mode* variable, and can be altered using the SET command (separate multiple modes with commas). Here's an example, which enables "strict" checking of values on all tables:

```
mysql> SET GLOBAL sql_mode = 'STRICT_ALL_TABLES';
Query OK, 0 rows affected (0.00 sec)

mysql> SELECT @@GLOBAL.sql_mode;
+-------------------+
| @@GLOBAL.sql_mode |
+-------------------+
| STRICT_ALL_TABLES |
+-------------------+
1 row in set (0.00 sec)
```

Here's another example, which forces the server to generate an error when a division-by-zero operation occurs:

```
mysql> SET sql_mode = '';
Query OK, 0 rows affected (0.00 sec)

mysql> CREATE TEMPORARY TABLE x (f INT);
Query OK, 0 rows affected (0.13 sec)

mysql> INSERT INTO x VALUES (1/0);
Query OK, 1 row affected (0.05 sec)

mysql> SET sql_mode = 'ERROR_FOR_DIVISION_BY_ZERO,STRICT_TRANS_TABLES';
Query OK, 0 rows affected (0.00 sec)

mysql> INSERT INTO x VALUES (1/0);
ERROR 1365 (22012): Division by 0
```

Troubleshooting with the Error Log

In case of difficulties starting the server, or if errors appear during its operation, it's always a good idea to check the MySQL error log in order to identify the cause(s) of the error. As the following brief sample illustrates, this log file stores information on server startup and shutdown, together with a list of critical error messages and warnings about corrupted tables:

```
090224  9:42:52  InnoDB: Database was not shut down normally!
InnoDB: Starting crash recovery.
InnoDB: Reading tablespace information from the .ibd files...
InnoDB: Restoring possible half-written data pages from the doublewrite
InnoDB: buffer...
```

```
090224   9:42:54   InnoDB: Started; log sequence number 0 359286
090224   9:42:54   [Note] Event Scheduler: Loaded 0 events
090224   9:42:54   [Note] C:\Program Files\MySQL\bin\mysqld.exe: ready for
connections.
Version: '5.1.30-community'   socket: ''   port: 3306   MySQL Community
Server (GPL)
```

By default, this file is called *hostname.err* in Windows and UNIX, and is always located in the MySQL *data/* directory. It's possible to specify a different location for the error log file by adding the *--log-error* argument to the MySQL server command line, as illustrated:

```
[root@host]# /usr/local/mysql/bin/mysqld_safe --log-error=/tmp/mysqld.errors
--user=mysql &
```

More information on how to repair corrupted tables is available in Chapter 12, as is information on other log files maintained by MySQL.

Obtaining Database Meta-Information

In this and previous chapters, you've seen various examples of MySQL's SHOW statement in action. This statement provides information on various aspects of a database and its tables. For example, the SHOW TABLES statement displays a list of all the tables in a database, while the SHOW CREATE PROCEDURE statement displays the internals of a particular stored procedure.

Up until MySQL 5.0, SHOW statements were the only way to access so-called "meta-information" about database objects. However, MySQL 5.0 introduced a new database, the *information_schema* database, which now serves as a central repository of information about all database objects, including tables, stored routines, triggers, events, views, system variables, user accounts … simply put, anything and everything related to the database server!

This central *information_schema* database can be accessed using standard SELECT statements, eliminating the need for SHOW statements and providing a consistent, standards-compliant interface to database meta-information. The information within this database is automatically updated by the MySQL server, and thus provides a snapshot of the database in operation at any given instant.

The *information_schema* database contains a number of tables, each holding information on a different type of database object. Table 10-5 has a list of the tables and a description of what each one contains.

Table Name	Type of Information
CHARACTER_SETS	Character sets
COLLATIONS	Collations
COLLATION_CHARACTER_SET_APLICABILITY	Mapping between character sets and collations

TABLE 10-5   Tables in the *information_schema* Database

Table Name	Type of Information
COLUMNS	Field names, data types, and modifiers
COLUMN_PRIVILEGES	Field-level privileges
ENGINES	Storage engines
EVENTS	Events
FILES	Files used by NDB (clustered) tables
GLOBAL_STATUS	Server status information (global variables)
GLOBAL_VARIABLES	Other global variables
KEY_COLUMN_USAGE	Index names, source fields, and types
PARTITIONS	User-defined table partitions
PLUGINS	Plug-ins
PROCESSLIST	Active server processes
PROFILING	Server profiling and benchmarking statistics
REFERENTIAL_CONSTRAINTS	Foreign keys
ROUTINES	Stored routines
SCHEMATA	Databases
SCHEMA_PRIVILEGES	Database-level privileges
SESSION_STATUS	Server status information (session variables)
SESSION_VARIABLES	Other session variables
STATISTICS	Index statistics
TABLES	Table names and types
TABLE_CONSTRAINTS	Table constraints
TABLE_PRIVILEGES	Table-level privileges
TRIGGERS	Triggers
USER_PRIVILEGES	User-level privileges
VIEWS	Views

TABLE 10-5 Tables in the *information_schema* Database *(continued)*

To illustrate, consider the next example, which produces a list of all the tables in the *db1* database by querying the *information_schema.TABLES* table (and generating output similar to that of the SHOW TABLES statement):

```
mysql> SELECT TABLE_NAME, TABLE_TYPE, ENGINE,
    -> TABLE_ROWS, AVG_ROW_LENGTH FROM TABLES
    -> WHERE TABLE_SCHEMA = 'db1';
```

```
+---------------+-------------+----------+--------------+-----------------+
| TABLE_NAME    | TABLE_TYPE  | ENGINE   | TABLE_ROWS   | AVG_ROW_LENGTH  |
+---------------+-------------+----------+--------------+-----------------+
| aircraft      | BASE TABLE  | MyISAM   |          16  |              32 |
| aircrafttype  | BASE TABLE  | MyISAM   |           6  |              20 |
| airport       | BASE TABLE  | MyISAM   |          15  |              47 |
| class         | BASE TABLE  | MyISAM   |           3  |              20 |
| flight        | BASE TABLE  | MyISAM   |          32  |               7 |
| flightclass   | BASE TABLE  | MyISAM   |           7  |              12 |
| flightdep     | BASE TABLE  | MyISAM   |         108  |               7 |
| log           | BASE TABLE  | MyISAM   |          13  |              60 |
| pax           | BASE TABLE  | MyISAM   |           3  |              45 |
| route         | BASE TABLE  | MyISAM   |          29  |              12 |
| stats         | BASE TABLE  | MyISAM   |           8  |              20 |
+---------------+-------------+----------+--------------+-----------------+
11 rows in set (0.00 sec)
```

Here's another example, which lists the triggers on *db1* by querying the *information_schema.TRIGGERS* table (producing output similar to that of the SHOW TRIGGERS FROM. . . statement):

```
mysql> SELECT TRIGGER_NAME, EVENT_MANIPULATION,
    -> ACTION_TIMING FROM TRIGGERS WHERE
    -> TRIGGER_SCHEMA = 'db1';
+---------------+--------------------+----------------+
| TRIGGER_NAME  | EVENT_MANIPULATION | ACTION_TIMING  |
+---------------+--------------------+----------------+
| flight_au     | UPDATE             | AFTER          |
| flight_ad     | DELETE             | AFTER          |
+---------------+--------------------+----------------+
2 rows in set (0.52 sec)
```

Want to obtain a list of user accounts and the privileges for each? Query the *information_schema.USER_PRIVILEGES* table, as shown:

```
mysql> SELECT GRANTEE, PRIVILEGE_TYPE FROM USER_PRIVILEGES;
+----------------------------+-------------------------+
| GRANTEE                    | PRIVILEGE_TYPE          |
+----------------------------+-------------------------+
| 'moodle'@'localhost'       | USAGE                   |
| 'propertysg'@'localhost'   | USAGE                   |
| 'metsons'@'localhost'      | USAGE                   |
| 'oxid'@'localhost'         | USAGE                   |
| 'goalee'@'localhost'       | USAGE                   |
| 'library'@'localhost'      | USAGE                   |
| 'root'@'127.0.0.1'         | SELECT                  |
| 'root'@'127.0.0.1'         | INSERT                  |
| 'root'@'127.0.0.1'         | UPDATE                  |
...
```

```
| ''@'localhost'                |  USAGE                         |
+-------------------------------+-------------------------------+
64 rows in set (0.00 sec)
```

To obtain a list of active client connections, such as that shown with the SHOW PROCESSLIST statement, query the *information_schema.PROCESSLIST* table, as shown:

```
mysql> SELECT ID, USER, HOST, DB, STATE FROM PROCESSLIST;
+----+--------+----------------+--------------------+----------+
| ID | USER   | HOST           | DB                 | STATE    |
+----+--------+----------------+--------------------+----------+
|  5 | gwl    | localhost:3131 | information_schema |          |
|  4 | moodle | localhost:3130 | information_schema |          |
|  3 | root   | localhost:3094 | information_schema | executing |
+----+--------+----------------+--------------------+----------+
3 rows in set (0.00 sec)
```

MySQL only permits reading data from tables within the *information_schema* database. Any attempt to insert new records or modify existing ones will be rejected:

```
mysql> INSERT INTO USER_PRIVILEGES
    -> VALUES ('dummy@localhost', NULL, 'INSERT', 'YES');
ERROR 1044 (42000): Access denied for user 'root'@'localhost' to database
'information_schema'
```

It's also important to note that MySQL will automatically take note of user privileges when displaying information from tables in the *information_schema* database. So, for example, if user *gwl@localhost* only has access privileges to database *gwl*, SELECT statements executed by this user on the *information_schema* database will only return information for the *gwl* database and not for any other. To illustrate, consider the following examples, which demonstrate how MySQL automatically restricts the information shown to *gwl@localhost* for various SELECT queries:

```
mysql> SELECT CURRENT_USER();
+----------------+
| CURRENT_USER() |
+----------------+
| gwl@localhost  |
+----------------+
1 row in set (0.00 sec)

mysql> SHOW GRANTS FOR 'gwl'@'localhost'\G
*************************** 1. row ***************************
Grants for gwl@localhost: GRANT USAGE ON *.* TO 'gwl'@'localhost'
*************************** 2. row ***************************
Grants for gwl@localhost: GRANT ALL PRIVILEGES ON `gwl`.* TO
'gwl'@'localhost'
2 rows in set (0.00 sec)
```

```
mysql> SELECT SCHEMA_NAME FROM SCHEMATA;
+--------------------+
| SCHEMA_NAME        |
+--------------------+
| information_schema |
| gwl                |
| test               |
+--------------------+
3 rows in set (0.00 sec)

mysql> SELECT GRANTEE, PRIVILEGE_TYPE FROM USER_PRIVILEGES;
+-------------------+----------------+
| GRANTEE           | PRIVILEGE_TYPE |
+-------------------+----------------+
| 'gwl'@'localhost' | USAGE          |
+-------------------+----------------+
1 row in set (0.00 sec)

mysql> SELECT ID, USER, HOST, DB, STATE FROM PROCESSLIST;
+----+------+----------------+--------------------+-----------+
| ID | USER | HOST           | DB                 | STATE     |
+----+------+----------------+--------------------+-----------+
|  5 | gwl  | localhost:3131 | information_schema | executing |
+----+------+----------------+--------------------+-----------+
1 row in set (0.02 sec)
```

Summary

This chapter offered a brief introduction to MySQL database administration, outlining the most common tasks database administrators are expected to perform and providing a brief look at the MySQL tools available to accomplish these tasks. Chief among these is the *mysqladmin* utility, which makes it possible to reload or shut down the server, view a list of active processes, and obtain current values of server variables—you'll be seeing a lot of this tool in your administrative role.

This chapter then proceeded to a discussion of the more basic tasks in the pantheon of MySQL administration, including starting and stopping the MySQL server, configuring the server to start automatically at boot time, obtaining server status, managing server processes, altering the server configuration through a configuration file or the SET command, and troubleshooting problems using the MySQL error log. It also discussed the new *information_schema* database that ships with MySQL 5.0 and later, and illustrates how this database could be used to obtain "live" information on various database objects.

Of course, this is just the tip of the iceberg. MySQL offers the database administrator a number of powerful features to help him or her maintain the server effectively and efficiently. The next few chapters will examine some of these features in greater depth. In the meanwhile, here are some links for further reading:

- The *mysqladmin* utility program, at http://dev.mysql.com/doc/refman/5.1/en/mysqladmin.html

- Server SQL modes, at http://dev.mysql.com/doc/refman/5.1/en/server-sql-mode.html

- Server options and variables, at http://dev.mysql.com/doc/refman/5.1/en/mysqld-option-tables.html

- The SET and SHOW statements, at http://dev.mysql.com/doc/refman/5.1/en/set-option.html and http://dev.mysql.com/doc/refman/4.1/en/show.html

- The *information_schema* database, at http://dev.mysql.com/doc/refman/5.1/en/information-schema.html

PART II

CHAPTER 11

Managing Users and Controlling Access

MySQL comes with a sophisticated access control and privilege system to prevent unauthorized clients from accessing the system. This system, implemented as a hierarchy, makes it possible to create comprehensive access rules that MySQL uses when deciding how to handle a particular client operation.

This chapter examines the MySQL access control system and throws some light on the MySQL grant tables. These tables, which are an integral part of the server's security system, offer database administrators a great deal of power and flexibility in deciding the rules that govern access to the system. In addition, this chapter discusses the management of user accounts and passwords in the MySQL access control system, explaining how passwords (especially the all-important root password) can be modified and how to reset a lost superuser password.

Understanding the Access Control System

The typical MySQL server installation has two levels of security in operation:

- Connections to the server are allowed only if they match the access rules laid down in the MySQL grant tables. These access rules can be specified on the basis of user and/or host, and can be used to restrict access from hosts outside a specific subnetwork or IP address range. Further, such connections to the server are permitted only after the user provides a valid password.

- Once a connection is established, MySQL checks every action performed by a user to verify whether the user has sufficient privileges to perform it. Users can be restricted to performing operations only on specified databases or fields, and MySQL even makes it possible to control which types of queries a user can run: at database, table, or field level.

The security of the system is further enhanced through the use of a one-way encryption scheme for user passwords. This encryption scheme, originally rather primitive, has been significantly improved since MySQL 4.1. Newer versions of MySQL also support SSL, which can be used to encrypt the data sent out over the MySQL client-server connection (such as query results) for greater security.

When MySQL is first installed, the MySQL installer automatically creates a database—the *mysql* database—which contains the six MySQL grant tables, as shown in Figure 11-1.

Each of these tables has a different role to play in deciding whether a user has access to a specific database, table, table field, or stored procedure. Access rules can be set up on the basis of username, connecting host, or database requested. The following sections examine each of these tables in greater detail.

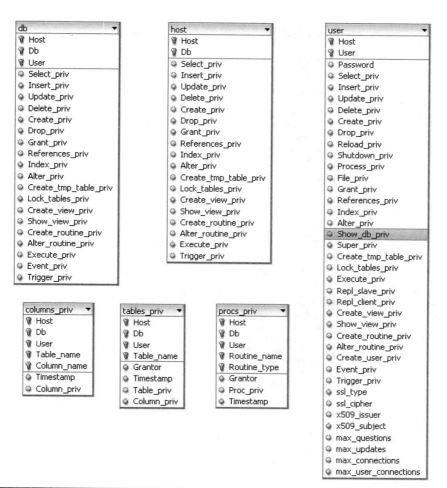

FIGURE 11-1   The MySQL grant tables

The user Table

MySQL uses a combination of both user and host identification as the basis for its security system. This identification information begins in the *user* table, which may be considered the most important of the six grant tables. Figure 11-2 illustrates what it looks like.

Within this table, the first three fields (referred to as *scope fields*) define which users are allowed to connect to the database server, their passwords, and the hosts from

FIGURE 11-2
The *user* table

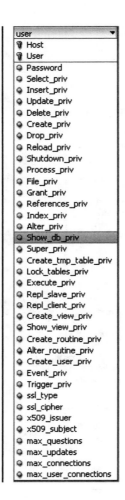

which they can connect. The remaining fields in the table (*privilege fields*) specify the global privileges available to each user. Table 11–1 specifies what each of these privilege fields represents.

Consider an example record in this table:

```
mysql> SELECT Host, User, Password,
    -> Event_priv FROM user WHERE User='joe'\G
*************************** 1. row ***************************
      Host: web.example.com
      User: joe
  Password: *0C23056193ED4CAE80DC86A535829C2BDE6688B6
Event_priv: Y
1 row in set (0.00 sec)
```

Field	Privilege Name	Users with This Privilege Can:
Select_priv	SELECT	Execute a SELECT query
Insert_priv	INSERT	Execute an INSERT query
Update_priv	UPDATE	Execute an UPDATE query
Delete_priv	DELETE	Execute a DELETE query
Create_priv	CREATE	Create databases and tables
Drop_priv	DROP	Delete databases and tables
Reload_priv	RELOAD	Reload/refresh the server
Shutdown_priv	SHUTDOWN	Shut down a running server
Process_priv	PROCESS	Track activity on the server
File_priv	FILE	Read and write files on the server
Grant_priv	GRANT OPTION	Grant other users the same privileges as the user
Index_priv	INDEX	Create, edit, and delete table indexes
Alter_priv	ALTER	Modify table structures
References_priv	REFERENCES	Create, edit, and delete foreign key references
Show_db_priv	SHOW DATABASES	View available databases on the server
Super_priv	SUPER	Execute administrative commands
Create_tmp_table_priv	CREATE TEMPORARY TABLES	Create temporary tables
Lock_tables_priv	LOCK TABLES	Create and delete table locks
Repl_slave_priv	REPLICATION SLAVE	Read master binary logs in a replication context
Repl_client_priv	REPLICATION CLIENT	Request information on masters and slaves in a replication context
Create_view_priv	CREATE VIEW	Create table views
Show_view_priv	SHOW VIEW	Execute the SHOW CREATE VIEW command
Create_routine_priv	CREATE ROUTINE	Create stored functions and procedures
Execute_priv	EXECUTE	Execute stored functions and procedures
Alter_routine_priv	ALTER ROUTINE	Modify or delete stored functions and procedures
Create_user_priv	CREATE USER	Create and delete MySQL user accounts
Event_priv	EVENT	Create, modify, and delete events
Trigger_priv	TRIGGER	Create and delete triggers

TABLE 11-1 MySQL Privilege Levels

This record allows clients authenticating as *joe@web.example.com* and supplying the correct password to connect to the MySQL server and create or modify MySQL events. Note that the password is not stored in cleartext, but as a hashed value.

IP addresses can be used instead of host names, and wildcards are also supported. Here's an example:

```
mysql> SELECT Host, User, Password,
    -> Select_priv FROM user WHERE User='joe'\G
*************************** 1. row ***************************
     Host: %.example.com
     User: joe
 Password: *0C23056193ED4CAE80DC86A535829C2BDE6688B6
Select_priv: Y
1 row in set (0.00 sec)
```

It's also possible to specify wildcards when setting up such access rules. The following example would allow access to both *joe@host.example.com* and *joe@web.example .com*, assuming the password was correctly supplied.

These security privileges, when assigned to a user in the *user* table, are globally valid; they apply to every database on the system. Consider the following user record:

```
mysql> SELECT Host, User, Password,
    -> Delete_priv FROM user WHERE User='joe'\G
*************************** 1. row ***************************
     Host: apple.example.com
     User: joe
 Password: *0C23056193ED4CAE80DC86A535829C2BDE6688B6
Delete_priv: Y
1 row in set (0.00 sec)
mysql> SHOW GRANTS FOR  'joe'@'apple.example.com'\G
*************************** 1. row ***************************
Grants for joe@apple.example.com: GRANT DELETE ON *.*
TO 'joe'@'apple.example.com' IDENTIFIED BY PASSWORD
'*667F407DE7C6AD07358FA38DAED7828A72014B4E'
1 row in set (0.00 sec)
```

This implies that user *joe@apple.example.com* has the ability to DELETE records from any table in any database on the server—a "lazy" setting that could result in massive data corruption if Joe's account was ever compromised. For this reason, the MySQL manual recommends leaving all privileges in this table to *N* (the default value) for each user, and instead using the *host* and *db* tables to set more specific access rules.

NOTE *The* user *table also includes some fields related to SSL encryption and resource usage limits per user; these are discussed in the section "Limiting Resource Usage."*

What Is the Relationship Between MySQL User Accounts and System User Accounts?

Absolutely none. MySQL users are not the same as system users on either Windows or UNIX. MySQL users exist only within the context of the MySQL RDBMS and need not have accounts or home directories on the system. While the MySQL command-line client on UNIX does default to using the currently logged-in user's name to connect to the server, this behavior can be overridden by specifying a username to the client via the *--user* parameter.

The db and host Tables

The *db* and *host* tables go together because they control which databases are available to which users and which operations are possible on those databases. Figure 11-3 illustrates what they look like.

Within the *db* table, the first three fields are scope fields, which specify the privileges available to a particular user/host combination on a particular database. The remaining privilege fields are used to specify the type of operations that user/host combination can perform on the named database. These fields have the same meaning as those in the *user* table, except that their effect is more "local" than "global."

FIGURE 11-3
The *db* and *host* tables

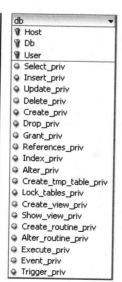
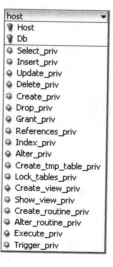

To illustrate, consider the following record:

```
mysql> SELECT * FROM db WHERE user='bill'\G
*************************** 1. row ***************************
                   Host: cranberry.example.com
                     Db: db1
                   User: bill
            Select_priv: Y
            Insert_priv: Y
            Update_priv: N
            Delete_priv: Y
            Create_priv: N
              Drop_priv: N
             Grant_priv: N
        References_priv: N
             Index_priv: N
             Alter_priv: N
  Create_tmp_table_priv: N
       Lock_tables_priv: N
       Create_view_priv: N
         Show_view_priv: N
    Create_routine_priv: N
     Alter_routine_priv: N
           Execute_priv: N
             Event_priv: Y
           Trigger_priv: N
```

A record like the previous one would imply that the client connecting as *bill@
cranberry.example.com* would be able to execute SELECT, INSERT, and DELETE queries
and manipulate events on the *db1* database only. This is verified by a quick call to
SHOW GRANTS:

```
mysql> SHOW GRANTS FOR  'bill'@'cranberry.example.com'\G
*************************** 1. row ***************************
Grants for bill@cranberry.example.com: GRANT USAGE ON *.* TO
'bill'@'cranberry.example.com' IDENTIFIED BY PASSWORD
'*667F407DE7C6AD07358FA38DAED7828A72014B4E'
*************************** 2. row ***************************
Grants for bill@cranberry.example.com: GRANT SELECT, INSERT, DELETE, EVENT
ON `db1`.* TO 'bill'@'cranberry.example.com'
2 rows in set (0.00 sec)
```

Here's another example:

```
mysql> SELECT * FROM db WHERE db='test'\G
*************************** 1. row ***************************
                   Host: %
                     Db: test
                   User:
            Select_priv: Y
            Insert_priv: Y
```

```
        Update_priv: Y
        Delete_priv: Y
        Create_priv: Y
          Drop_priv: Y
         Grant_priv: N
    References_priv: Y
         Index_priv: Y
         Alter_priv: Y
Create_tmp_table_priv: Y
    Lock_tables_priv: Y
    Create_view_priv: Y
      Show_view_priv: Y
 Create_routine_priv: Y
  Alter_routine_priv: N
        Execute_priv: N
          Event_priv: Y
        Trigger_priv: Y
1 row in set (0.00 sec)
```

This would imply that any user, connecting from any host, would have reasonably complete access to the *test* database.

If the *Host* field for a particular user/database combination in the *db* table is empty, MySQL will automatically look up the *host* table for host-specific privilege information. Only those privileges that are enabled in both tables will then be granted access to the connecting client. To illustrate, consider the following records:

```
mysql> SELECT Host, User, Db, Select_priv,
    -> Insert_priv FROM db WHERE user='bill'\G
*************************** 1. row ***************************
      Host:
      User: bill
        Db: db1
Select_priv: Y
Insert_priv: Y
1 row in set (0.01 sec)

mysql> SELECT Host, Db, Select_priv,
    -> Insert_priv FROM host
    -> WHERE db='db1'\G
*************************** 1. row ***************************
      Host: banana.example.com
        Db: db1
Select_priv: Y
Insert_priv: N
*************************** 2. row ***************************
      Host: cranberry.example.com
        Db: db1
Select_priv: Y
Insert_priv: Y
2 rows in set (0.00 sec)
```

This structure implies that clients connecting as *bill@banana.example.com* and *bill@ cranberry.example.com* will both be able to connect to the MySQL server. However, the client connecting as *bill@banana.example.com* will only be able to execute SELECT queries, while the client connecting as *bill@cranberry.example.com* will be able to execute both SELECT and INSERT queries.

This separation between the *host* and *db* tables is more useful than it appears at first glance. In the absence of the *host* table, if the same user needed different privileges based on the host from which he or she was connecting, a separate record for each host, with appropriate privileges, would need to be maintained in the *db* table (this, incidentally, is what the GRANT command does). However, because the *host* table exists, there's an alternative approach: The various host names can be maintained as separate records in the *host* table, each with its own privilege settings, and linked to a single entry in the *db* table. When a connection is attempted from one of the named hosts, MySQL will first look up the *db* table, then the *host* table, and assign privileges based on the intersection of the two tables.

**Why Do the db and host Tables Not Include All
the Privilege Fields Seen in the user Table?**
Some of the privilege fields in the *user* table—for example, *user.Shutdown_priv, user .Reload_priv,* and *user.Super_priv*—are related to server administration and are not specific to a particular database or table. Therefore, these fields are only available in the *user* table and not in other grant tables.

The tables_priv and columns_priv Tables

For even more fine-grained control, MySQL offers the *tables_priv* and *columns_priv* tables. These allow a database administrator to restrict access to specific tables in a database and to specific fields of a table, respectively. Figure 11-4 illustrates the structure of these tables.

FIGURE 11-4
The *tables_priv* and
columns_priv tables

Within the *tables_priv* table, the *Table_priv* field contains the table-level privileges for a particular user/host/database combination. The privileges are specified as a comma-separated list. Here's an example that restricts the user *joe@localhost* to only performing SELECT queries on the *airport* table:

```
mysql> SELECT * FROM tables_priv WHERE db='db1'\G
*************************** 1. row ***************************
       Host: localhost
         Db: db1
       User: joe
 Table_name: airport
    Grantor: root@localhost
  Timestamp: 2008-11-13 21:15:34
 Table_priv: Select
Column_priv:
1 row in set (0.01 sec)

mysql> SHOW GRANTS FOR 'joe'@'localhost'\G
*************************** 1. row ***************************
Grants for joe@localhost: GRANT USAGE ON *.* TO 'joe'@'localhost'
*************************** 2. row ***************************
Grants for joe@localhost: GRANT SELECT ON `db1`.`airport` TO 'joe'@
'localhost'
2 rows in set (0.00 sec)
```

Similarly, the following record indicates that the user *writer@localhost* can perform SELECT, INSERT, and UPDATE (but not DELETE) queries on the *db1.flight* table:

```
mysql> SELECT * FROM tables_priv WHERE db='db1'\G
*************************** 1. row ***************************
       Host: localhost
         Db: db1
       User: writer
 Table_name: flight
    Grantor: root@localhost
  Timestamp: 2008-11-13 21:58:31
 Table_priv: Select,Insert,Update
Column_priv:
1 row in set (0.02 sec)

mysql> SHOW GRANTS FOR 'writer'@'localhost'\G
*************************** 1. row ***************************
Grants for writer@localhost: GRANT USAGE ON *.* TO 'writer'@'localhost'
*************************** 2. row ***************************
Grants for writer@localhost: GRANT SELECT, INSERT, UPDATE ON `db1`.`flight`
TO 'writer'@'localhost'
2 rows in set (0.00 sec)
```

It's possible to specify access rules at the field level with the *columns_priv* table. Consider the following example, which allows clients logging in as *editor@localhost* to only read the aircraft number and last maintenance date, and clients logging in as *supervisor@localhost* to view and update the next maintenance date:

```
mysql> SELECT * FROM columns_priv\G
*************************** 1. row ***************************
      Host: localhost
        Db: db1
      User: editor
Table_name: aircraft
Column_name: RegNum
 Timestamp: 2008-11-13 22:23:23
Column_priv: Select
*************************** 2. row ***************************
      Host: localhost
        Db: db1
      User: editor
Table_name: aircraft
Column_name: LastMaintEnd
 Timestamp: 2008-11-13 22:23:23
Column_priv: Select
*************************** 3. row ***************************
      Host: localhost
        Db: db1
      User: supervisor
Table_name: aircraft
Column_name: RegNum
 Timestamp: 2008-11-13 22:24:15
Column_priv: Select
*************************** 4. row ***************************
      Host: localhost
        Db: db1
      User: supervisor
Table_name: aircraft
Column_name: LastMaintEnd
 Timestamp: 2008-11-13 22:24:15
Column_priv: Select
*************************** 5. row ***************************
      Host: localhost
        Db: db1
      User: supervisor
Table_name: aircraft
Column_name: NextMaintBegin
 Timestamp: 2008-11-13 22:24:15
Column_priv: Select,Update
*************************** 6. row ***************************
      Host: localhost
        Db: db1
      User: supervisor
```

```
  Table_name: aircraft
 Column_name: NextMaintEnd
   Timestamp: 2008-11-13 22:24:15
 Column_priv: Select,Update
6 rows in set (0.00 sec)
```

```
mysql> SHOW GRANTS FOR 'editor'@'localhost'\G
*************************** 1. row ***************************
Grants for editor@localhost: GRANT USAGE ON *.* TO 'editor'@'localhost'
*************************** 2. row ***************************
Grants for editor@localhost: GRANT SELECT (LastMaintEnd, RegNum) ON
`db1`.`aircraft` TO 'editor'@'localhost'
2 rows in set (0.00 sec)
```

```
mysql> SHOW GRANTS FOR 'supervisor'@'localhost'\G
*************************** 1. row ***************************
Grants for supervisor@localhost: GRANT USAGE ON *.* TO
'supervisor'@'localhost'
*************************** 2. row ***************************
Grants for supervisor@localhost: GRANT SELECT (NextMaintBegin, RegNum,
NextMaintEnd, LastMaintEnd), UPDATE (NextMaintBegin, NextMaintEnd) ON
`db1`.`aircraft` TO 'supervisor'@'localhost'
2 rows in set (0.00 sec)
```

And look what happens if an editor tries to read or modify a field to which he or she hasn't been given access:

```
mysql> SELECT AircraftID FROM aircraft\G
ERROR 1143 (42000): SELECT command denied to user 'editor'@'localhost'
for column 'AircraftID' in table 'aircraft'
mysql> UPDATE aircraft SET RegNum='ZX6822' WHERE RegNum='ZX6821'\G
ERROR 1142 (42000): UPDATE command denied to user 'editor'@'localhost'
for table 'aircraft'
```

The procs_priv Table

A new addition to MySQL 5.0 is the *procs_priv* table (Figure 11-5). Largely independent of the other five grant tables, this table specifies which stored procedures a particular user/host/database combination can call or modify. Within this table, the *Proc_priv* field specifies privileges as a comma-separated list; allowed privileges are EXECUTE, ALTER ROUTINE, and GRANT.

FIGURE 11-5
The *procs_priv* table

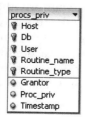

Here's an example rule, which allows *editor@localhost* to run the *getFlightsPerDay()* stored procedure:

```
mysql> SELECT * FROM procs_priv\G
*************************** 1. row ***************************
        Host: localhost
          Db: db1
        User: editor
Routine_name: getflightsperday
Routine_type: FUNCTION
     Grantor: root@localhost
   Proc_priv: Execute
   Timestamp: 2008-11-13 22:47:59
1 row in set (0.00 sec)

mysql> SHOW GRANTS FOR 'editor'@'localhost'\G
*************************** 1. row ***************************
Grants for editor@localhost: GRANT USAGE ON *.* TO 'editor'@'localhost'
*************************** 2. row ***************************
Grants for editor@localhost: GRANT EXECUTE ON FUNCTION
`db1`.`getflightsperday` TO 'editor'@'localhost'
2 rows in set (0.00 sec)
```

Interaction Between the Grant Tables

The various grant tables discussed in the previous sections interact with each other to create comprehensive access rules that MySQL uses when deciding how to handle a particular user request. In the hierarchy of the MySQL grant tables, the *user* table comes first, with the *db* and *host* tables below it, and the *tables_priv, columns_priv,* and *procs_priv* tables at the bottom. A table at a lower level is referred to only if a higher-level table fails to provide the necessary scope or privileges.

Access control takes place at two stages: the connection stage and the request stage.

- **The connection stage**   When a user requests a connection to the database server from a specific host, MySQL will first check whether an entry exists for the user in the user table, if the user's password is correct, and if the user is allowed to connect from that specific host. If the check is successful, a connection will be allowed to the server.

- **The request stage**   Once a connection is allowed, every subsequent request to the server—SELECT, DELETE, UPDATE, and other queries—will first be vetted to ensure that the user has the privileges necessary to perform the corresponding action. To make an appropriate decision, MySQL takes the privilege fields in all six grant tables into account, beginning with the *user* table and proceeding downwards through the grant table hierarchy until it reaches the *columns_priv* and *procs_priv* tables. Only after performing a logical intersection of the privileges listed in these different tables does MySQL allow or disallow a specific operation.

When MySQL encounters a request for an administrative action—RELOAD, PROCESS, and so forth—by a user, it decides whether to permit that action based solely on the corresponding permissions for that user in the *user* table. None of the other grant tables are consulted to make this determination. This is because these administrative privileges apply to the system as a whole and not to specific databases or tables; therefore, the corresponding columns make an appearance in the *user* table only.

What Default Privileges Does MySQL Come With?
Out of the box, MySQL:

- Gives the client connecting as *root@localhost* complete access to all databases on the system

- Gives clients connecting as *%@localhost* complete access to the *test* database

- Denies access to all clients connecting from other hosts

Managing User Privileges

MySQL offers two methods of altering user privileges in the grant tables—you can either use INSERT, UPDATE, and DELETE DML queries to hand-alter the information in the tables or you can use the GRANT and REVOKE commands. The latter is the preferred method; direct modification of the grant tables is advisable only for unusual tasks or situations, and is generally not recommended.

Granting and Revoking Privileges

To illustrate the GRANT command in action, consider the following example, which assigns SELECT, INSERT, UPDATE, and DELETE privileges on the table *db1.airport* to the user *supervisor@localhost* with password "timber":

```
mysql> GRANT SELECT, INSERT, UPDATE ON db1.airport
    -> TO 'supervisor'@'localhost' IDENTIFIED BY 'timber';
Query OK, 0 rows affected (0.01 sec)
```

MySQL allows the use of the * wildcard when referring to databases and tables. This next example assigns RELOAD, PROCESS, SELECT, DELETE, and INSERT privileges on all databases to the user *admin@medusa.example.com*:

```
mysql> GRANT RELOAD, PROCESS, SELECT, DELETE, INSERT ON *.*
    -> TO 'admin'@'medusa.example.com' IDENTIFIED BY 'secret';
Query OK, 0 rows affected (0.01 sec)
```

This next example assigns SELECT privileges on the table *db1.flightdep* to the supervisor user only:

```
mysql> GRANT SELECT ON db1.employees TO 'supervisor'@'localhost';
Query OK, 0 rows affected (0.01 sec)
```

This next example takes things one step further, assigning SELECT and UPDATE privileges to specific fields of the *airport* table to *editor@localhost* and *supervisor@localhost*, respectively:

```
mysql> GRANT SELECT (RegNum, LastMaintEnd)
    -> ON db1.aircraft TO 'editor'@'localhost';
Query OK, 0 rows affected (0.01 sec)
mysql> GRANT
    -> SELECT (RegNum, LastMaintEnd, NextMaintBegin, NextMaintEnd),
    -> UPDATE (NextMaintBegin, NextMaintEnd) ON db1.aircraft
    -> TO 'supervisor'@'localhost';
Query OK, 0 rows affected (0.01 sec)
```

The GRANT command can also be used to grant or deny access to stored procedures and functions. Here's an example, which allows *editor@localhost* to execute the *getFlightsPerDay()* function:

```
mysql> GRANT EXECUTE ON FUNCTION db1.getFlightsPerDay
    -> TO 'editor'@'localhost';
Query OK, 0 rows affected (0.01 sec)
```

NOTE *The tables, fields, and procedures named in the GRANT command must exist prior to assigning corresponding table-level, field-level, and procedure-level privileges. However, this rule does not hold true when dealing with database-level privileges. MySQL permits you to assign database-level privileges, even if the corresponding database does not exist. This difference in treatment of table- and database-level privileges is a common cause of error, so be forewarned!*

The REVOKE command does the opposite of the GRANT command, making it possible to revoke privileges assigned to a user. Consider the following example, which rescinds the INSERT and UPDATE privileges granted to *supervisor@localhost*:

```
mysql> REVOKE INSERT, UPDATE ON db1.airport
    -> FROM 'supervisor'@'localhost';
Query OK, 0 rows affected (0.01 sec)
```

The following command rescinds *tim@localhost*'s CREATE and DROP rights on the *db1* database:

```
mysql> REVOKE CREATE, DROP ON db1.* FROM 'tim'@'localhost';
Query OK, 0 rows affected (0.01 sec)
```

And this one takes away the UPDATE rights to the *aircraft* table previously granted to *supervisor@localhost*:

```
mysql> REVOKE UPDATE (NextMaintBegin, NextMaintEnd)
    -> ON db1.aircraft FROM 'supervisor'@'localhost';
Query OK, 0 rows affected (0.01 sec)
```

There's one other important point to note about the GRANT and REVOKE commands. When the GRANT command is invoked for a particular user, it automatically creates an entry for that user in the *user* table, if one does not already exist. However, a REVOKE command does not delete that entry from the *user* table, even if its invocation results in all the user's privileges being stripped. Thus, though a user record can be automatically added to the system via GRANT, it is never automatically removed using REVOKE. To remove a user record, use the DROP USER command, explained in the section "Working with User Accounts and Passwords."

The ALL and USAGE Privileges

MySQL provides the ALL privilege level as shorthand for "all privileges," and the USAGE privilege level as shorthand for "no privileges." These can help to make your GRANT and REVOKE statements more compact. Consider the next example, which assigns all privileges on the *web* database to the user *admin* connecting from any host in the *melonfire.com* domain:

```
mysql> GRANT ALL ON web.* TO 'admin'@'%.melonfire.com';
Query OK, 0 rows affected (0.01 sec)
```

In contrast, the following command would assign no privileges to the user *test* (and is, therefore, equivalent to running a simple CREATE USER command):

```
mysql> GRANT USAGE ON web.* TO 'test'@'%.melonfire.com';
Query OK, 0 rows affected (0.01 sec)
```

The GRANT Privilege

MySQL lets users grant other users the same privileges they themselves possess via the special WITH GRANT OPTION clause of the GRANT command. When this clause is added to a GRANT command, users to whom it applies can assign the privileges they have to other users. Consider the following example, which illustrates this by allowing *supervisor@localhost* to give other users the same rights he has:

```
mysql> GRANT SELECT, DELETE, INSERT, UPDATE, CREATE, DROP, INDEX
    -> ON db1.* TO 'supervisor'@'localhost' WITH GRANT OPTION;
Query OK, 0 rows affected (0.01 sec)
mysql> SHOW GRANTS FOR 'supervisor'@'localhost'\G
*************************** 1. row ***************************
Grants for supervisor@localhost: GRANT USAGE ON *.* TO
'supervisor'@'localhost'
*************************** 2. row ***************************
Grants for supervisor@localhost: GRANT SELECT, INSERT, UPDATE, DELETE,
CREATE, DROP, INDEX ON `db1`.* TO 'supervisor'@'localhost' WITH GRANT OPTION
2 rows in set (0.00 sec)
```

The user *supervisor@localhost* can now log in to MySQL and GRANT other users all or some of the privileges he possesses, as the following shows:

```
mysql> GRANT SELECT ON db1.* TO 'joe'@'localhost';
Query OK, 0 rows affected (0.01 sec)
```

The GRANT privilege can be reversed by using the GRANT OPTION clause in a standard REVOKE command, as the following shows:

```
mysql> REVOKE GRANT OPTION ON db1.* FROM 'supervisor'@'localhost';
Query OK, 0 rows affected (0.01 sec)
```

CAUTION *Care should be taken when assigning users the GRANT privilege. Users with different access levels can combine them and thereby obtain a higher level of access than they are normally allowed.*

The SUPER and PROCESS Privileges

The SUPER and PROCESS privileges are noteworthy because they allow administrative control over server processes. Users with the PROCESS privilege can view the commands being executed by connecting clients in real time, while users with the SUPER privilege can terminate client connections and alter global server settings.

Here's an example of assigning a user the SUPER privilege:

```
mysql> GRANT SUPER ON *.* TO 'admin'@'localhost';
Query OK, 0 rows affected (0.01 sec)
```

CAUTION *Care should be taken when assigning the SUPER and PROCESS privileges, as they permit users to exercise a high degree of control over almost all aspects of server operation.*

Limiting Resource Usage

MySQL also allows administrators to limit resource usage on the MySQL server on a per-user basis. This is accomplished via four optional clauses to the GRANT command.

The first of these is the MAX_QUERIES_PER_HOUR clause, which limits the number of queries that can be run by a user in an hour. Here's an example:

```
mysql> GRANT SELECT ON *.* TO 'supervisor'@'localhost'
    -> WITH MAX_QUERIES_PER_HOUR 5;
Query OK, 0 rows affected (0.00 sec)
```

The MAX_QUERIES_PER_HOUR clause controls the total number of queries permitted per hour, regardless of whether these are SELECT, INSERT, UPDATE, DELETE, or other queries. If this is too all-encompassing, an alternative is to set a limit on the number of queries that change the data in the database via the MAX_UPDATES_PER_HOUR clause, as in the following:

```
mysql> GRANT SELECT, INSERT, UPDATE ON *.*
    -> TO 'supervisor'@'localhost' WITH MAX_UPDATES_PER_HOUR 5;
Query OK, 0 rows affected (0.00 sec)
```

The number of new connections opened by the named user(s) in an hour can be controlled via the MAX_CONNECTIONS_PER_HOUR clause, as the following shows.

```
mysql> GRANT USAGE ON *.* TO 'supervisor'@'localhost'
    -> WITH MAX_CONNECTIONS_PER_HOUR 3;
Query OK, 0 rows affected (0.00 sec)
```

The maximum number of simultaneous connections that the same user may have open at any one time is specified via the MAX_USER_CONNECTIONS clause, as in the following example:

```
mysql> GRANT USAGE ON *.* TO 'supervisor'@'localhost'
    -> WITH MAX_USER_CONNECTIONS 1;
Query OK, 0 rows affected (0.00 sec)
```

These clauses can also be used in combination with each other. The following is a perfectly valid GRANT:

```
mysql> GRANT SELECT, INSERT, UPDATE, DELETE ON *.*
    -> TO 'supervisor'@'localhost' WITH
    -> MAX_QUERIES_PER_HOUR 50
    -> MAX_UPDATES_PER_HOUR 10
    -> MAX_CONNECTIONS_PER_HOUR 4;
Query OK, 0 rows affected (0.00 sec)
```

It's important to realize that these usage limits cannot be specified per-database or per-table. They can only be specified in the global context by using an ON *.* clause in the GRANT command. A value of 0 for any of these clauses removes the corresponding limitation.

The server maintains internal counters on a per-user basis for each of these three resource limits. These counters could be reset at any time with the new FLUSH USER_RESOURCES command, as in the following:

```
mysql> FLUSH USER_RESOURCES;
Query OK, 0 rows affected (0.00 sec)
```

Note that you need the RELOAD privilege to execute the FLUSH command.

Viewing Privileges

To view the privileges assigned to a particular user, use the SHOW GRANTS command, which accepts a username as argument and displays a list of all the privileges granted to that user. There are numerous examples of this command in previous sections, but here's another one:

```
mysql> SHOW GRANTS FOR 'supervisor'@'localhost'\G
*************************** 1. row ***************************
Grants for supervisor@localhost: GRANT USAGE ON *.* TO
'supervisor'@'localhost'
```

```
*************************** 2. row ***************************
Grants for supervisor@localhost: GRANT SELECT, INSERT, UPDATE, DELETE,
CREATE, DROP, INDEX ON `db1`.* TO 'supervisor'@'localhost'
WITH GRANT OPTION
2 rows in set (0.00 sec)
```

Restoring Default Privileges

If you want to reset the grant tables to their initial default settings, the process is as follows:

1. If the server is running, stop it in the usual manner:

   ```
   [root@host]# /usr/local/mysql/support-files/mysql.server stop
   ```

2. Change to the data directory of your MySQL installation, and then delete the *mysql/* folder. Because databases in MySQL are represented as directories on the file system, this will effectively erase the grant tables.

   ```
   [root@host]# rm -rf /usr/local/mysql/data/mysql
   ```

   On UNIX, reinstall the grant tables by running the initialization script, *mysql_install_db*, which ships with the program:

   ```
   [root@host]# /usr/local/mysql/scripts/mysql_install_db
   ```

   Then, change back to the data directory of your MySQL installation and alter the ownership of the newly created MySQL directory so it is owned by the *mysql* user:

   ```
   [root@host]# chown -R mysql.mysql /usr/local/mysql/data/mysql
   ```

   On Windows, because this initialization script is not part of the binary distribution, you need to reinstall the package into the same directory to revert to the original grant tables.

3. Restart the server.

   ```
   [root@host]# /usr/local/mysql/support-files/mysql.server stop
   ```

The MySQL grant tables should now be reset to their default values. You can now log in as *root@localhost* and make changes to them using the GRANT and REVOKE commands.

Working with User Accounts and Passwords

To simplify the task of user account management, MySQL offers the CREATE USER and DROP USER commands. A password for the user can be specified with the optional IDENTIFIED BY clause. Here's an example:

```
mysql> CREATE USER 'joe'@'localhost'
    -> IDENTIFIED BY 'guessme';
Query OK, 0 rows affected (0.02 sec)
```

The GRANT command will also automatically create user accounts, if they don't already exist at the time of specifying the grant. Again, the optional IDENTIFIED BY clause can be used to set the user password. Here's an example:

```
mysql> GRANT SELECT ON *.*
    -> TO 'joe'@'localhost'
    -> IDENTIFIED BY 'guessme';
Query OK, 0 rows affected (0.01 sec)
```

The IDENTIFIED BY clause of the GRANT command is optional, and creating a grant for a new user without this clause will set an empty password for that user. This opens a security hole in the system, so administrators should always make it a point to assign a password to new users. Alternatively, setting the NO_AUTO_CREATE_USER SQL mode will ensure that the GRANT command only creates new user accounts if they are accompanied by a password (see Chapter 10 for more information on SQL modes).

Passwords can also be set with the MySQL SET PASSWORD command. In its most basic form, this command changes the password for the currently logged-in user. Here's an example:

```
mysql> SET PASSWORD = PASSWORD('secret');
Query OK, 0 rows affected (0.01 sec)
```

To change the password for another user on the system, add the FOR clause and specify the target user account, as in the following example:

```
mysql> SET PASSWORD FOR 'joe'@'localhost' = PASSWORD('1rock');
Query OK, 0 rows affected (0.01 sec)
```

Note, however, that the ability to change the passwords of other users is restricted to those user accounts that have been granted UPDATE privileges on the *mysql* database.

When setting a password using the IDENTIFIED BY clause of the GRANT or CREATE USER commands, or via the *mysqladmin* tool, MySQL will automatically encrypt the password string for you. However, this does not apply to passwords set with the SET PASSWORD command, which requires you to manually encrypt the password. Therefore, the following three commands are equivalent:

```
mysql> SET PASSWORD FOR 'joe'@'localhost' = PASSWORD('1rock');
mysql> CREATE USER 'joe'@'localhost' IDENTIFIED BY '1rock';
mysql> GRANT USAGE ON *.* TO 'joe'@'localhost' IDENTIFIED BY '1rock';
```

How Does MySQL Password Authentication Work?

Passwords are stored in the *Password* field of the *user* grant table, and are encrypted with the MySQL PASSWORD() function. When a user logs in to the MySQL server and provides a password, MySQL first encrypts the supplied password string using the PASSWORD() function, and then compares the resulting value with the value in the *Password* field of the corresponding user record in the *user* table.

If the two values match (and other access rules permit it), the user is granted access. If the values do not match, access is denied.

CAUTION *The* PASSWORD() *function in MySQL 4.1 and later generates a longer, 41-byte hash value that is not compatible with older versions (which used a 16-byte value). Therefore, when you upgrade a pre-4.1 MySQL server installation to MySQL 4.1 or better, you must run the* mysql_fix_privilege_ tables *script in the* scripts/ *directory of your MySQL installation to update the grant tables so they can handle the longer hash value.*

The Administrator Password

For both UNIX and Windows systems, when MySQL is first installed, the administrative account *root@localhost* is initialized with an empty password. This default setting implies that any one could log in as *root* without a password, and would be granted administrative privileges on the server. Needless to say, this is a significant security hole.

To rectify this, set a password for *root@localhost* as soon as possible using any of the following commands:

```
[root@host]# /usr/local/mysql/bin/mysqladmin -u root password 'secret'

mysql> SET PASSWORD FOR 'root'@'localhost' = PASSWORD('secret');
```

This password change goes into effect immediately, with no need to restart the server or reload the grant tables.

If you later forget the password for *root@localhost* and are locked out of the grant tables, take a deep breath, and then follow these steps to get things up and running again:

1. Log in to the system as the system administrator (*root* on UNIX) and stop the MySQL server. This can be accomplished via the *mysql.server* startup and shutdown script in the *support-files/* directory of your MySQL installation, as follows:

   ```
   [root@host]# /usr/local/mysql/support-files/mysql.server stop
   ```

   On UNIX systems that come with MySQL preinstalled, an alternative is to stop (and start) MySQL with the */etc/rc.d/init.d/mysqld* scripts.

2. Start MySQL again with the special *--skip-grant-tables* startup option.

   ```
   [root@host]# /usr/local/mysql/bin/safe_mysqld --skip-grant-tables
                   --skip-networking
   ```

   This bypasses the grant tables, enabling server login as the MySQL *root* user without providing a password. The additional *--skip-networking* option tells MySQL not to listen for TCP/IP connections and ensures that no one can break in over the network while you are resetting the password.

3. Use the SET PASSWORD command, as described in the preceding section, to set a new password for the MySQL *root* user:

```
mysql> SET PASSWORD FOR 'root'@'localhost' = PASSWORD('secret');
```

4. Log out of the server, stop it, and restart it again in the normal manner:

```
[root@host]# /usr/local/mysql/support-files/mysql.server stop
[root@host]# /usr/local/mysql/support-files/mysql.server start
```

This procedure should reset the password for the *root@localhost* account and permit logins with the new password set in step 3.

Summary

MySQL comes with a hierarchical access control system that allows administrators to precisely define which clients and hosts can access which parts of the database server. This access control system, implemented through six grant tables, was discussed in detail throughout this chapter. The chapter also examined the topics of limiting server resource usage, changing user passwords, recovering from a lost administrator password, and resetting the grant tables.

To learn more about the topics discussed in this chapter, consider visiting the following links:

- The MySQL access control system, at http://dev.mysql.com/doc/refman/5.1/en/privilege-system.html

- MySQL privilege levels, at http://dev.mysql.com/doc/refman/5.1/en/privileges-provided.html

- The CREATE USER, DROP USER, and SET PASSWORD commands, at http://dev.mysql.com/doc/refman/5.1/en/account-management-sql.html

- The GRANT and REVOKE commands, at http://dev.mysql.com/doc/refman/5.1/en/grant.html

CHAPTER 12

Performing Maintenance, Backup, and Recovery

A s you've discovered by now, MySQL is relatively easy to use, which makes it an ideal database tool for many types of production environments where a dedicated database administrator is neither feasible nor desired. Despite this, a certain amount of basic maintenance needs to be done, regardless of the size of your installation. This chapter will introduce you to MySQL's tools for table maintenance and data backup, and prepare you for when disaster strikes (and yes, that's "when," not "if").

Using Database Log Files

A significant amount of maintenance needed by MySQL is done through the various log files. Logging is essential for situations where troubleshooting is necessary, or where you want to be proactive and avoid problems in advance.

When the MySQL server starts up, it checks which logging options are marked for activation. If indicated, the server starts the logs as part of the startup process. Log files provide the information necessary to manage your server. Analyzing performance and investigating problems are some of the main reasons for consulting these logs. The files are stored in the same directory as the MySQL data files.

Although these are all standard text files, several different types of logs are available:

- The error log
- The general query log
- The slow query log
- The binary log

The Error Log

The error log does exactly what you think it would do—it keeps a record of every error that occurs on the server. As such, this is a basic diagnostic tool, and one that comes in handy when troubleshooting hard-to-diagnose problems.

To activate the error log, add the --*log-error* option to the server's startup command line or option file, as shown:

```
[root@host]# /usr/local/mysql/bin/mysqld_safe --log-error
```

Here's a sample snippet from the error log:

```
Version: '5.1.30-community'  socket: ''  port: 3306  MySQL Community Server
(GPL)
InnoDB: The log sequence number in ibdata files does not match
InnoDB: the log sequence number in the ib_logfiles!
090309 20:02:55  InnoDB: Database was not shut down normally!
InnoDB: Starting crash recovery.
InnoDB: Reading tablespace information from the .ibd files...
InnoDB: Restoring possible half-written data pages from the doublewrite
InnoDB: buffer...
090309 20:02:57  InnoDB: Started; log sequence number 0 389374
```

By default, this file is called *hostname.err* and is located in the MySQL *data/* directory. You can specify a different filename and location by passing it to the *--log-error* option as an argument, as in the following example:

```
[root@host]# /usr/local/mysql/bin/mysqld_safe --log-error=/tmp/mysql.errors
```

The General Query Log

The general query log is another useful log because it (surprise, surprise!) keeps track of every query sent to the server by a client. It also displays details about which clients are connected to the server and what these clients are doing. If you want to monitor activity for the purpose of troubleshooting, you should activate the query log by adding the *--general_log* option to the server's startup command line or option file:

```
[root@host]# /usr/local/mysql/bin/mysqld_safe --general_log
```

Here's a sample snippet from the query log:

```
090310 15:32:15     1 Query      SELECT DATABASE()
                 1 Init DB       db1
090310 15:32:17     1 Query      SELECT DATABASE()
                 1 Init DB       gwl
090310 15:32:19     1 Query      select 8 from users
090310 15:32:24     1 Query      select * from user
090310 15:32:27     1 Query      select * from userdataset
090310 15:32:35     1 Query      select * from userfielddataset
090310 15:34:25     1 Query      SELECT DATABASE()
                 1 Init DB       db1
090310 15:34:43     1 Query      select * from route left join flight on
routeid
090310 15:34:51     1 Query      select * from route left join flight on
route.routeid
```

By default, this file is called *hostname.log*, and it, too, is located in the MySQL *data/* directory. You can specify a different filename and location by passing it to the *--general_ log* option as an argument, as explained earlier.

The Slow Query Log

A related log is the slow query log, which lists all the queries that exceed a predefined amount of time (specified by the *long_query_time* variable). Any query that takes longer than this value is listed in this log. If you're looking for a way to optimize performance, this log is a good place to start.

NOTE *Query optimization is discussed in detail in Chapter 9.*

Typically, you would look at the queries in this log as candidates for revision to lessen the impact on your server's performance. Remember, though, the length of time a query takes can be the result of factors other than poorly written code. Queries that usually run under the "long" threshold can appear in this log if the server is tied up elsewhere.

The slow query log is activated by using the *--slow-query-log* option at server startup, as in the example shown:

```
[root@host]# /usr/local/mysql/bin/mysqld_safe --slow-query-log
```

The default filename for the log is *hostname-slow.log*, also located in the MySQL *data/* directory. As specified earlier, you can specify a custom name and location for this log by passing it to the *--slow-query-log* option.

The Binary Log

MySQL 3.23.14 and later also support logging of all the commands that make changes to a table's data. Commands such as INSERT, REPLACE, DELETE, GRANT, and REVOKE, along with UPDATE, CREATE TABLE, and DROP TABLE are all in this category. This information is stored in a binary log, which provides a more efficient storage format for data and also records a larger amount of information. A utility named *mysqlbinlog* converts the binary log back to text so you can read it. The binary log can be activated by using the *--log-bin* option when starting MySQL, as shown:

```
[root@host]# /usr/local/mysql/bin/mysqld_safe --log-bin
```

The default filename for the log is *hostname-bin*, with the file extension containing a number identifying the log in the sequence. You can specify a different location for the binary log by passing it to the *--log-bin* option as an argument.

TIP *Because the binary log is critical for crash recovery, it's always a good idea to save it to a different drive or device than the one which holds the MySQL database files.*

NOTE *Versions of MySQL prior to MySQL 5.0 used a more primitive version of the binary log, the "update log," which recorded all the queries that changed a table's data. Statements such as INSERT, REPLACE, DELETE, GRANT, and REVOKE, along with UPDATE, CREATE TABLE, and DROP TABLE, were all recorded in this log. However, this update log is no longer supported in MySQL 5.0 and later, and is instead replaced by the binary log.*

Why Would I Need to Use the Binary Log?

Updates that are part of a transaction are not executed immediately; they are kept in a cache until the transaction is committed. Once a COMMIT command is received by the MySQL server, the entire transaction is first written to the binary log, and then the changes are saved to the database. If a part of the transaction fails for whatever reason, the whole transaction is rolled back and no changes are written to the binary log. Also, if you're setting up master and slave servers for replication, you must enable the binary log (more about replication in Chapter 13).

To refresh the logs, use the FLUSH LOGS command. This command causes the server to close and then reopen the log files. For the binary logs, this command closes the current log and creates a new log with a new sequence number so the old one can be archived, if desired.

The value of log flushing becomes more evident when you consider issues of log rotation, which are covered in the next section.

Rotating Logs

Your logs will become huge quickly (and your disks full) if your server is busy. So logs must be managed via expiration dates and rotation to keep them from becoming a hindrance rather than a help.

Log rotation is one method used to alleviate this problem. *Log rotation* works by creating a finite number of log files and then overwriting them in succession so the oldest one is dropped in each cycle. For example, if you have a file named *hostname.log*, the first time rotation takes place, it's renamed *hostname.log.1* and a new *hostname.log* file is created. At the next rotation, *hostname.log.1* is renamed *hostname.log.2*, *hostname.log* is renamed *hostname.log.1*, and a new file named (you guessed it!) *hostname.log* is created. When the last rotation in the cycle is reached, the oldest file is overwritten.

How much log information you keep depends on how often you rotate and how many files you create. These numbers vary, depending on your circumstances, but a common arrangement is to create new logs daily and rotate them seven times through a cycle, one for each day of the week.

Sending Log Output to a Table

If writing data to log files isn't your style, MySQL also lets you redirect the output of the general query log and the slow query log to a database table instead of, or in addition to, a disk file. To do this, add the *--log-output* argument to the server command line, followed by one or more of the options FILE, TABLE, or NONE in a comma-separated list. The default value is FILE, which writes log messages to the corresponding log file; TABLE tells MySQL to write log messages to the *general_log* or *slow_log* table in the *mysql* database, while NONE disables logging.

Here's an example, which logs queries to both the *mysql.general_log* table and the *hostname.log* file:

```
[root@host]# /usr/local/mysql/bin/mysqld_safe --general_log --log-
output=FILE,TABLE
```

Here's an example of what the *mysql.general_log* table might then contain:

```
mysql> SELECT event_time, command_type, argument
    -> FROM mysql.general_log LIMIT 0,6;
+---------------------+--------------+---------------------------+
| event_time          | command_type | argument                  |
+---------------------+--------------+---------------------------+
| 2009-03-10 20:14:53 | Connect      | root@localhost on gwl     |
| 2009-03-10 20:14:53 | Query        | desc post                 |
| 2009-03-10 20:14:59 | Query        | desc forumpost            |
```

```
|  2009-03-10 20:15:03  |  Query      |  select * from forumpost  |
|  2009-03-10 20:15:05  |  Query      |  SELECT DATABASE()        |
|  2009-03-10 20:15:05  |  Init DB    |  db1                      |
+----------------------+-------------+---------------------------+
6 rows in set (0.00 sec)
```

Checking and Repairing Tables

You might need to restore corrupted tables (or even an entire database) from your backups and use the update logs if a table gets damaged or deleted by accident. In case of relatively minor damage, however, MySQL provides several options for table repair. This next section deals with what you can do if this is the case.

Checking Tables for Errors

The first thing to do if you suspect something is wrong is to check the table for errors. The *myisamchk* utility is one way to check a table. To invoke this utility, execute the command *myisamchk table-file*.

Because *myisamchk* requires exclusive access to the tables, a good idea is to take the server offline before running it. This way, you needn't worry about coordinating access between clients. In addition, you can run several options when you check a table for errors, as shown in Table 12-1.

The following example runs *myisamchk* with the extended option enabled. If you're following along, don't use a large table to see how this works because you'll tie up your server for quite a while. If no errors are detected using the extended option, you can be certain the specified table isn't the problem.

```
[root@production ~]# /usr/local/bin/myisamchk --extend-check
/usr/local/mysql/data/db1/airport.MYI
Checking MyISAM file: /usr/local/mysql/data/db1/airport.MYI
Data records:        15    Deleted blocks:        0
myisamchk: warning: 1 client is using or hasn't closed the table properly
- check file-size
- check record delete-chain
- check key delete-chain
- check index reference
- check data record references index: 1
- check record links
MyISAM-table '/usr/local/mysql/data/db1/airport.MYI' is usable but should be
fixed
```

The downside of *myisamchk* is this database-checking tool requires locking out clients while the diagnosis is performed. Moreover, no client can hold a lock on the table being checked while *myisamchk* is running. On a big table, where *myisamchk* can take a few minutes to perform its checks, this can be a problem.

Option	Name	Description
--fast	Fast check	Only checks irregularly closed files
--medium-check	Medium check	A more detailed check
--extend-check	Extended check	Slowest, most thorough check
--check	Basic check	Basic table check

TABLE 12-1 Additional *myisamchk* Table Check Options

One alternative here is to set *myisamchk* to use large buffers (use *myisamchk --help* to see the options for changing the various buffers). Another alternative is to use a different method to check your tables: the CHECK TABLE command.

The *myisamchk* utility requires exclusive access to the tables it's checking because it works directly with the table files. The CHECK TABLE command, on the other hand, has the server check the tables. This means less work for you, as you don't have to take the server down and remove all the locks from the table. Here's an example of it in action:

```
mysql> CHECK TABLE airport;
+--------------+-------+----------+----------+
| Table        | Op    | Msg_type | Msg_text |
+--------------+-------+----------+----------+
| db1.airport  | check | status   | OK       |
+--------------+-------+----------+----------+
1 row in set (0.08 sec)
```

In case you were wondering, you can also add the keywords FAST, MEDIUM, and EXTENDED to the CHECK TABLE command to perform the desired type of check.

Why not run CHECK TABLE all the time then, instead of *myisamchk*, you might ask? The main reason is this: The server does all the work when using CHECK TABLE. If your server is down, CHECK TABLE isn't an option. On the other hand, *myisamchk* works at the file level and, therefore, can work even if the server is down. Since CHECK TABLE is a SQL command that can only be sent via a client, the server must be running to accept it. If you have a choice, however, by all means let MySQL do the work.

CAUTION myisamchk *only works with the MyISAM storage engine. To check InnoDB tables, use the* CHECK TABLE *command instead.*

Repairing Tables

If you find errors exist after checking a table, you must repair the table. The best practice is to make a copy of the table in question before you try to repair it. This gives you the option of trying a different way to recover it if your first solution doesn't work.

The *myisamchk* tool discussed previously can also be used to repair a damaged table. Use the *--recover* option with the table filename to start this process. Here's an example:

```
[root@host]# /usr/local/mysql/bin/myisamchk --recover
/usr/local/mysql/data/db1/airport.MYI
- recovering (with sort) MyISAM-table
'/usr/local/mysql/data/db1/airport.MYI'
Data records: 15
- Fixing index 1
```

If the *--recover* option fails to take care of the problem, the *--safe-recover* option attempts a slow recovery of the table. Other options are also available, and Table 12-2 explains what they mean.

As noted in the preceding section, keep in mind that the *myisamchk* tool works at the file level and, therefore, requires that all locks be removed and all clients be excluded.

As when checking a table, you should try the fastest options first and move to the slower, more thorough, options only if needed. You might find many common problems are fixed without having to resort to the slower options. If you still have a problem after running even the most intensive repair possibilities, you'll have to restore the table from your backups. Restoring is covered in detail in the section "Restoring Databases and Tables from Backup."

The other option you have when repairing a table is the REPAIR TABLE command, coupled with the table name. Similar to *myisamchk,* you have the option of using the QUICK or EXTENDED keyword to set the type of repair. Simply add the option name to the end of the REPAIR TABLE statement, as in the example shown:

```
mysql> REPAIR TABLE airport QUICK;
+--------------+--------+----------+----------+
| Table        | Op     | Msg_type | Msg_text |
+--------------+--------+----------+----------+
| db1.airport  | repair | status   | OK       |
+--------------+--------+----------+----------+
1 row in set (0.00 sec)
```

TIP *You can use either* myisamchk *or* REPAIR TABLE *to fix a damaged table, but remember (as discussed earlier in the context of the* CHECK TABLE *command), the server must be running in order to use* REPAIR TABLE, *while you must only use* myisamchk *if the server is down.*

Option	Name	Description
–recover	Repair and recover	Standard recovery
-safe-recover	Safe mode for recovery	Slow, thorough recovery
–quick	Quick recovery	Only checks index and not data files

TABLE 12-2 Additional *myisamchk* Table Repair Options

Optimizing Tables

There are a number of times when optimizing a table is a good idea. A common example is if a table gets considerable activity, especially many deletions. In such a situation, it can quickly get fragmented, resulting in performance degradation. Running the OPTIMIZE TABLE command flushes these deleted records and frees up space.

For example, the following command optimizes the *route* table:

```
mysql> OPTIMIZE TABLE route;
+------------+----------+----------+----------+
| Table      | Op       | Msg_type | Msg_text |
+------------+----------+----------+----------+
| db1.route  | optimize | status   | OK       |
+------------+----------+----------+----------+
1 row in set (0.06 sec)
```

The OPTIMIZE TABLE command is like your mother coming in and tidying your room. In addition to getting rid of old, deleted files, it sorts indexed files, places the contents of variable table rows into contiguous spaces, and updates table statistics. Remember, though, that the table is locked and can't be accessed by clients while it's being serviced.

Backing Up and Restoring Data

In addition to logging and table optimization, the other essential task of any database administrator is to make sure the data is protected from loss. This is accomplished by regular backup and test restorations of your database. When disaster strikes (and it will, make no mistake about that), you will be better equipped to deal with it if you perform the steps suggested in this next section.

Backing Up Databases and Tables

The MySQL distribution comes with a utility called *mysqldump* that can be used to back up an entire database and/or individual tables from a database to a text file. Besides the obvious need to back up your data, this action is also useful if you need to export your database contents to a different RDBMS, or if you simply need to move certain information from one system to another quickly and easily. Chapter 8 has an example of this, using *mysqldump* to export the contents of a database in XML format.

```
[user@host]# /usr/local/mysql/bin/mysqldump --user=john --password=hoonose
db1
```

This procedure displays the contents of the entire example database, *db1*, on your screen. The output should look similar to Figure 12-1.

Notice from Figure 12-1 that SQL statements are included in the output of *mysqldump* to facilitate rebuilding tables. As with the *mysql* command, you need to use the *--user* and *--password* options to designate an authorized user and password to perform the dump function.

```
--

DROP TABLE IF EXISTS `route`;
CREATE TABLE `route` (
  `RouteID` smallint(4) unsigned NOT NULL auto_increment,
  `From` smallint(4) unsigned NOT NULL,
  `To` smallint(4) unsigned NOT NULL,
  `Distance` smallint(4) unsigned NOT NULL,
  `Duration` smallint(4) unsigned NOT NULL,
  `Status` tinyint(1) NOT NULL,
  PRIMARY KEY  (`RouteID`),
  KEY `Duration` (`Duration`)
) ENGINE=MyISAM AUTO_INCREMENT=1210 DEFAULT CHARSET=utf8;


--
-- Dumping data for table `route`
--

LOCK TABLES `route` WRITE;
/*!40000 ALTER TABLE `route` DISABLE KEYS */;
INSERT INTO `route` VALUES (1003,126,56,7200,550,1),(1005,34,48,343,85,1),(1176,
56,132,1267,150,1),(1175,132,56,1267,150,1),(1018,34,87,1248,135,1),(1023,48,59,
1434,150,1),(1008,34,165,686,60,1),(1009,34,92,489,70,1),(1165,92,59,683,50,1),(
1167,92,56,777,70,0),(1123,92,48,777,60,1),(1133,74,126,6336,470,1),(1141,126,20
```

FIGURE 12-1   The output of the *mysqldump* command

TIP   *If the data you are backing up has been corrupted, it is a best practice to execute a*
DROP TABLE *or a* DROP DATABASE *command before restoration. This creates a clean*
slate for your restoration. Fortunately, the mysqldump *utility does this for you; if you*
look at the SQL statements resulting from a call to mysqldump, *you will see these*
commands included.

What if you don't need the entire database to be dumped? A simple change enables
you to specify which tables from within the database should be backed up. Here's an
example:

```
[user@host]# /usr/local/mysql/bin/mysqldump --user=john --password=hoonose
db1 route flight
```

This command dumps only the contents of the *db1.name* and *db1.address* tables.
In the real world, you'll want to save the output of *mysqldump* to a file, not watch it
scroll by on a console. On both UNIX and Windows, this can be accomplished via the >
redirection operator, as shown in the following example:

```
[user@host]# /usr/local/mysql/bin/mysqldump --user=john --password=hoonose
db1 route flight > mydump.sql
```

The result of this command will be a text file, called *mydump.sql,* containing the SQL
commands needed to re-create the *db1.name* and *db1.address* tables.

Backing Up Multiple Databases

To back up more than one database at a time, use the *–B* option, as in the following example:

```
[user@host]# /usr/local/mysql/bin/mysqldump --user=john --password=hoonose
-B db1 db2
```

Note that no tables are specified in this case, because when you use the *-B* option to back up more than one database, the entire database will be dumped. Individual tables cannot be designated in this operation.

To back up all the databases on the system, use the shortcut *--all-databases* option, as shown:

```
[user@host]# /usr/local/mysql/bin/mysqldump --user=john --password=hoonose
--all-databases
```

TIP *When using the* mysqldump *utility, you can control the characters used to enclose and separate the fields from the column output by adding any or all of the options --fields-enclosed-by, --fields-terminated-by, --fields-escaped-by, and --lines-terminated-by. This is similar to the features provided by the* LOAD DATA INFILE, *and* SELECT ... INTO OUTFILE *commands discussed in Chapter 8, and it is particularly useful if you need to port the dumped data into a system that requires records to be encoded in a custom format before importing them.*

Backing Up Table Structures

What if you want to create a table with the same structure but different data from the one you have? Again, the *mysqldump* utility comes to the rescue. The *--no-data* option produces the same table in form, but empty of content. To see this in action, try the following command:

```
[user@host]# /usr/local/mysql/bin/mysqldump --user=john --password=hoonose
--no-data db1 airport > airport.sql
```

This generates a dump file containing SQL commands to create an empty copy of the *db1.airport* table.

Backing Up Table Contents

The other side of the coin is a situation where you only need the contents of a table—for example, to dump them into a different table. Again you use *mysqldump*, but with the *--no-create-info* option. This yields a file containing all the INSERT statements that have been executed on the table. What doesn't get duplicated are the instructions for creating the table.

Here's an example:

```
[user@host]# /usr/local/mysql/bin/mysqldump --user=john --password=hoonose
--no-create-info db1 flight > flight.sql
```

The records from the *flight* table are now ready to be imported into any other application that understands SQL.

Backing Up Other Database Objects

It's worth noting that, by default, *mysqldump* does not back up database events or stored routines. To add these database objects to the output of a *mysqldump* run, add the *--events* and *--routines* options, as shown:

```
[user@host]# /usr/local/mysql/bin/mysqldump --user=john --password=hoonose
--events --routines db1 > db1.sql
```

Triggers and views are, however, automatically included in the output of *mysqldump*. To skip these, use the *--skip-triggers* and *--ignore-table* options, as shown:

```
[user@host]# /usr/local/mysql/bin/mysqldump --user=john --password=hoonose
--skip-triggers --ignore-table=db1.v_small_airports_gb db1 > db1.sql
```

Restoring Databases and Tables from Backup

Most books on the subject emphasize the importance of backing up your data regularly (and rightly so), but restoring the data is an often-overlooked aspect of this process. Backed-up files are useless if they can't be accessed. Accordingly, you should regularly restore your files from backup to make certain they can be used in an emergency. In fact, it might not be too much to say that a backup job isn't complete until you've confirmed that the backup files can be restored. Besides the peace of mind you'll achieve, it pays to be thoroughly familiar with the process, because you certainly don't want to waste time learning the restore procedure *after* the system goes down.

In the preceding section, you learned that the output of the *mysqldump* utility includes SQL statements such as CREATE TABLE to simplify the process of rebuilding lost data. Because of this, you can take a file generated by *mysqldump* and pipe it through the *mysql* command-line client to quickly re-create a lost database or table.

Here's an example:

```
[user@host]# /usr/local/mysql/bin/mysql db1 < mydump.sql
```

In this example, *mydump.sql* is the text file containing the output of a previous *mysqldump* run. The contents of this file (SQL commands) are executed through the *mysql* command-line client using standard input redirection. Note that the database must exist prior to piping the contents of the backup file through it.

CAUTION *The user who performs the restoration must have permission to create tables and databases. Accordingly, you might need to use the --user, --password, or --host options with the previous command.*

If you don't have access to (or don't like) the command line, another option is to use the SOURCE command, as shown:

```
mysql> SOURCE mydump.sql
```

The SOURCE command uses the SQL instructions in the named text file to rebuild the database(s) or table(s) specified. To see the results of the restoration, use a simple SELECT statement to verify that the data has been successfully restored.

Another option is to use the LOAD DATA INFILE command to import data from a text file. Here's an example:

```
mysql> LOAD DATA LOCAL INFILE '/tmp/mydump.sql'
    -> INTO TABLE p
    -> FIELDS TERMINATED BY ','
    -> ENCLOSED BY '"'
    -> LINES TERMINATED BY '\r\n';
Query OK, 5 rows affected (0.00 sec)
Records: 5  Deleted: 0  Skipped: 0  Warnings: 0
```

See Chapter 8 for more details on the LOAD DATA INFILE command.

Once you're comfortable with the procedures to back up and restore your data, you'll likely want to set up a regular schedule of backups for your organization. Both Windows and UNIX come with built-in tools that you can use for this purpose.

- The *cron* tool is a UNIX scheduling utility that can be used for this purpose. It allows you to schedule the *mysqldump* utility to run at designated times and dates. Type *man cron* at your UNIX command prompt to find out more about how to use this tool.

- In Windows NT, Windows 2000, or Windows XP, you can use either the AT command from the command prompt or the Task Scheduler (Start | Control Panel | Scheduled Tasks) to automate backups.

Summary

One of the qualities that has made MySQL popular is its ease of use; however, it won't do everything for you. Basic maintenance and an established backup and restoration process are required from the administrator in any production environment. This chapter has focused on the minimum steps you should take to ensure smooth performance of your installation, such as using the various logs to monitor the database and pinpoint areas of potential trouble. Methods of checking and repairing tables were reviewed. Finally, the all-important topics of backup and restoration were considered using various utilities that MySQL provides.

To learn more about the topics discussed in this chapter, consider visiting the following links from the MySQL manual:

- Types of server logs, at http://dev.mysql.com/doc/refman/5.1/en/log-files.html
- Log file maintenance, at http://dev.mysql.com/doc/refman/5.1/en/log-file-maintenance.html
- Table maintenance, at http://dev.mysql.com/doc/refman/5.1/en/table-maintenance-sql.html
- Example backup and recovery strategy, at http://dev.mysql.com/doc/refman/5.1/en/backup-strategy-example.html

CHAPTER 13

Replicating Data

A s discussed in the previous chapter, backing up a database involves taking a snapshot of the database and copying it to another location. This kind of backup is suited for databases that are not in constant use, or where server uptime isn't a business-critical requirement.

For companies that live and die by their databases, however, this kind of one-shot backup isn't really the perfect solution. Typically for such companies (think Yahoo! or Google), database access is a near-constant process, and database content changes continually, often on a second-by-second basis. Data replication, which involves continual data transfer between two (or more) servers to maintain a replica of the original database, is a better backup solution for these situations.

This chapter discusses the basics of data replication, demonstrating how to set up a master-slave replication system with MySQL and introducing the commands needed to manage it.

Understanding Replication

Replication in MySQL is the dynamic process of synchronizing data between a primary (master) database server and one or more secondary (slave) database servers in near-real time. Using this process, it's possible to create copies of one or more databases so that even if the primary server fails, data can still be recovered from one of the secondary servers.

Replication is essential for many applications, and the lack of replication support was a major drawback to MySQL compared to other relational database management systems (RDBMSs). MySQL 3.23 was the first version to introduce replication support, and support has improved continually in subsequent versions. However, MySQL is still best suited for one-way replication, where you have one master and one or more slaves.

TIP *As much as possible, try to use the same version of MySQL for both the master and slave server(s). A version mismatch can sometimes result in erratic replication behavior.*

Why replication? There are four common reasons.

- To create a standby database server. If the primary server fails, the standby can step in, take over, and immediately be current. For any organization that has mission-critical, time-sensitive tasks involving its database, this is a must!

- To enable backups without having to bring down or lock out the master server. After replication takes place, backups are done on the slave, rather than on the master. This way, the master can be left to do its job without disturbance.

- To keep data current across multiple locations. Replication is necessary if several branches of an organization need to work from a current copy of the same database.

- To balance the workload of multiple servers. By making it possible to create mirror images of one database on multiple servers, replication can help alleviate the woes of a single overloaded database server by splitting queries between multiple servers, each running on separate hardware.

Now that you have an idea why you might want to set up replication, let's look at some of the concepts on which it's based.

The Master-Slave Relationship

As previously stated, replication requires at least two servers. The servers are set up such that the first server, called the *master,* enters into a relationship with the other server, called the *slave.* Periodically, the latest changes to the database on the master are transferred to the slave. Through this replication relationship, an updated database can be propagated throughout an enterprise into multiple slave servers, but only one master can be in a replication relationship at any one time. It's also possible to "promote" a slave to a master, if necessary.

As a necessary prelude to configuring servers for replication, both master and slave servers must be synchronized so that the databases being replicated are the same at both ends of the replication connection. Once this is accomplished, it becomes critical for all updates to be done on the master, and *not* on the slave(s), to avoid confusion about the sequence of the updates.

In addition, binary update logging must be enabled on the master for replication to take place. This is because updates are transferred from the master to the slave via the master server's binary update logs. Replication is based on the concept that the master keeps track of the changes to the database through the binary logs and the slave updates its copy of the database by executing the changes recorded on the same logs.

Once the master and slave servers are configured, the process begins with the slave contacting the master and requesting updates. Permissions for this must be enabled on the slave server(s). The slave informs the master of the point in the binary log where the last update occurred, and then it begins the process of adding the new updates. Once completed, the slave notes where it left off and connects periodically to the master, checking for the next round of changes. This process continues for as long as replication is enabled. Figure 13-1 illustrates this relationship.

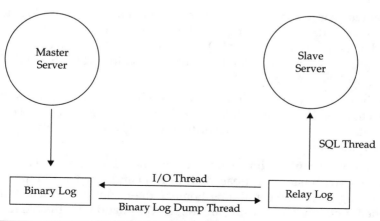

FIGURE 13-1 The master-slave replication relationship

Replication Threads

Three threads are involved in replication: one on the master and two on the slave. The I/O thread on the slave connects to the master and requests the binary update log. The binary log dump thread on the master sends the binary update log to the slave on request. Once on the slave, the I/O thread reads the data sent by the master and copies it to the relay log in the slave's data directory. The third thread, also on the slave, is the SQL thread, which reads and executes the queries from the relay log to bring the slave in alignment with the master.

The relay logs on the slave are in the same format as binary logs. Once all the events in the relay log are executed, the SQL thread automatically deletes the log. A new relay log is automatically created when an I/O thread starts. It's worth pointing out that MySQL replication is asynchronous and so the slave needn't be connected to the master all the time; it has the capability to keep track of where it left off and automatically get itself current, regardless of how much time has passed since the last update took place.

> **NOTE** *The reason for two separate slave threads? Performance! By being independent of each other, the processes of reading and writing on the slave can occur simultaneously. Because the execution of the SQL commands on the slave takes longer than reading and copying the binary logs to the relay logs, splitting these two functions also makes sense in terms of efficiency on the master. The binary logs can be safely purged from the master because a copy of them already exists on the slave, even if all the updates to the slave haven't yet been committed.*

Replication Methods

MySQL supports two (or three, depending on how you look at it) different methods of replicating databases from master to slave. All of these methods use the binary log; however, they differ in the type of data that is written to the master's binary log.

- **Statement-based replication**   Under this method, the binary log stores the SQL statements used to change databases on the master server. The slave reads this data and reexecutes these SQL statements to produce a copy of the master database. This is the default replication method in MySQL 5.1.11 and earlier and MySQL 5.1.29 onwards.

- **Row-based replication**   Under this method, the binary log stores the record-level changes that occur to database tables on the master server. The slave reads this data and manipulates its records accordingly to produce a copy of the master database.

- **Mixed-format replication**   Under this method, the server can dynamically choose between statement-based replication and row-based replication, depending on certain conditions. Some of these conditions include using a user-defined function (UDF), using an INSERT command with the DELAYED clause, using temporary tables, or using a statement that uses system variables. This is the default replication method in MySQL 5.1.12 to MySQL 5.1.28.

If you're unsure which replication method to use and your replication needs aren't complex, it's best to stick to statement-based replication, as it's been around longest and therefore has had the most time to have its kinks worked out. That said, certain types of statements cannot be replicated using this method, and it also tends to require a higher number of table locks. Row-based replication is useful for these situations. Because it replicates changes to rows, any change can be replicated, and it also requires fewer table locks. The summary section of this chapter includes links for a detailed comparison of the two methods.

The replication method currently in use on the server is listed in the *binlog_format* server variable.

```
mysql> SHOW VARIABLES LIKE 'binlog_format';
+---------------+-----------+
| Variable_name | Value     |
+---------------+-----------+
| binlog_format | STATEMENT |
+---------------+-----------+
1 row in set (0.08 sec)
```

To alter the replication method, set a new value for this variable, as shown, using the SET command with either GLOBAL or SESSION scope. Note that using GLOBAL scope requires a server restart for the change in method to take effect.

```
mysql> SET binlog_format = 'MIXED';
Query OK, 0 rows affected (0.02 sec)
mysql> SELECT @@SESSION.binlog_format;
+-------------------------+
| @@SESSION.binlog_format |
+-------------------------+
| MIXED                   |
+-------------------------+
1 row in set (0.00 sec)

mysql> SET GLOBAL binlog_format = 'ROW';
Query OK, 0 rows affected (0.00 sec)
mysql> SELECT @@GLOBAL.binlog_format;;
+------------------------+
| @@GLOBAL.binlog_format |
+------------------------+
| ROW                    |
+------------------------+
1 row in set (0.00 sec)
```

Configuring Master-Slave Replication

The process of creating master and slave servers, and then configuring them is fairly straightforward. This section will discuss the steps involved, under the assumption that the *db1* database on the master server (*cerberus*) should be replicated to the slave server (*achilles*).

1. The first step is to grant permission for the slave server to contact the master server for updates. This is done on the master server by creating a user account for the slave server and issuing it with the necessary privileges. Here's an example, which grants the appropriate privileges to *db1-slave@achilles* with the password "rosebud":

   ```
   (Master server)
   mysql> GRANT REPLICATION SLAVE ON *.*
       -> TO 'db1-slave'@'achilles' IDENTIFIED BY 'rosebud';
   Query OK, 0 rows affected (0.00 sec)
   ```

2. The next step involves configuring the master server's replication ID, activating its binary log, and (optionally) specifying which databases should be replicated. The easiest way to do this is to add the following directives to the *my.cnf* option file and then restart the MySQL server. On restart, these new options should take effect, and all updates should now be written to the binary update log.

   ```
   (Master server)
   [mysqld]
   server-id = 10
   log-bin = mysql-bin
   replicate-do-db = db1
   ```

   Note that both master and slave server(s) must have replication IDs, which are unique values in the range 1 to 4294967295.

TIP *If binary logging has already been enabled on the master server, make a backup of the binary logs before shutting down and restarting. Then, when you restart, use the* RESET MASTER *statement to clear the existing binary logs.*

3. The next step is to copy the database from the master server to the slave. As previously mentioned, you must start with an exact duplicate to assure proper replication. One way to do this is by exporting data to a backup file on the master server using the *mysqldump* command, as discussed in Chapter 12.

   Before doing this, you need to determine the current position of the master server's binary log by running the SHOW MASTER STATUS command on the master server. Note that you should lock tables prior to executing this command to ensure that no changes take place and produce inaccurate information.

```
(Master server)
mysql> FLUSH TABLES WITH READ LOCK;
Query OK, 0 rows affected (0.00 sec)
mysql> SHOW MASTER STATUS;
+-------------------+----------+---------------+------------------+
| File              | Position | Binlog_Do_DB  | Binlog_Ignore_DB |
+-------------------+----------+---------------+------------------+
| mysql-bin.000001  |    106   |               |                  |
+-------------------+----------+---------------+------------------+
1 row in set (0.00 sec)
```

The output of this command reveals that the master server is on binary log #1, position 106.

In a different window, export the contents of the database to a text file:

```
(Master server)
[user@cerberus]# /usr/local/mysql/bin/mysqldump --user=root
--password=guessme db1 > /tmp/db1.sql
```

Release the table locks to return the server to normal operation:

```
mysql> UNLOCK TABLES;
Query OK, 0 rows affected (0.00 sec)
```

4. Next, copy the exported database to the slave server using the *mysql* command, as discussed in Chapter 12:

```
(Slave server)
mysql> CREATE DATABASE db1;
Query OK, 1 row affected (0.00 sec)
[user@cerberus]# /usr/local/mysql/bin/mysql --user=root
--host=achilles --password=root db1 < /tmp/db1.sql
```

NOTE *Earlier versions of MySQL provided a* LOAD DATA FROM MASTER *command to transfer the database from the master to the slave server. However, several restrictions were involved in using this command. It was usually only suitable when the source database was small and used the MyISAM engine, and having a read lock on the master server for a long time wasn't a problem. In real-world implementations, these conditions were found too restrictive and the command was deprecated in MySQL 4.1. Currently, the MySQL manual recommends transferring the master database with the* mysqldump *command, as explained previously.*

---

5. The next step is to update the slave server's configuration. All that's needed is to assign each slave a unique replication ID and then restart the server for the change to take effect. Here's an example of a slave server's option file:

```
(Slave server)
[mysqld]
server-id = 7
```

6. It's necessary to tell the slave server the position of the binary log to begin processing from by running the CHANGE MASTER TO command on the slave server:

```
(Slave server)
mysql> CHANGE MASTER TO
    -> MASTER_HOST='cerberus',
    -> MASTER_USER='db1-slave',
    -> MASTER_PASSWORD='rosebud',
    -> MASTER_LOG_FILE='mysql-bin.000001',
    -> MASTER_LOG_POS=106;
Query OK, 0 rows affected (0.00 sec)
```

7. The final step is to start the replication threads on the slave server by issuing the START SLAVE command. The slave will use the options in the CHANGE MASTER command to determine how to connect to the master and will also create *master.info* and *relay-log.info* files in the data directory to store information about the replication process.

```
(Slave server)
mysql> START SLAVE;
Query OK, 0 rows affected (0.00 sec)
```

If you decide later to change the replication options, you must again execute the CHANGE MASTER TO command to update the slave with new information.

Configuring Master-Master Replication

It's also possible to configure replication with two (or more) master servers, such that changes to data on any one of them are automatically replicated to the other(s). This is referred to as master-master replication or, if there are only two master servers involved, bi-directional replication.

The usual problem that occurs in this type of replication is related to AUTO_INCREMENT PRIMARY KEY fields. Consider the following situation: A new record is added to a table containing this field type on the first master server. Simultaneously, a new record (with different field values) is added to the same table on the second master server. Both records will share the same auto-generated record ID, as the insertions have occurred on two independent servers. Replication will fail in this case, as the record added on one master server will be blocked from insertion on the second due to a primary key conflict.

CAUTION *While master-master replication is technically possible under MySQL, it's certainly not the recommended configuration. The very nature of this type of replication makes it inherently risky, with significant data loss possible if any of the servers in the relationship fails. There's also a high risk of duplicate data when both master servers write to the same table. As far as possible, stick to regular master-slave replication and use master-master replication only if you have a full understanding of the risks involved, as well as adequate redundancies that will take over in case of problems.*

Fortunately, MySQL comes with a solution to this problem, wherein each master "knows" about other masters in the relationship and automatically avoids such primary key conflicts. This section will discuss the steps involved, under the assumption that the *db1* database is to be replicated between two master servers (*cerberus* and *achilles*).

1. The first step is to grant permission for each master server to contact the other for updates, as though it were a slave. This is done by creating a user account on each master server and issuing it the necessary privileges. Here's an example:

```
(Master server 'cerberus')
mysql> GRANT REPLICATION SLAVE ON *.*
    -> TO 'master'@'achilles' IDENTIFIED BY 'rosebud';
Query OK, 0 rows affected (0.00 sec)

(Master server 'achilles')
mysql> GRANT REPLICATION SLAVE ON *.*
    -> TO 'master'@'cerberus' IDENTIFIED BY 'twilight';
Query OK, 0 rows affected (0.00 sec)
```

2. The next step involves configuring replication IDs and binary logs on each master server. The easiest way to do this is to add the following directives to the *my.cnf* option file on each server and then restart them. On restart, these new options should take effect, and all updates should now be written to the binary update log.

```
(Master server 'cerberus')
[mysqld]
server-id = 10
log-bin = mysql-bin
replicate-do-db = db1
auto-increment-increment = 2
auto-increment-offset = 1

(Master server 'achilles')
[mysqld]
server-id = 20
log-bin = mysql-bin
replicate-do-db = db1
auto-increment-increment = 2
auto-increment-offset = 2
```

The *auto-increment-increment* option specifies the interval between auto-generated values for AUTO_INCREMENT fields, while the *auto-increment-offset* option specifies the starting value. In a master-master relationship, the *auto-increment-increment* option should be set to the total number of master servers, while the *auto-increment-offset* should hold a different value, beginning with 1 and ending with the value of *auto-increment-increment*, on each master server. Note also that each master server must have a unique replication ID.

3. The next step is to copy the database from either one of the master servers to the other. It doesn't really matter which one you use as the source; all that matters is that both servers exactly mirror each other's data prior to starting the replication process. One way to do this is by exporting data to a backup file on the source server using the *mysqldump* command, as discussed in Chapter 12.

Before doing this, you need to determine the current position of the source master server's binary log by running the SHOW MASTER STATUS command. Note that you should lock tables prior to executing this command to ensure that no changes take place and produce inaccurate information.

```
(Master server 'cerberus')
mysql> FLUSH TABLES WITH READ LOCK;
Query OK, 0 rows affected (0.00 sec)
mysql> SHOW MASTER STATUS;
+-------------------+----------+--------------+------------------+
| File              | Position | Binlog_Do_DB | Binlog_Ignore_DB |
+-------------------+----------+--------------+------------------+
| mysql-bin.000006  |    213   |              |                  |
+-------------------+----------+--------------+------------------+
1 row in set (0.01 sec)
```

The output of this command reveals that the source server is on binary log #6, position 213.

In a different window, export the contents of the database to a text file:

```
(Master server 'cerberus')
[user@cerberus]# /usr/local/mysql/bin/mysqldump --user=root
--password=guessme db1 > /tmp/db1.sql
```

Release the table locks to return the server to normal operation:

```
mysql> UNLOCK TABLES;
Query OK, 0 rows affected (0.00 sec)
```

4. Next, copy the exported database to the second master server(s) using the *mysql* command, as discussed in Chapter 12:

```
(Master server 'achilles')
mysql> CREATE DATABASE db1;
Query OK, 1 row affected (0.00 sec)
[user@cerberus]# /usr/local/mysql/bin/mysql --user=root
--host=achilles --password=root db1 < /tmp/db1.sql
```

At this point, you need to determine the current position of the second master server's binary log by running the SHOW MASTER STATUS command. Note that you should lock tables prior to executing this command to ensure that no changes take place and produce inaccurate information.

```
(Master server 'achilles')
mysql> FLUSH TABLES WITH READ LOCK;
Query OK, 0 rows affected (0.00 sec)
mysql> SHOW MASTER STATUS;
```

```
+-------------------+----------+--------------+------------------+
| File              | Position | Binlog_Do_DB | Binlog_Ignore_DB |
+-------------------+----------+--------------+------------------+
| mysql-bin.000001  |   106    |              |                  |
+-------------------+----------+--------------+------------------+
1 row in set (0.00 sec)
```

The output of this command reveals that the second server is on binary log #1, position 106.

Release the table locks to return the server to normal operation:

```
mysql> UNLOCK TABLES;
Query OK, 0 rows affected (0.00 sec)
```

5. It's necessary to tell each master server the position of the other's binary log by running the CHANGE MASTER TO command:

```
(Master server 'cerberus')
mysql> CHANGE MASTER TO
    -> MASTER_HOST='achilles',
    -> MASTER_USER='master',
    -> MASTER_PASSWORD='twilight',
    -> MASTER_LOG_FILE='mysql-bin.000001',
    -> MASTER_LOG_POS=106;
Query OK, 0 rows affected (0.00 sec)
(Master server 'achilles')
mysql> CHANGE MASTER TO
    -> MASTER_HOST='cerberus',
    -> MASTER_USER='master',
    -> MASTER_PASSWORD='rosebud',
    -> MASTER_LOG_FILE='mysql-bin.000006',
    -> MASTER_LOG_POS=213;
Query OK, 0 rows affected (0.00 sec)
```

6. The final step is to start the replication threads on each master server by issuing the START SLAVE command:

```
(Master server 'cerberus')
mysql> START SLAVE;
Query OK, 0 rows affected (0.00 sec)
(Master server 'achilles')
mysql> START SLAVE;
Query OK, 0 rows affected (0.00 sec)
```

Changes made on any one of the two servers should now be replicated to the other. If you take a close look, you'll also see that auto-generated primary keys on *cerberus* are odd numbers, while those on *achilles* are even numbers. This is entirely due to the *auto-increment-increment* and *auto-increment-offset* options specified earlier and ensures that primary key conflicts do not occur.

Managing the Replication Process

Now that your master and slave servers are running smoothly, some commands exist that let you manage their relationship. All these commands are executed within the MySQL interface. In the process of examining these statements, you'll learn more about the details of replication.

Changing Replication Parameters

The CHANGE MASTER TO command instructs the slave to check a different binary log in the master server for updates and/or to write to a different relay log in the slave. This statement also is used to change the connection and binary log parameters. For example, let's say your company just bought a brand-new, super-big, super-fast dedicated server (since you're imagining, you might as well make it interesting!) for the database. You want to change masters from the old server to the new one. Here's an example of the command you'd use:

```
(Slave server)
mysql> STOP SLAVE;
Query OK, 0 rows affected (0.00 sec)
mysql> CHANGE MASTER TO
    -> MASTER_HOST ='cerberus',
    -> MASTER_USER = 'slave',
    -> MASTER_PASSWORD = 'slavepass',
    -> MASTER_PORT = '3306',
    -> MASTER_LOG_FILE = 'mysql-bin.001',
    -> MASTER_LOG_POS = 7,
    -> MASTER_CONNECT_RETRY = 15;
    -> RELAY_LOG_FILE = 'slave-relay-bin.010',
    -> RELAY_LOG_POS = 6084;
Query OK, 0 rows affected (0.00 sec)
mysql> START SLAVE;
Query OK, 0 rows affected (0.00 sec)
```

Table 13-1 contains a quick reference chart for these parameters. Only the parameters specified will change; if a parameter is unspecified, the existing value remains as is. The exceptions to this rule are the host name and the port number. If either of these changes, MySQL assumes you're changing master servers and it automatically drops the binary update log name and position values; you'll need to remember to specify these values.

Starting and Stopping Slave Servers

The START SLAVE command is used to begin or resume replication, while the STOP SLAVE command is used to pause or end replication. Note that executing the START SLAVE command in itself is no guarantee that replication has begun. If the slave is unable to connect to the master or read the binary logs, it might stop on its own without providing an error message.

Parameter	What It Means
MASTER_HOST	Host name for the master server
MASTER_USER	Slave name to use when connecting to the master
MASTER_PASSWORD	Slave's password to connection to master
MASTER_PORT	Port number to connect to master
MASTER_LOG_FILE	Name of master's binary log file from which to start reading when replication begins
MASTER_LOG_POS	Position in the master's binary log file from which to start reading when replication begins
MASTER_CONNECT_RETRY	Number of seconds to wait between connection attempts
RELAY_LOG_FILE	Name of the slave relay log from which to begin execution when replication begins
RELAY_LOG_POS	Position in slave relay log from which to begin execution when replication begins
MASTER_SSL	Whether to connect to the master server using SSL

TABLE 13-1 Common Options for the CHANGE MASTER TO Command

TIP *Don't assume everything is fine because you issued the START SLAVE command successfully—monitor the slave's activities by using the SHOW SLAVE STATUS command. You can also read the slave's error log to make sure everything is okay.*

Checking Replication Status

The SHOW SLAVE STATUS command provides information about the slave server's status. It should be run on the slave database server. Here's what it looks like:

```
(Slave server)
mysql> SHOW SLAVE STATUS\G
*************************** 1. row ***************************
               Slave_IO_State: Waiting for master to send event
                  Master_Host: cerberus
                  Master_User: db1-slave
                  Master_Port: 3306
                Connect_Retry: 60
              Master_Log_File: mysql-bin.000004
          Read_Master_Log_Pos: 106
               Relay_Log_File: ACHILLES-relay-bin.000006
                Relay_Log_Pos: 251
        Relay_Master_Log_File: mysql-bin.000004
             Slave_IO_Running: Yes
            Slave_SQL_Running: Yes
              Replicate_Do_DB:
```

```
          Replicate_Ignore_DB:
        Replicate_Do_Table:
     Replicate_Ignore_Table:
    Replicate_Wild_Do_Table:
 Replicate_Wild_Ignore_Table:
                   Last_Errno: 0
                   Last_Error:
                 Skip_Counter: 0
          Exec_Master_Log_Pos: 106
             Relay_Log_Space: 554
             Until_Condition: None
              Until_Log_File:
               Until_Log_Pos: 0
                  ...
1 row in set (0.00 sec)
```

In addition to displaying information on the current server and user credentials, the SHOW SLAVE STATUS command provides information on how many times the slave server will attempt to connect to the master server, the status of slave I/O and SQL threads, the name and position in the master's binary log, the name and position in the slave's relay log, the size of relay log files, the databases and tables excluded from replication, and whether SSL connections are in use.

The SHOW PROCESSLIST command displays information about the threads on the server, and was discussed in Chapter 10. In a replication context, it can be used to obtain status information on both the master and the slave. For each thread, the output is shown in various fields, as illustrated:

```
(Master server)
mysql> SHOW PROCESSLIST\G
*************************** 1. row ***************************
     Id: 2
   User: db1-slave
   Host: ACHILLES:43424
     db: NULL
Command: Binlog Dump
   Time: 2128
  State: Has sent all binlog to slave; waiting for binlog to be updated
   Info: NULL
*************************** 2. row ***************************
     Id: 6
   User: root
   Host: localhost:1302
     db: NULL
Command: Query
   Time: 0
  State: NULL
   Info: show processlist
2 rows in set (0.00 sec)
```

```
(Slave server)
mysql> SHOW PROCESSLIST\G
*************************** 1. row ***************************
     Id: 12
   User: root
   Host: localhost:43422
     db: NULL
Command: Sleep
   Time: 1937
  State:
   Info: NULL
*************************** 2. row ***************************
     Id: 13
   User: system user
   Host:
     db: NULL
Command: Connect
   Time: 1941
  State: Waiting for master to send event
   Info: NULL
*************************** 3. row ***************************
     Id: 14
   User: system user
   Host:
     db: NULL
Command: Connect
   Time: 1941
  State: Has read all relay log; waiting for the slave I/O thread to
update it
   Info: NULL
*************************** 4. row ***************************
     Id: 16
   User: root
   Host: CERBERUS:1294
     db: NULL
Command: Query
   Time: 0
  State: NULL
   Info: SHOW PROCESSLIST
4 rows in set (0.03 sec)
```

Of these various fields, the one you'll usually be most interested in is the *State* field, which contains information about what the server is doing. For example, on the master server, you could see something like 'Sending binlog event to slave.' On the slave's I/O thread, you might see 'Connecting to master' or 'Requesting binlog dump.' On the slave's SQL thread, a common state is 'Reading event from the relay log.' You'll also find information (where appropriate) about which database the thread is accessing, the statement it's currently executing, and how long (in seconds) the thread has been executing.

Working with Master Server Binary Logs

As discussed earlier, when replicating, everything is based on the binary log on the master server. To display events in this log, the SHOW BINLOG EVENTS command can be used. Here's an example:

```
(Master server)
mysql> SHOW BINLOG EVENTS FROM 4 LIMIT 0,10\G
*************************** 1. row ***************************
   Log_name: mysql-bin.000001
        Pos: 4
 Event_type: Format_desc
  Server_id: 10
End_log_pos: 106
       Info: Server ver: 5.1.30-community-log, Binlog ver: 4
*************************** 2. row ***************************
   Log_name: mysql-bin.000001
        Pos: 106
 Event_type: Query
  Server_id: 10
End_log_pos: 203
       Info: use `db1`; delete from log where RecordID = 37
2 rows in set (0.00 sec)
```

By itself, this command displays all events in the binary log. This can be a time-consuming process when dealing with large binary logs. Therefore, the MySQL manual suggests limiting the output of this command by only showing events starting from a specific position in the log (the FROM clause) and displaying a specified number of events (the LIMIT clause), as in the previous example.

The PURGE MASTER command deletes all binary logs on the master server prior to a specified date or log number. As an example, suppose you want to purge all the master binary update logs prior to the one named *bin_log.999*. You would execute the following:

```
(Master server)
mysql> PURGE MASTER LOGS TO mysql-bin.000999;
Query OK, 0 rows affected (0.00 sec)
```

Note that this statement requires the SUPER privilege.

For additional information about the master server's binary logs, use the SHOW MASTER STATUS command, which displays the current binary log name and position being written to. Here's an example:

```
(Master server)
mysql> SHOW MASTER STATUS\G
*************************** 1. row ***************************
            File: mysql-bin.000004
        Position: 106
    Binlog_Do_DB:
Binlog_Ignore_DB:
1 row in set (0.00 sec)
```

Summary

This chapter introduced many of the basic replication concepts, such as the master-slave relationship, binary logging, and relay logging. It reviewed and analyzed the three threads that carry out replication on the master and slave servers, and provided step-by-step instructions for taking two servers and configuring them for ongoing replication in two different configurations. Finally, it looked at various SQL commands that are useful for configuring and troubleshooting replication, and that provide considerable information about the processes involved.

To learn more about the topics discussed in this chapter, consider visiting the following links:

- A comparison of replication methods, at http://dev.mysql.com/doc/refman/5.1/en/replication-sbr-rbr.html

- Replication variables and options, at http://dev.mysql.com/doc/refman/5.1/en/replication-options.html

- Replication thread states, at http://dev.mysql.com/doc/refman/5.1/en/master-thread-states.html

- Replication tips, at http://dev.mysql.com/doc/refman/5.1/en/replication-notes.html

APPENDIX

Installing MySQL and the Sample Database

T his book discusses the MySQL RDBMS and the tools and commands it provides to store, manipulate, and retrieve data in databases. In case you're new to MySQL and don't already have a working installation of the software, this appendix guides you through the process of obtaining, installing, configuring, and testing the MySQL server. It discusses the different versions of MySQL, covers installation of binary versions on both UNIX and Microsoft Windows, and helps create a server environment suitable for running the code examples in this book.

CAUTION *This appendix is intended to provide an overview and general guide to the process of installing and configuring MySQL on UNIX and Windows. It is not intended as a replacement for the installation instructions that ship with MySQL. If you encounter difficulties installing or configuring MySQL, visit the online MySQL manual or search the Web for detailed troubleshooting information and advice (some links are provided at the end of this chapter).*

Obtaining MySQL

The first order of business is to drop by the official MySQL website at www.mysql.com and get a copy of the most current release of the software. This isn't necessarily as easy as it sounds—like ice-cream, MySQL comes in many flavors, and you'll need to select the one that's most appropriate for your needs.

There are two primary decisions to be made when selecting which MySQL distribution to download and use.

- Choosing which version to install
- Choosing between binary and source distributions

Choosing Which Version to Install

Sun Microsystems currently makes two versions of the MySQL database server available on their website.

- **MySQL Community Server**   This is the General Public License (GPL) version of the MySQL database server, which includes support for both regular, nontransactional storage engines and transaction-safe tables. It is suited for production environments requiring a stable, flexible, and robust database engine, and can be downloaded free of charge.

- **MySQL Enterprise Server**   This version is only available as part of the MySQL Enterprise platform, a commercial offering aimed at enterprise customers with business-critical applications. It includes all the features of the Community Server, along with automated updates and hot fixes, consulting support, and monitoring services.

So long as you're willing to put in the time and effort needed to manage the MySQL database server and don't mind resolving technical issues yourself, the

MySQL Community Server is the most appropriate choice. It's the version used in all the examples in this book, and it's stable, feature-rich, and suited for most common applications. However, business customers who need automated updates, continuous system monitoring, and access to 24/7 technical and consulting support would probably be better served by a MySQL Enterprise subscription.

Choosing Between Binary and Source Distributions

Sun Microsystems makes both source and binary distributions of the MySQL database server available for download on their website. As of this writing, binary distributions are available for Linux (Red Hat, SuSE, and generic distributions), Solaris, FreeBSD, Mac OS X, 32-bit and 64-bit Windows, HP-UX, and IBM AIX and IBM i5, and source distributions are available for both Windows and UNIX platforms.

Windows users must further choose between three different binary distributions: the "Essentials" distribution, which includes the minimum set of files and an automated installer; the "Complete" distribution, which includes everything in the "Essentials" distribution plus additional tools such as the MySQL Benchmark Suite; and the "Noinstall" distribution, which includes everything in the "Complete" distribution *except* the automated installer.

In most cases, it's preferable to use a precompiled binary distribution rather than a source distribution, for two reasons: It is easier to install, and it has been optimized for maximum performance on different platforms by the MySQL development team. That said, there are a number of possible situations where a source distribution might be preferable to a binary distribution.

- You need to recompile MySQL with different compile-time options from the defaults provided by the MySQL team (for example, to set a different value for the default installation path).

- You need to compile a smaller, lighter version of MySQL that doesn't include all the features (and overhead) of the standard binary distribution.

- You need newer, experimental features that are disabled by default in the standard binaries.

- You need to make modifications to the server's source code.

Source distributions are typically used only by experienced developers who either need to tweak MySQL's default values for their own purposes or who are interested in studying the source code to see how it works. Such users usually also have the time, inclination, and expertise to diagnose and troubleshoot compilation and configuration issues that may arise during the installation process.

MySQL versions that don't come with an automated installer are usually packaged in either TGZ or ZIP format. Therefore, users on both UNIX and Windows platforms will need a decompression tool capable of dealing with Tape Archive (TAR) and GNU Zip (GZ) files. On UNIX, the *tar* and *gzip* utilities are appropriate, and are usually included with the operating system. On Windows, a good decompression tool is WinZip, available from www.winzip.com.

The instructions in the following sections assume that you will be using a binary distribution of MySQL Community Server. This distribution can be downloaded from the MySQL website. The MySQL software is also mirrored on a number of other sites around the world, and you can make your download more efficient by selecting the site that is geographically closest to you. Once downloaded, move to the section titled "Installing and Configuring MySQL."

Installing and Configuring MySQL

The next step is to install and configure MySQL for your specific platform. The following sections outline the steps for both Windows and UNIX platforms.

Installing on UNIX

MySQL is available in binary form for almost all versions of UNIX, and can be compiled from source for those UNIX variants for which no binary distribution exists. This section will discuss installing and configuring MySQL on Linux using a binary distribution; the process for other UNIX variants is similar, though you should refer to the documentation included with the MySQL distribution for platform-specific notes.

To install MySQL from a binary distribution, use the following steps:

1. Ensure that you are logged in as the system's "root" user.

   ```
   [user@host]# su - root
   ```

2. Extract the contents of the MySQL binary archive to an appropriate directory on your system—for example, *usr/local/*:

   ```
   [root@host]# cd /usr/local
   [root@host]# tar -xzvf /tmp/mysql-5.1.30-linux-i686-glibc23.tar.gz
   ```

   The MySQL files should get extracted into a directory named according to the format *mysql-version-os-architecture*—for example, *mysql-5.1.30-linux-i686-glibc23*.

3. For ease of use, set a shorter name for the directory created in the previous step by creating a soft link named *mysql* pointing to this directory in the same location:

   ```
   [root@host]# ln -s mysql-5.1.30-linux-i686-glibc23 mysql
   ```

4. For security reasons, the MySQL database server process should never run as the system superuser. Therefore, it is necessary to create a special "mysql" user and group for this purpose. Do this with the *groupadd* and *useradd* commands, and then change the ownership of the MySQL installation directory to this user and group:

   ```
   [root@host]# groupadd mysql
   [root@host]# useradd -g mysql mysql
   [root@host]# chown -R mysql /usr/local/mysql
   [root@host]# chgrp -R mysql /usr/local/mysql
   ```

5. Initialize the MySQL tables with the *mysql_install_db* initialization script, included in the distribution:

```
[root@host]# /usr/local/mysql/scripts/mysql_install_db --user=mysql
```

Figure A-1 demonstrates what you should see when you do this.

As this output suggests, this initialization script prepares and installs the various MySQL base tables and sets up default access permissions for MySQL.

6. Alter the ownership of the MySQL binaries so that they are owned by "root":

```
[root@host]# chown -R root /usr/local/mysql
```

and ensure that the "mysql" user created in step 4 has read/write privileges to the MySQL data directory:

```
[root@host]# chown -R mysql /usr/local/mysql/data
```

7. Start the MySQL server by manually running the *mysqld_safe* script:

```
[root@host]# /usr/local/mysql/bin/mysqld_safe --user=mysql &
```

MySQL should now start up normally.

Once installation has been successfully completed and the server has started up, move down to the section entitled "Testing MySQL" to verify that it is functioning as it should.

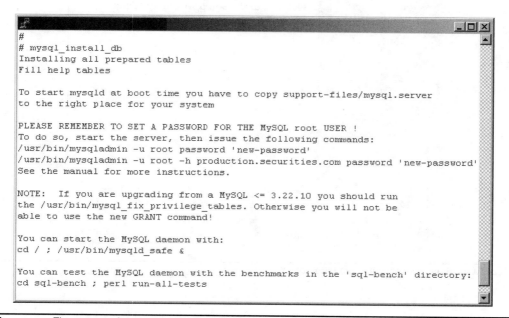

```
#
# mysql_install_db
Installing all prepared tables
Fill help tables

To start mysqld at boot time you have to copy support-files/mysql.server
to the right place for your system

PLEASE REMEMBER TO SET A PASSWORD FOR THE MySQL root USER !
To do so, start the server, then issue the following commands:
/usr/bin/mysqladmin -u root password 'new-password'
/usr/bin/mysqladmin -u root -h production.securities.com password 'new-password'
See the manual for more instructions.

NOTE:  If you are upgrading from a MySQL <= 3.22.10 you should run
the /usr/bin/mysql_fix_privilege_tables. Otherwise you will not be
able to use the new GRANT command!

You can start the MySQL daemon with:
cd / ; /usr/bin/mysqld_safe &

You can test the MySQL daemon with the benchmarks in the 'sql-bench' directory:
cd sql-bench ; perl run-all-tests
```

FIGURE A-1 The output of the *mysql_install_db* script

Installing on Windows

MySQL is available in both source and binary forms for both 32-bit and 64-bit versions of Microsoft Windows. Most often, you will want to use either the "Essentials" or "Complete" binary distribution, which includes an automated installer to get MySQL up and running in just a few minutes.

To install MySQL from a binary distribution, use the following steps:

1. Log in as an administrator (if you're using Windows NT/2000/XP/Vista).

2. Double-click the *mysql-*.msi* file to begin the installation process. You should see a welcome screen (Figure A-2).

3. Select the type of installation required (Figure A-3).

   Most often, a Typical Installation will do; however, if you're the kind who likes tweaking default settings, or if you're just short of disk space, select the Custom Installation option, and decide which components of the package should be installed.

4. MySQL should now begin installing to your system (Figure A-4).

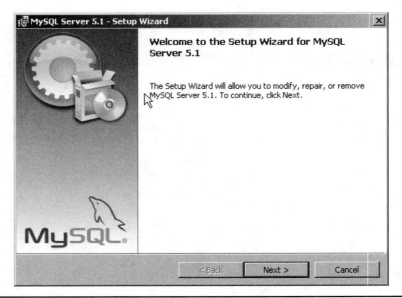

FIGURE A-2   Beginning MySQL installation on Windows

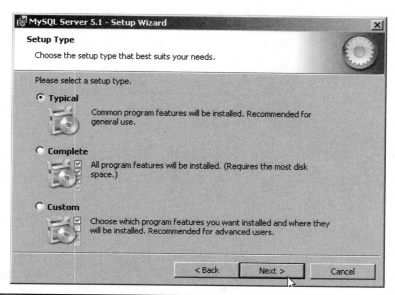

FIGURE A-3   Selecting the MySQL installation type

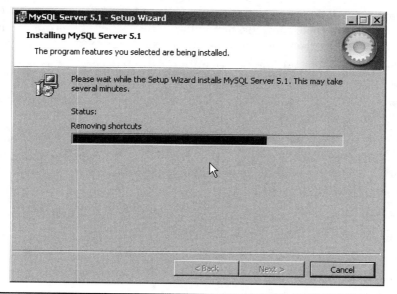

FIGURE A-4   MySQL installation in progress

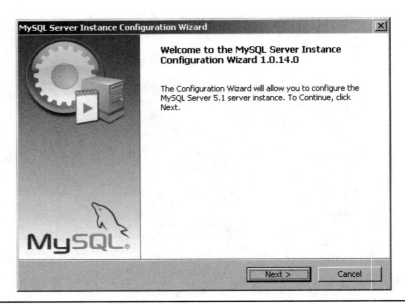

Figure A-5 Beginning MySQL configuration on Windows

5. Once installation is complete, you should see a success notification. At this point, you will have the option to launch the MySQL Server Instance Config Wizard to complete configuration of the software. Select this option, and you should see the corresponding welcome screen (Figure A-5).

6. Select the type of configuration (Figure A-6). In most cases, the Standard Configuration will suffice.

7. Install MySQL as a Windows service, such that it starts and stops automatically with Windows (Figure A-7).

8. Enter a password for the MySQL administrator ("root") account (Figure A-8).

9. The server will now be configured with your specified settings and automatically started. You will be presented with a success notification once all required tasks are complete (Figure A-9).

You can now proceed to test the server, as described in the section "Testing MySQL," to ensure that everything is working as it should.

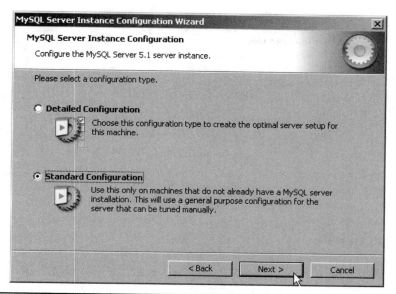

FIGURE A-6   Selecting the configuration type

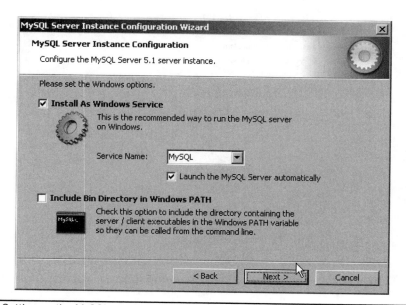

FIGURE A-7   Setting up the MySQL service

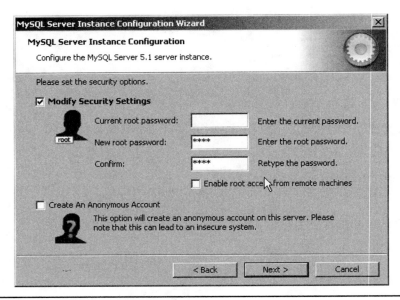

FIGURE A-8 Setting the administrator password

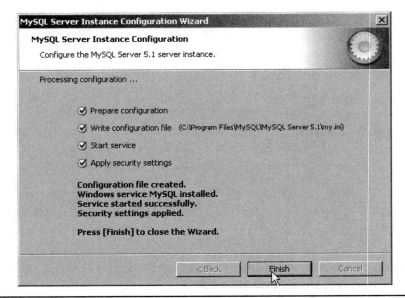

FIGURE A-9 MySQL configuration successfully completed

Testing MySQL

First, start up the MySQL command-line client by changing to the *bin/* subdirectory of your MySQL installation directory and typing the following command:

```
prompt# mysql -u root
```

You should be rewarded with a prompt, as shown:

```
Welcome to the MySQL monitor.  Commands end with ; or \g.
Your MySQL connection id is 1
Server version: 5.1.30-community MySQL Community Server (GPL)
Type 'help;' or '\h' for help. Type '\c' to clear the buffer.
mysql>
```

At this point, you are connected to the MySQL server and can begin executing SQL commands or queries to test whether the server is working as it should. Here are a few examples, with their output:

```
mysql> SHOW DATABASES;
+----------+
| Database |
+----------+
| mysql    |
| test     |
+----------+
2 rows in set (0.13 sec)
mysql> USE mysql;
Database changed
mysql> SHOW TABLES;
+-------------------------+
| Tables_in_mysql         |
+-------------------------+
| columns_priv            |
| db                      |
| event                   |
| func                    |
| general_log             |
| help_category           |
| help_keyword            |
| help_relation           |
| help_topic              |
| host                    |
| ndb_binlog_index        |
```

```
| plugin                      |
| proc                        |
| procs_priv                  |
| servers                     |
| slow_log                    |
| tables_priv                 |
| time_zone                   |
| time_zone_leap_second       |
| time_zone_name              |
| time_zone_transition        |
| time_zone_transition_type   |
| user                        |
+-----------------------------+
23 rows in set (0.23 sec)
mysql> SELECT VERSION();
+------------------+
| VERSION()        |
+------------------+
| 5.1.30-community |
+------------------+
1 row in set (0.00 sec)
```

If you see output similar to that, your MySQL installation is working as it should. Exit the command-line client by typing the following command, and you'll be returned to your command prompt:

```
mysql> exit
```

If you don't see output like that shown here, or if MySQL throws warnings and errors at you, review the installation procedure in the previous section, as well as the documents that shipped with your version of MySQL, to see what went wrong.

Performing Post-Installation Steps

Once testing is complete, you may wish to perform the following two tasks.

Setting the MySQL Superuser Password

On UNIX, when MySQL is first installed, access to the database server is restricted to the MySQL administrator, aka "root." By default, this user is initialized with a blank password, which is generally considered a Bad Thing. You should, therefore, rectify this as soon as possible by setting a password for this user via the included *mysqladmin* utility, using the following syntax in UNIX:

```
[root@host]# /usr/local/mysql/bin/mysqladmin -u root password 'new-password'
```

In Windows, you can use the MySQL Server Instance Config Wizard, which allows you to set or reset the MySQL administrator password (see the section entitled "Installing on Windows" for more details).

This password change goes into effect immediately, with no requirement to restart the server.

NOTE *The MySQL "root" user is not the same as the system superuser ("root") on UNIX, so altering one password does not affect the other.*

Configuring MySQL and Apache to Start Automatically

On UNIX, MySQL comes with startup/shutdown scripts, which can be used to start and stop the server. These scripts are located within the MySQL installation hierarchy. Here's an example of how to use the MySQL server control script:

```
[root@host]# /usr/local/mysql/support-files/mysql.server start
[root@host]# /usr/local/mysql/support-files/mysql.server stop
```

- To have MySQL start automatically at boot time on UNIX, simply invoke the respective control scripts with appropriate parameters from your system's bootup and shutdown scripts in the /etc/rc.d/* hierarchy.

- To start MySQL automatically on Windows, simply add a link to the *mysqld.exe* server binary to your Startup group. You can also start MySQL automatically by installing it as a Windows service (see the section entitled "Installing on Windows" for instructions).

TIP *In case you have problems starting the MySQL server, you can obtain fairly detailed information on what went wrong by looking at the MySQL error log. By default, this file is called* hostname.err *in Windows and UNIX, and is always located in the MySQL data/ directory. Other common problems, such as a forgotten superuser password or incorrect path settings, can also be discovered and resolved via a close study of this error log.*

Setting Up the Example Database

The code listings in this book all make use of a sample database containing flight, route, and passenger information for a fictitious airline. The following sections discuss how to re-create this sample database on your development system and take a closer look at the tables that make up this database.

Re-creating the Example Database

The SQL commands needed to re-create the example database can be found in a single file, available from this book's website, at www.mysql-usage.com. Once you've downloaded this file, drop to your shell prompt, fire up the MySQL command-line client, and execute the following commands:

```
prompt# mysql -u root -p
Enter password: ***
Welcome to the MySQL monitor.  Commands end with ; or \g.
Your MySQL connection id is 14
Server version: 5.1.30-community MySQL Community Server (GPL)
Type 'help;' or '\h' for help. Type '\c' to clear the buffer.
mysql> CREATE DATABASE db1;
Query OK, 1 row affected (0.00 sec)
mysql> exit
Bye
prompt# mysql -u root -p -D db1 < db1.sql
Enter password: ***
```

These commands will create a new, empty database and then read in the SQL commands from the source file to create the example database (see Chapter 12 for more information on these commands).

You can verify that the database has been correctly created by issuing a few quick SELECT commands and checking the output, as shown:

```
mysql> SHOW TABLES;
+---------------+
| Tables_in_db1 |
+---------------+
| aircraft      |
| aircrafttype  |
| airport       |
| class         |
| flight        |
| flightclass   |
| flightdep     |
| log           |
| pax           |
| route         |
| stats         |
+---------------+
11 rows in set (0.02 sec)
```

```
mysql> SELECT COUNT(*) FROM flightdep;
+----------+
| COUNT(*) |
+----------+
|      108 |
+----------+
1 row in set (0.09 sec)
```

Understanding the Example Database

It's worthwhile spending a few minutes to understand the structure of the example database. Table A-1 provides a concise summary of the tables in this database, together with an explanation of what each table contains.

The relationships between these tables can be visually understood from the entity-relationship (E-R) diagram in Figure A-10.

PART II

Table Name	Description
airport	Master list of airports serviced by the airline. For each airport, specifies information on the host country, number of runways, and number of terminals.
route	Master list of routes between airport pairs. For each route, specifies flying time, distance, and route status (active or inactive).
flight	Master list of flight numbers servicing each route
flightdep	Departure schedule for each flight (weekday and time)
aircraft	Master list of aircraft used for each flight number. For each aircraft, specifies aircraft registration number, type, and maintenance cycle.
aircrafttype	Master list of aircraft types in use
class	Master list of seating classes
flightclass	Master list of seating classes available on each flight. For each class, specifies maximum number of available seats and base price per seat.
pax	Master list of passengers on each flight
stats	Current inventory of seat availability and price per seat on each flight
log	Activity log

TABLE A-1   Tables in the Example Database

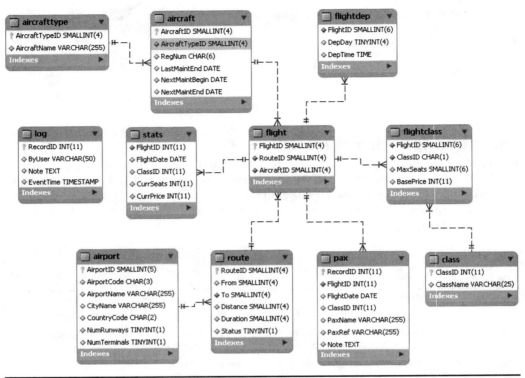

Figure A-10   E-R diagram for the example database

Summary

As a popular open-source application, MySQL is available for a wide variety of platforms and architectures, in both binary and source forms. This chapter explained the differences between the different versions of MySQL and demonstrated the process of installing a binary version of MySQL on the two most common platforms, UNIX and Windows. It also provided information on testing, securing, and automatically starting the MySQL server on both platforms.

For more detailed installation and troubleshooting information, consider visiting the following links:

- General installation notes, at http://dev.mysql.com/doc/refman/5.1/en/ general-installation-issues.html

- MySQL installation from binary tarballs on UNIX/Linux, at http://dev.mysql .com/doc/refman/5.1/en/installing-binary.html

- MySQL installation from RPM packages on UNIX/Linux, at http://dev.mysql .com/doc/refman/5.1/en/linux-rpm.html

- MySQL installation on Windows, at http://dev.mysql.com/doc/refman/5.1/ en/windows-installation.html

Index